Gender Perspectives in Law

Volume 5

Series Editors

Dragica Vujadinović, Faculty of Law, University of Belgrade, Belgrade, Serbia

Ivana Krstić, Faculty of Law, University of Belgrade, Belgrade, Serbia

The series 'Gender Perspectives in Law' discusses all-encompassing gender-competent legal questions. Having a gender-competent approach is required when considering the highest values and normative standards of modern international, European, and national law. Raising awareness about gender equality issues means investing in the creation, interpretation, and implementation of legislation that is more fair, just, and equitable and will also contribute to a comprehensive understanding of social reality, as well as to gender-competent political, legal and economic decision-making and public policies.

The series accepts monographs focusing on a specific topic, as well as edited collections of articles covering a specific theme or collections of articles.

Nicola Lacey • Miodrag A. Jovanović •
Bojan Spaic • Ana Zdravković
Editors

Reassessing Feminist Legal Theories

Springer

Editors
Nicola Lacey
Law
London School of Economics
London, UK

Miodrag A. Jovanović
Faculty of Law
University of Belgrade
Beograd, Serbia

Bojan Spaic
Faculty of Law
University of Belgrade
Beograd, Serbia

Ana Zdravković
Institute of Comparative Law
Belgrade, Serbia

ISSN 2731-8346 ISSN 2731-8354 (electronic)
Gender Perspectives in Law
ISBN 978-3-031-75422-7 ISBN 978-3-031-75423-4 (eBook)
https://doi.org/10.1007/978-3-031-75423-4

This Springer imprint is published by the registered company Springer Nature Switzerland AG
The registered company address is: Gewerbestrasse 11, 6330 Cham, Switzerland

Contents

Reassessing Feminist Legal Theories: Introduction

Miodrag A. Jovanović and Ana Zdravković

The latest book in the Springer series *Gender Perspectives in Law*, which is entitled *Reassessing Feminist Legal Theories*, offers a perspective on theoretical/philosophical grounding of some of the dominant themes from the disciplinary field. The title of the volume, however, already pinpoints some of the intricate and harshly debated meta-theoretical issues of the scholarship. First of them concerns the adjective 'feminist' in correlation to law. By deliberately merging and contrasting some of the classical works in the field with fresh scholarly contributions, the volume problematizes the very meaning of concepts 'feminism/feminist' and 'gender', their mutual relation, as well as their correlation with 'law'.

To begin with, even if we assume, which is not in itself uncontroversial, that a 'feminist' perspective necessarily depicts the connexion between 'gender' and 'law', it is far from clear how one should think of the resultant disciplinary endeavour. Namely, does this perspective enable grounding of a discipline labelled 'law and gender', akin to similar scholarly fields, such as 'law and society', or 'law and religion'? This seems to be Conaghan's approach, who states at the beginning of her book with that exact title, that it is about "exploring the relationship between law and gender."[1] Alternatively, a feminist perspective may serve the purpose of devising a

[1]Conaghan (2013), p. 5. By the end of the book, she offers some tentative conclusions. Namely, while "gender is not *inherent* in law in any absolute sense", that is, "the law–gender relationship is contingent rather than necessary", this alone "does not preclude a determination that gender is indeed built into the very forms of law", Conaghan (2013), p. 245. Hence, when arguing that "law is gendered", Conaghan is interested in "deploying gender as an evaluative tool in legal contexts", that

M. A. Jovanović
Faculty of Law, University of Belgrade, Beograd, Serbia
e-mail: miodrag@ius.bg.ac.rs

A. Zdravković (✉)
Institute of Comparative Law, Belgrade, Serbia
e-mail: a.zdravkovic@iup.rs

N. Lacey et al. (eds.), *Reassessing Feminist Legal Theories*, Gender Perspectives in Law 5, https://doi.org/10.1007/978-3-031-75423-4_1

distinctive area of law, called 'law on gender'/'gender law', akin to 'law on contracts and torts', or 'criminal law'. In order for something to count as an 'area of law', it should form "a subset of the legal norms in the system", which is as such "intersubjectively recognised by the legal complex in that system",[2] that is, by "a cluster of legal actors",[3] such as "judges, legislators, legal academics, private and government lawyers, civil servants, law reform movements, legal services regulators, law commissions, legal advisors, academic publishers, conference organisers, law journal editors, legal associations, court registries, casebook and textbook writers, case reporters, and the like."[4] It is important to note that, even if the dominant classification system of norms does not contain particular area of law (e.g. gender law'), one of the tasks of legal scholarship may be to try to "inaugurate" such area.[5] A feminist perspective may serve exactly this purpose.

Indeterminacy with respect to what a 'feminist perspective' amounts to has a further implication. Hence, by using 'legal theory' in plural, the volume's title indicates that different theoretical approaches towards the subject matter are possible. Indeed, a cursory overview of the literature demonstrates the lack of consensus when it comes to *the* adequate disciplinary methodology. Feminist jurisprudence is often depicted as a parcel of the wider project of critical legal studies, thereby belonging to what Bentham famously characterized as "censorial jurisprudence".[6] Such is, for example, the understanding of "feminist philosophy of law" as the discipline which "identifies the pervasive influence of patriarchy and masculinist norms on legal structures and demonstrates their effects on the material conditions of women and girls and those who may not conform to cisgender norms. It also considers problems at the intersection of sexuality and law and develops reforms to correct gender injustice, exploitation, or restriction."[7] As such, it "is an effort to

is, in "prompt[ing] a better (more inclusive) understanding of law in which gender considerations come more easily to the fore." See Conaghan (2013), p. 247.

[2] Khaitan and Steel (2023), p. 78.

[3] They are "related to each other in dynamic structures and constituted and reconstituted through a variety of processes", most important of them being "drafting, representing, advising, judging, prosecuting, teaching, and writing law." Karpik and Halliday (2011), pp. 220–221.

[4] Khaitan and Steel emphasize that, "[w]hile legal scholars are part of the legal complex, they matter with respect to determining the existence of an area of law only to the extent that their research and teaching interacts with and influences the practice of law", Khaitan and Steel (2023), p. 80.

[5] Khaitan and Steel (2023), p. 79.

[6] Whereas "expository jurisprudence" is the investigation of what the law is, "censorial jurisprudence" is the investigation of whether the existing law ought to be in line with a certain assumed standard, Bentham (1780/1789) (Kitchener: Batoche Books, 2000), p. 234. *Cf.* Bentham (1891), p. 99.

[7] "To these ends, feminist philosophy of law applies insights from feminist epistemology, relational metaphysics and progressive social ontology, feminist political theory, and other developments in feminist philosophy to understand how legal institutions enforce dominant gendered and masculinist norms. Contemporary feminist philosophy of law also draws from diverse scholarly perspectives such as international human rights theory, postcolonial theory, critical legal studies, critical race theory, queer theory, and disability studies", Francis and Smith (2021). The pressing need to

examine and reformulate legal doctrine to overcome entrenched bias and enforced inequality of the past as it structures human concepts and institutions for the future."[8]

Conaghan is not satisfied with the thus conceived methodological orientation of feminist jurisprudence. She finds it "striking . . . that although feminism and critical legal theory have together produced vast reams of literature which contest virtually every aspect of how law is traditionally conceived, mainstream legal scholarship remains strangely immune to the contamination which such a challenge presents." Therefore, she urges for "a gendered analysis",[9] a seemingly much needed methodological approach for elucidating the relation between gender and law.

Green is, however, unpersuaded by this attempt at providing a feminist analytical jurisprudence. He says that "to establish that the very forms of law are 'gendered' would take an explanation of those forms and an account of the sense in which they are masculine (or feminine)." In Green's opinion, "Conaghan does not undertake that analysis."[10] His ultimate conclusion is that, while "gender is of no relevance to general jurisprudence", it is "highly relevant to law because gender norms shape the content and application of the law." Therefore, gender warrants a familiar normative methodological approach of critical evaluation, but it is also relevant "to some problems in special jurisprudence",[11] understood as a discipline concerned with conceptual problems about some specific doctrinary issues (e.g. in family law, anti-discrimination law, labour law, etc.).[12]

***

The contributions to this volume include papers written by Nicola M. Lacey, Duncan Kennedy, Dragica Vujadinović and Adriana Zaharijević, Duška Franeta, Lídia Balogh, Francesca Poggi, Zara Saeizadeh, Fabio Macioce, Wojciech Załuski and Antonio Álvarez del Cuvillo. The volume opens with the reprints of two remarkable papers that has firstly been published more than two decades ago yet have not lost their relevance.

Nicola M. Lacey addresses the fact that feminism, while challenging the concept of gender or sexual neutrality, questions the very existence of such neutrality—an

---

enhance the legal and factual status of women and girls, including through theoretical considerations of these matters, can also be understood in light of the fact that the prohibition of (gender) discrimination can be regarded as a *jus cogens* norm, see Zdravković (2021), p. 155.

[8] Francis and Smith (2021).

[9] Conaghan (2013), p. 15.

[10] Green (2020), p. 898. And indeed, when defining what she means by the preferred analytical method, Conaghan admits that "a truly gendered analysis turns out to require a layer of investigation not generally considered to be part of legal enquiry. Unearthing the normative premises which support legal rules and doctrines and considering their impact and effects in a wider social, political and cultural context requires a penetration of the boundaries of the strictly legal and a reframing of the legal landscape in terms which threaten the integrity of law as a discrete sphere of operation." Conaghan (2013), pp. 82–83.

[11] Green (2020), p. 911.

[12] Green (2020), p. 894. For reviewing approaches to the gender perspective in Public International Law, see Zdravković (2023) and the reviewed book.

ideal deeply ingrained in the self-conception of a liberal legal order and a crucial methodological tenet of good scholarship. Starting from the position that sex or gender plays a significant role in determining and thus elucidating the structure of social practices such as law, as well as that the impact of gender on society is inherently politically contentious, in the sense that gender serves as a focal point for oppression and inequality rather than just a form of distinction, the paper outlines the evolution of feminist legal thought. Lacey contrasts "liberal feminism" perspective, which highlights the exclusion of women from complete legal subjectivity, focusing on achieving inclusion through sex-blind equality, from "difference feminism", in which the analytical emphasis is on the assimilation of women into a male-centric understanding of legal subjectivity and which advocates for embracing and accommodating gender differences. The paper delves into the 'doble binds' that feminism encounters as it seemingly diverges from the neutrality that plays a central role in contemporary thought and the modern vision of the rule of law, while attempting to explore the implications of difference feminism on feminist practices and answer how this perspective intersects with other critical theories, particularly those addressing class and race issues, together with the question of how the concept of law influences these debates.

Duncan Kennedy offers an in-depth analysis of the complex issues surrounding male sexual abuse of women and provocative dressing, while highlighting two conflicting viewpoints: the "conventional view" which perceives provocative female attire as a trigger for abuse; and "radical feminism" which views sexual abuse as a foundational element of the patriarchal system. Through a thorough examination of how legal systems and mainstream culture eroticize dominance, violence, and abuse, the author recognizes that according to radical feminists, patriarchy manifests itself in the realm of fashion, utilizing sexual abuse as a tool for male disciplinary terror against women. This power dynamic is further entrenched by the integration of erotic pleasures of male dominance in all aspects of society. The paper concludes that abuse is harmful for both genders, not solely due to the imperative of safeguarding human rights, but also because abuse discourages risking different forms of pleasure found in the imagery of anything that abuts the real-life sites of oppression.

First originally published contribution in the book is the one co-authored by Dragica Vujadinović and Adriana Zaharijević, which represents feminist critical reconsideration of justice, identifying that it is necessary to include family justice and gender justice within the inclusive understanding of justice and equality within constitutional democracies and the context of global justice. In addition, it draws attention to the disputable nature of the mainstream separation between the public and private spheres and the ensuing reduction of justice to the public sphere. By challenging the conventional portrayal of justice as a female figure and examining the origins and interpretations of justice, particularly in relation to family and gender dynamics, this chapter delves into the evolving discourse on gender justice within contemporary justice theories. In that regard, John Rawls's idea of justice is specifically examined, together with two other mainstream theories of justice, Michael Walzer's communitarian theory and Philip Green's social-democratic theory, both of which incorporate aspects of family and gender equality. Furthermore, the paper leans on the perspectives of liberal feminist thought on justice of Susan Moller Okin, the feminist socialist thought on justice of Nancy Fraser, and the social justice conception of Iris Marion Young.

Duška Franeta explores the common applications of the concept of human dignity within feminist discussions, particularly the concept of objectification which stems from the Kantian idea that people should not be treated as means to an end. Specifically, this concept is applied to social practices or behaviours that dehumanize women, particularly in contexts related to sex. The paper reminds that certain authors within feminist discourse advocate for the legal abolition of sexual harassment and exploitation, viewing them as forms of objectification, while for others, human dignity is critically examined as an element of (in Peter Sloterdijk's terms) the *thymotic* conceptual arsenal that closely links it to independence, autonomy, impartiality, justice, etc. When viewed in this light, human dignity is seen as disruptive to the acknowledgment of important moral values, potentially reinforcing male dominance over women. A third perspective on the usage of human dignity concentrates on shame societies and the relationship between shame and dignity, while contrasting ancient *dignitas*, shaming practices, patriarchal rank and honour with societies that respect the human dignity of women. These varying interpretations of human dignity in feminist discourse differently reflect on contemporary morality, law, and practical philosophy. Finally, Franeta elucidates ways in which they advocate for a more consistent safeguarding of human dignity, a more nuanced understanding of dignity, and challenge certain foundational aspects of contemporary law and morality.

In the next chapter, Lídia Balogh provokingly questions the role of gender as a legal concept for advancing women's rights, by trying to underline the need to separate law from the realm of activism. By recalling the constructivist understanding of gender in legal and public policy realms, which meant that it primarily served as an analytical concept that encompassed the social roles of women and men, along with the associated social expectations, stereotypes and power dynamics, it is shown that the interpretation of the notion has recently changed, since it has evolved into an activist concept, and this shift may not serve the promotion of women's issues. The analysis suggests that viewing gender as an analytical concept remains valuable in social science research for understanding gender dynamics and addressing social issues. Nonetheless, as a legal concept, gender is shown to be less relevant to women's rights than anticipated and as a political and movement slogan, it may be detrimental to women's causes. The study delves into the complex history of the Istanbul Convention and the contentious debates surrounding gender and women's rights. To contextualize gender as a legal concept, the Balogh draws parallels with the evolution of intersectionality, prompting reflection on whether a concept should be adopted in legal frameworks purely based on its success in academic analysis and activism.

Francesca Poggi conceptually analyses gender-based violence, since the concept is vague and lacks final definition, yet it is still crucial for the feminist movement. Even though the concept of gender-based violence is perhaps one of the most important contributions that feminist thought has made to legal theory and its political and social significance is demonstrated by its widespread adoption in both theory and practice, it still raises several challenges. The theoretical aspect is particularly complex, as there are multiple interpretations of the concept within literature and legal frameworks, leading to ambiguity. From the political perspective, the feminist movement's struggle to assert gender violence has reinforced societal stereotypes by portraying women as weak and as victims. Poggi also recognizes that there has simultaneously been an overemphasis on adopting new gender-oriented criminal offences. The conceptual analysis such as the one included in this chapter should precede the identified debate in order to clarify the notions of violence and gender and their interplay.

Zara Saeizadeh deals with the citizenship of trans* individuals. Feminist perspectives on citizenship have long critiqued the traditional focus on male, white, heterosexual, and able-bodied citizenship. However, many feminist theories on citizenship uphold the gender binary system and the concept of universal rights for all, which often overlooks differences and systemic inequalities. Saeizadeh focuses on how feminist politics address the citizenship of trans* individuals through the framework of trans* citizenship as proposed by Surya Monro, while also considering Nancy Fraser's ideas on recognition. She focuses on the politics of recognition, which highlights the status and needs of citizens as crucial for achieving social justice and also illuminates the limitations of identity-based politics of recognition in feminist theories and practices which have led to social injustices and affected trans* people's needs, directly impacting their citizenship. It is argued that trans* citizenship demands the attention of feminist socio-legal researchers, practitioners, and policy makers to address the social status and needs of trans* individuals, recognizing the diversity of their knowledge and experiences.

In the paper by Fabio Macioce, the notion of vulnerability is reassessed from a feminist perspective, bearing in mind the connection between privilege and gender oppression. Within the feminist debate, it was developed in light of women's status and the issue of gender-based violence. In this later context, the notion of vulnerability has faced significant criticism for being seen as promoting unjustified essentialism and potentially reinforcing exclusion and victimhood. The paper aims to demonstrate how re-evaluating the concept of vulnerability, especially group vulnerability, can be both theoretically coherent and politically beneficial. By fostering forms of collective agency that are politically constructive, Macioce suggests that reconsideration of vulnerability can serve as a prerequisite for contesting prevailing power hierarchies, fostering new dialogues, introducing alternative narratives and uniting otherwise marginalized interests and needs.

Wojciech Załuski reflects on whether the "reasonable person standard" should be "genderized", since some courts have already adopted the "reasonable woman standard" within sexual harassment law, assuming that women have a lower threshold for identifying conduct as sexual harassment compared to men. The analysis identifies the most common arguments against such change, together with its normative implications. The main criticisms are that it may reinforce gender stereotypes and lacks a solid scientific foundation. However, it is argued in this paper that the latter objection is not as strong, since scientific theories, such as evolutionary theory and neuroscience, support the idea of gender differences in the perception of sexual misconduct, as well as in other mental traits like attitude to risk, dominance assertion, and empathy. This suggests a following normative implication: instead of confining the reasonable woman standard to sexual harassment cases alone, it is proposed for consistency reasons either to completely discard gender differentiation in the standard (if one agrees with the first objection and/or believes that 'reasonableness' should be defined by mental faculties common to both genders), or to apply it in more legal contexts beyond sexual harassment law. The paper advocates for the former option, which involves embracing a personalist (i.e. based on philosophical view called "personalism") interpretation of the reasonable person standard, as a more convincing approach.

In the final chapter, Antonio Álvarez del Cuvillo recalls that certain feminist authors claimed that individualist notion of discrimination, derived from Aristotelian concept of equality, ineffectively address women's oppression. This concept is closely related to the idea of substantial equality prevalent in modern democracies. However, the regulations against discrimination often rely on individualistic legal frameworks, which can be narrowly interpreted by legal practitioners, reducing marginalized groups to abstract reasons for differentiated treatment. In order to reconstruct a group-based understanding of sex discrimination, it is essential to develop a theory on the damage caused by discriminatory conduct, articulating both individual and social harm. The paper claims that such an approach sheds light on various issues, including justifying affirmative action, the possibility of reverse discrimination, applying discrimination by association, distinguishing discrimination from stigmatization, and considering whether men can challenge indirect discrimination that harms them individually and women globally.

***

Volumes of this sort are rarely expected to solve all the open issues in the given disciplinary field. In that respect, this volume is no exception. Although at times it may appear to reinforce some of the aforementioned divisions within the scholarship, it nonetheless strives to open the room for distinctive methodological approaches to various gender issues. In doing so, the volume fosters the idea that feminist scholarship is—to paraphrase Julie Dickson's dictum for general jurisprudence—"a broad church",[13] insofar as it welcomes all theoretical accounts that can elucidate various complex aspects of the relation between gender and law.

References

Bentham J (1780/1789) An introduction to the principles of morals and legislation. Batoche Books (2000)

[13] Dickson (2015), pp. 207–230.

Bentham J (1891) A fragment on government (with an introduction by F. C. Montague). Clarendon Press, Oxford
Conaghan J (2013) Law and gender. Oxford University Press
Dickson J (2015) Ours is a broad church: indirectly evaluative legal philosophy as a facet of jurisprudential inquiry. Jurisprudence Int J Legal Polit Thought 6(2):207–230
Francis L, Smith P (2021) Feminist Philosophy of Law. In: Zalta EN (ed) The Stanford Encyclopedia of Philosophy. At https://plato.stanford.edu/archives/fall2021/entries/feminism-law/. Accessed 1 June 2024
Green L (2020) Gender and the analytical jurisprudential mind. Mod Law Rev 83(4):893–912
Karpik L, Halliday TC (2011) The legal complex. Ann Rev Law Soc Sci 7:217–236
Khaitan T, Steel S (2023) Areas of law: three questions in special jurisprudence. Oxf J Leg Stud 43(1):76–96
Zdravković A (2021) Finding the core of international law - Jus Cogens in the work of international law commission. SEE EU Cluster of Excellence in European and International Law, Series of Papers. Europa Institut, University of Saarbrücken, pp 141–158
Zdravković A (2023) Krstić, Ivana, Marco Evola, Maria Isabel Ribes Moreno (eds) 2023. Legal issues of international law from a gender perspective. Springer, Cham, p 224. Annals of the Faculty of Law in Belgrade 71(3):629–642

Feminist Legal Theory Beyond Neutrality

Nicola Lacey

Contents

Abstract The paper explores the intersection of feminist legal theory and the concept of neutrality, addressing the challenges contemporary feminist legal scholarship faces in reconciling the ideal of gender or sexual neutrality with the realities of legal practice. It examines the evolution from liberal feminism, which emphasises sex-blind equality, to difference feminism, which highlights the importance of recognising and accommodating differences. Through a critical analysis of supposed 'double binds' confronting difference feminism, the paper investigates the

I should like to acknowledge with very warm thanks the importance of the discussions I had with David Soskice whilst I was writing this paper; the openness and generosity with which he entered into dialogue was a mark of the possibility of the exchange across disciplines to which the paper seeks to contribute. I should also like to thank the audience to whom the lecture was delivered, whose questions helped me to develop its argument; Anton Schütz, who engaged me in critical dialogue about its contents; and Peter Goodrich, with whom I had thought-provoking discussions of Irigaray.

N. Lacey (✉)
London School of Economics, London, UK
e-mail: n.m.lacey@lse.ac.uk

N. Lacey et al. (eds.), *Reassessing Feminist Legal Theories*, Gender Perspectives in Law 5, https://doi.org/10.1007/978-3-031-75423-4_2

implications of contextualising legal subjects within broader social and relational contexts. It also evaluates the interplay between feminist legal theory and other critical theories, particularly concerning class and race. By delving into current debates on legal subject conceptualisation, the role of psychoanalysis in feminist thought, and the advocacy for special rights for women, the paper aims to provide a nuanced understanding of how feminist strategies can navigate and potentially subvert entrenched stereotypes and power dynamics within the legal system.

> *Le neutre est suppose representer un ni-l'un-ni-l'autre. Avant que ce ni-l'un-ni-l'autre puisse se signifier, il importe que l'un et l'autre existent, que deux identites soient definies differement que comme poles artificiellement opposes d'un modele humain unique'.* (Luce Irigaray, *J'aime à toi*, Paris, Grasset 1992, p. 198.)

1 Introduction

The figure of neutrality stands in many ways as a powerful symbol for the challenges faced by contemporary feminist legal scholarship. For in questioning not only the reality but the very possibility of gender or sexual neutrality, feminism has pitched itself against both an ideal which lies at the heart of the ideological self-conception of a liberal legal order, and a key methodological tenet of what has been taken to be good scholarship. In this paper, my focus will be on some supposed 'double binds' which confront feminism as it appears to turn away from the neutrality which has a central place in the framework of modern thought and in the modern ideal of the rule of law. But I could hardly fail to be aware of the second problem, writing, as I am, a paper to be delivered on a platform from which, as a student, I was lectured on the overweening importance of understanding the difference between the law as it is and as it ought to be, and in terms which generally assumed the autonomy and integrity of law and legal method. This positivist stance did not invariably preclude a certain reflexivity about the lecturer's standpoint. I remember being advised, on one particularly memorable occasion, that the ensuing lecture would be based on two premises: first, that the Oxford English Dictionary was always right; and second, that whatever the Queen in Parliament enacted was law. Following and indeed expanding on this good example, I should begin by stating that my lecture is based not on two but on three premises: first, that sex or gender is one important factor in determining and hence in explaining the shape of social practices such as law; second, that the ways in which gender shapes the social world are presumptively politically problematic—that is, that gender has marked an axis of oppression and injustice rather than a mere differentiation; and third, that writing, as I shall, in the first person, does not undermine any value which there may be in what I have to say.[1]

[1] Beyond this minimal statement of what I take to be the modest premises of feminism, I shall not occupy myself with questions about the status of feminist or other critical projects in relation to law,

I want to begin by sketching, in a necessarily caricatured way, the development of feminist legal thought from one position to another.[2] The first position-I shall call it 'liberal feminism'-is one in which the analytic emphasis is on the implicit and explicit exclusion of women from the full status of legal subject, whilst the normative emphasis is on our inclusion via a strategy of sex-blind equality. The second, which I shall label 'difference feminism', is one in which the analytic focus is on a problematic assimilation of women to a substantially male conception of legal subjectivity, and in which the normative emphasis is on the recognition and accommodation of difference. After colouring these sketches in, I shall go on to consider a number of apparent 'double binds' which are thought to confront difference feminism. The particular questions which I want to address are these. First, what sort of feminist practice does difference feminism imply, and under what conditions can the practices which it engenders avoid reproducing images of sexual difference as, if not 'essential', at least shaped in relatively intractable ways? Secondly, how does this issue affect the relationship between difference feminism and other critical theories, particularly those concerned with questions of class and race? And thirdly, how is the structure of these problems affected by the ways in which we conceptualise law or the legal? I shall think through these questions in relation to three current debates: first, a debate about how the legal subject is conceptualised; second, a debate about the place of psychoanalysis in feminist thought; and third, a debate about the desirability of special rights for women.

2 Feminist Legal Theory: From the Age of Innocence to the Color Purple?

The premises which informed liberal feminism and what might be called feminist legal theory's age of innocence are well known and can be very simply stated. In a variety of ways, implicitly and explicitly, women had been excluded from

many of which I take to have been resolved by the 'interpretive turn' in social theory. I do, however, want to record my pleasure in the Faculty's invitation to me to speak on a specifically feminist theme, and my gratitude to Helena Kennedy for her generosity in chairing the lecture. The invitation was one which I was only too happy to accept, conscious as I am of what it meant to me to be both student and teacher in a university with radical traditions and in which a woman's sex has never been institutionalised as a barrier to membership of the intellectual community. It is also a pleasure to have this occasion to express my appreciation of the intellectual companionship and the personal support and encouragement which several of my teachers and later colleagues at U.C.L. provided.

[2] The characterisation is schematic and does not attempt to incorporate every position associated with feminist legal thought: it is designed rather to point up the particular trajectory which will be the main focus of my discussion. Similarly, the labels are used as a matter of expositional convenience: I do not mean to imply, for example, that all exponents of positions within the spectrum of 'difference feminism' see themselves as moving beyond the ambit of liberal politics, broadly understood. Whilst some of the questions raised by difference feminism about liberalism and about the philosophical discourse of modernity are addressed indirectly later in the paper, a full analysis of these issues runs well beyond its scope.

membership of the community of legal subjects. Whilst explicit discrimination such as the exclusion of women from political suffrage and from rights of ownership had largely been swept away by the time of feminism's rebirth in the 1960s, feminist lawyers pointed out a myriad of subtler and more indirect ways in which the constitution of legal rules and categories in fact excluded or disadvantaged women, and expressed a view of the world which reflected male interests.[3] This feminist analysis drew on a distinction between sex and gender, and, in doing so, sought to undermine received views about the importance of 'natural' differences between the sexes. Since the ancient disadvantages and exclusions which had marked the legal status of women had generally been justified in terms of supposedly 'natural' characteristics and incapacities, the interpretation of many, if not most, of these differences as social constructs-as matters of gender rather than of 'given' sex-assumed a distinctive political importance. For if the social meanings of gender were contingent, albeit powerful, this entailed first, that they could no longer feature as counters in the justification for differential treatment; and second, that they could be changed by changing powerful social practices such as law. Notwithstanding references to biological differences such as reproductive capacities which would call for appropriately but exceptionally different treatment, sex difference per se was accorded little importance: what mattered to liberal feminism was the way the meaning of sex-i.e. gender-had been constructed. And if sex difference was unimportant, it could hardly he a barrier to a sexually universal-or neutral- conception of citizenship and legal subjecthood.

The task of constructing this feminist critique was, of course, a laborious one. It entailed an elaboration of the detailed ways in which the shape and enforcement of, for example, laws on rape, child custody, part time work, or marital property, in fact had an adverse impact on women.[4] But the politics which informed the task was relatively unproblematic. For it was, in essence, the very same politics which informed the ideological self-conception of the liberal and democratic legal order which it took itself to be criticising. The argument was simply this: if, as a liberal society, you profess to accord women the full rights of citizenship, then you are logically committed to attending to the various ways in which your legal framework in fact falls short of this universalist ideal. Give women the same rights and entitlements as you give to men; treat women equally; dispense your justice even-handedly. Live up, in other words, to the ideal of neutrality between persons which is a central component of the modern imaginary. The clearest symbol of this brand of legal feminism's political achievement in the UK is probably therefore the Sex Discrimination Act 1975, which prohibits not discrimination against women, but rather discrimination *on grounds of sex.*[5]

---

[3] For an example of this kind of work, see Atkins and Hoggett (1984).

[4] It also, crucially, entailed a careful analysis of the general patterns of legal intervention and non-intervention.

[5] It is interesting to note that this was, even formally, a commitment to sex neutrality but not, strictly speaking, to gender neutrality. For if gender is defined as that set of social practices and discourses

The position I have just described is often characterised in later feminist work as the call for formal as opposed to substantive equality.[6] This is something of a misdescription, because even this early liberal feminism went well beyond a call for formally equal status. For example, in deciding what would count as equal treatment, the present effects of past discrimination, which marked sexually the impact of sexually neutral rules, could be taken into account-as in the SDA's conception of indirect discrimination. And this concern not just with the formal surfaces of law but with its impact entailed a strong affinity between feminist scholarship and detailed socio-legal research which reached beyond the bounds of legal doctrine-cases and statutes-to comprehend enforcement practices, broadly understood.[7] This is an affinity which characterises feminist legal research to this day, and it is one which, as I shall argue in more detail later, we forget at our peril. Furthermore, the caricature of liberal equality as inevitably premised on 'sameness' is an exaggeration: liberal theorists such as Ronald Dworkin, for example, have been concerned to emphasise the notion of equality as 'treatment as an equal' rather than as 'equal treatment'.[8]

Nonetheless, it is clear that in several important respects liberal feminism contained the seeds of its own deconstruction, and these were quickly identified by difference feminism. The basic problems of liberal feminism were as intimately linked with its conceptual framework as the form/substance distinction which I have mentioned. One set of problems had to do with a particular configuration of the division between public and private, which feminists questioned in a way which began to take their feminism beyond the bounds of the liberalism which had given it birth.[9] This important subject has been very fully analysed and I will not address it in this paper.

The problem on which I do want to focus is the simple fact that liberal feminism's central ideal amounted to a strategy of assimilation of women to a standard set by and for men.[10] The rights assigned to men as legal subjects had to be made available to women wherever a comparison between the treatment of the two revealed a disparity: but the equalisation was almost invariably in one direction-towards a male norm. The radical potential inherent in the idea of 'treatment as an equal'

which determine the meaning of a woman's or a man's sexual identity, it can hardly be doubted to include our sexual orientation. And the SDA does not straightforwardly encompass discrimination on grounds of sexuality as opposed to sex. Cf. Drucilla Cornell's argument for encompassing discrimination on grounds of sexual orientation within Title VII of the U.S. Civil Rights Act: 'Gender, Sex and Equivalent Rights', in Butler and Scott (1992), p. 280. For further discussion, see below at fn. 62.

[6]See for example Katherine O'Donovan (1985), Chapter 7; Smart (1989), pp. 82–5, 139–44.

[7]A good example is Carol Smart's *The Ties that Bind*, Routledge (1984).

[8]Dworkin (1977), p. 227. This is not to imply that Dworkin's theory in general is satisfactory from a feminist point of view: see Frazer and Lacey (1993), pp. 53–77; Hunt and Kerruish (1992).

[9]Lacey (1993), O'Donovan (1985), Olsen (1983).

[10]Lacey (1986), Cornell (1992a), p. 280: O'Donovan (1985), Chapter 7; O'Donovan and Szyszczak (1988).

was not realised, because the political debate issued in by liberal feminism was highly circumscribed. Far from engendering a substantial reconsideration of the way in which the world was organised, the public standards already in place were assumed to be valid, and the feminist conceptual tools of bias, discrimination, equal worth measured against them. To borrow Katherine O'Donovan's formulation, the general tendency was simply to assume that 'a woman could be more like a man'. And even the occasionally converse strategy-that of 'making a man more like a woman'-left in place prevailing views about sexual difference and, crucially, about its specific shape.[11] On the view emerging in the difference feminism which challenged liberal feminism, the SDA was toppled from its position at the summit of feminist achievement. With its symmetrical and comparative method and its sex-neutral conceptual framework, it became instead the symbol of the effacement of the feminine, of women, from legal discourse-an effacement which was all the more problematic because it was effected in the name of sexual equality.

The general shape of difference feminism entailed, of course, its own set of laborious and detailed analytic tasks. It brought with it a shift of emphasis beyond a concern with the differential impact of laws on subjects pre-formed as women and men to the recognition and explication of a more dynamic role for law in constructing and underpinning gender hierarchies.[12] It entailed the need to focus not just on law's construction of images of women and femininity but also its constitutions of men and masculinity. If the argument about the pitfalls of the liberal/comparative approach was to be made out, we had to substantiate the central claim that the legal subjecthood to which women had been assimilated was implicitly male, and possibly that the very methods of legal practices were masculine. Our focus shifted-in common with broader developments in critical legal theory-from the instrumental aspects of law to its symbolic aspects. The messages about women and men transmitted by law; the role of law as a discursive practice into which the material realities of women's and men's embodied lives are inserted, and in which the assumptions underlying law's conceptualisation of subjecthood are constructed as (T)ruths; the subtle role of law in categorising and disciplining its subjects: all these became the stuff of critical legal analysis, accompanying and sometimes displacing the more materialist focus of earlier critical traditions informed by Marxism.[13] As befitted the focus on discourse, the main emphasis of this feminist scholarship was on critical analysis. But an underlying normative commitment to the recognition of differently constituted subjectivities could be perceived from very early on and has become both more insistent and more explicit with time. A new set of utopias began to emerge, and they were oriented to the construction or imagination of a more polyphonous and inclusive law, and to thinking beyond a law whose dominant mode is to fix its subjects' sexual or other identities within rigid categories.

[11] O'Donovan (1985), Chapter 7 and 8.

[12] For a variety of work representing this kind of development, see Naffine (1990), Smart (1989), Graycar and Morgan (1990), Cornell (1991), Frug (1992).

[13] See Collins (1982).

3 More on the Subject of Sex

I now want to give a somewhat more detailed account of just how the critique associated with difference feminism conceptualises the legal subject and argues for its maleness. The basic argument is that the paradigm legal subject has been constructed as an individual, and moreover as an individual abstracted from its social context, including the context of its own body, and of the dependence of its own identity on its relationship towards and affective ties with others.[14] The features of the subject to which legal rules and methods attach importance is characterised in terms of a number of distinctive capacities, foremost among which is reason: paradigm legal subjects are those who have the capacities for rational understanding, reflection and control of their own actions. It is this emphasis on reason and the capacity for self-control which underpins the equation of individual rational subjectivity with masculinity.

The argument depends on an assertion of the power of a number of binary oppositions within (and indeed prior to) modern Western thought. Important examples include reason and emotion, self and other, individual and community, mind and body, public and private, male and female. The crucial step in the feminist deployment of this argument depends on three assertions: first, that these oppositions are dichotomous-in other words that each member of the pair is defined in opposition to, and is hence inconsistent with, the other: second, that the dichotomies are marked by hierarchy-in other words, that one member of the pair has been privileged in modern western thought and social practice; and third, that the hierarchies are marked, among other things, by sex-in other words, that the feminine has been associated with the less valued members of each pair.[15] The feminine, and hence women, have been associated with emotion, the body, the private; masculinity, and hence men, with reason, the mind, the public. To the extent, then, that the conceptualisation of subjects within legal doctrine, and the insertion of embodied women and men into those frameworks via legal discourse, are genuinely marked by the features of reason and individuality and by the repression or forgetting of the body and affectivity, and to the extent that these hallmarks of subjecthood are elevated to the status of objectivity or universality, women will find themselves constructed as non-standard, as other.

This is not to say, however, that the feminine has no role to play within the legal construction of subjecthood. On the contrary, according to this argument woman's role as other is integral to man's constitution as one: the woman as other acts as the support which gives back to man, in a mirror image, his sense of the integrity of his own identity. This function is poetically evoked by Luce Irigaray in the following passage from her letter to Nietzsche:

---

[14] See Naffine (1990, 1994); for analogous arguments in philosophy and political theory see Jaggar (1983), Chapters 3 and 7; Lloyd (1984); Frazer and Lacey (1993), Chapters 2 and 3; Taylor (1985), pp. 187–210.

[15] For an elegant statement of these arguments, see Olsen (1990), pp. 199–215.

'Learn what was the foundation of everything you have built up. If you want to rise up once more, remember the earth you take flight from. For if she were to fail you, you would lose the very sensation of height.[16]

And should you [here the addressee is female] stir even ever so slightly, that tightrope walker up there may fall into the abyss! That is how he manages to stay up there alone-if you don't remain the prisoner of his lack of freedom, he falls! And as (he) takes each next step, (he) suffers from the risk that it entails! And each time (he) plunges back into the depths of the flesh, her stillness exalts him and (he) thrills at the brilliance of his new exploit! As with her subterranean and submarine strength she keeps the rope secure for his glorious ascent.'[17]

The point is made more directly by Ngaire Naffine:

'Officially, the legal subject is potentially anyone, anywhere. And it is this any-person ness of the legal person which is supposed to ensure that the law is at the disposal of us all, equally-without fear, favour or affection. This book, however, has found the legal subject to be someone with a quite specific set of distinguishing characteristics. But these characteristics do not sit easily together. On the one hand our man of law is assumed to be a freestanding, autonomous creature, rationally self-interested and hard- headed; on the other hand he is a being who is assumed both to have and to need access to the values of Gemeinschaft, the family values, though he must not display them in his public, legal Gesellschaft life. The legal person described here is thus essentially a paradox . . .

The argument of this volume has been that the law . . . assigns to women the job of holding the two worlds together . . . As the courts continue to tell us, the Gemeinschaft functions are vital and necessary ones, but they are most appropriately performed by dutiful wives and mothers-not by the man of law. Women's domestic labours sustain the paradox of the man of law.'[18]

The unacknowledged feminine, then, operates as a necessary complement to the in fact partial constitution of the masculine subject of legal doctrine: its hidden existence is essential to the conjuring trick which sustains the illusion of the (masculine) subject's self-identity.

4 Mapping the (Apparent) Double Binds

I now want to sketch what are often thought to be double binds for difference feminism. I have already observed that one of the beauties of early liberal legal feminism was the relative simplicity of its politics: essentially, its politics was not

[16]Irigaray (1991), p. 20.

[17]Irigaray (1991), p. 24.

[18]Naffine (1990), pp. 148–149. The difference in written style of Naffine's and Irigaray's overlapping arguments is itself significant. Whilst Irigary speaks to us directly, Naffine's subjectivity is distanced by the use of the neutral, and hence, according to the logic of her own argument, masculine third person. I shall take up the question of written style and feminist theory in the final section of the paper.

oppositional, except at the level of challenging men's self interest. Its analysis was the quintessential expression of the philosophical discourse of modernity; its ideology was liberal; and, on the assumption that that liberal ideology was widely shared, its strategy was simply to appeal to the good faith of those in political and legal power. Doubtless, given the strength of those interests and the short supply of good faith, this in itself was rarely a directly effective approach. But, in principle, there was an easy and very direct inference from theory or analysis to policy or strategy. And this was highly sympathetic for feminism, which has always affirmed the intimacy of theory and practice.

With the move away from liberal feminism, this simplicity disappeared. And a more sophisticated and complex analysis seemed to entail a far more complicated politics. This 'loss of innocence' is perhaps most graphically and simply evoked in Audre Lorde's famous metaphor: one cannot use the master's tools to destroy the master's house.[19] Once law itself, and indeed the very framework of liberal politics, had been argued to be part of the problem, it no longer represented a straightforwardly usable tool for feminist legal strategy.[20] But the problem was not merely strategic: it was also conceptual. In the liberal feminist critique, feminists were able to draw on a rich set of normative and conceptual resources: the language of rights, justice and equality was readily and unproblematically available as the medium for the articulation of feminist criticisms and claims. But since, according to later feminism, these concepts too were marked by masculinity, they could no longer be appealed to in the construction of feminist utopias-or they could only be appealed to once they had been substantially reconstructed.[21] This seemed to locate an important part of the feminist critical enterprise at the level of conceptual and hence linguistic reconstruction. But here we seemed to be stuck in another cul de sac-and, worse, one constructed by the very theories which had helped us to form our feminist critique. For language, too, was being reinterpreted as a social practice which itself reflects and reproduces gendered configurations of power.[22] This is the first double bind which appears to confront difference feminism.

A further problem arose from the fact that the practices which we sought to criticise had already developed to accommodate significant elements of liberal feminism. Our successes in shifting the borders between sex and gender-in interpreting more and more differences between women's and men's lives as matters of constructed gender rather than given sex-had drawn us into a politics which assumed that the positing of gender neutrality would engender sexual equality. Persisting inequalities could be legitimated as determined by the choices of autonomous liberal individuals. In law, this had made the problem of sexual difference all

[19] Lorde (1984).

[20] This problem is most insistently expressed in Carol Smart's argument for the 'decentring' of law: Smart (1989), Chapters 1, 4, 7 & 8.

[21] See Fudge (1989), p. 445; Kingdom (1991); Smart (1989), Chapter 7. On reconstruction, see for example Littleton (1987); Cornell (1991); Nedelsky (1989), p. 7.

[22] Cornell (1991), Chapter 2.

but invisible, thus arguably engendering an even more difficult struggle-that to recover our sexed bodies, demand that they be taken notice of, and, most difficult of all, articulate that demand in terms which do not invite response in terms of the very stereotypes about women which we tried to overcome with the strategy of neutrality. The problem was simply that whilst gender-the social meaning of sex-was indeed contingent, the mapping of gender onto sexed bodies was, as a matter of history, distinctly patterned. Yet in tracing the ways in which laws and other social practices involved in imagining and discursively constructing reality consistently mapped certain configurations of gender onto particular sexed bodies, we appeared to be open to precisely the charge of sex essentialism which it had been the project of early feminism to deconstruct.[23] And here emerges a second, apparent, double bind.

5 The Subject of Criminalisation

5.1 Contextualisation as Critique

I now want to take a closer look at difference feminism's critique of the legal subject by locating it within some specific debates in criminal law. I want to suggest that, although the supposed double binds which I have identified can indeed be loosened, our ability to do so has been hampered by a failure to distinguish between two different arguments. The first is a critical analysis of the conceptual framework of legal doctrine; the second is an argument about the basically extra-legal assumptions about masculinity and femininity which mark the insertion of women and men into that conceptual framework via legal discourse. I shall argue that we have sometimes been too quick to map a philosophical argument about the conceptual construction of subjecthood in legal doctrine onto a broader set of discourses whose assumptions about gendered subjecthood are in fact more open and fragmented, and even less stable and consistent, than those of the doctrinal framework itself.

There is a striking affinity between the feminist argument about the contours of the legal subject and that developed within critical legal theory such as that in the criminal law sphere. Consider for a moment the standard conceptualisation of the responsible subject in criminal law, as encapsulated within H. L. A. Hart's influential theory.[24] The subject who is fairly held accountable for his actions is one who has standard cognitive and volitional capacities: only if he understands the nature of his action, and had a fair opportunity to act otherwise than he did, will it be appropriate

[23] For there was always a lurking question which our opponents wanted us to answer: if gender was constructed and contingent, why was the pattern so consistent? My point here is basically a tactical one. A politics which insists on both the contingency and the power and patterning of gender is engaged in something akin to a tightrope walk, in which its balance may easily be knocked by its opponents. For a thoughtful discussion of the problems confronting use of the sex/gender distinction, see Williams (1989), p. 797.

[24] Hart (1968).

to hold him responsible for it. In terms of legal doctrine, this theory issues in a paradigm conception of fault or 'mens rea' as intention or subjective recklessness: choosing to do an act or bring about a consequence in so far as it is within your power to do so, or acting in awareness of the likely consequences of your actions. To the extent that objective forms of liability can be accommodated on this view, it is on the basis that the subject's normal capacities imply that he could have reached a 'reasonable' standard of care or behaviour had he chosen to do so. The contortions undertaken by both judges and scholars to accommodate strict and more fully objective standards of liability within this essentially liberal account have been analysed at length elsewhere, and I shall not consider them here.[25] What I shall do is to sketch an influential critique—that of Alan Norrie-and to trace its continuities with the feminist argument that the legal subject is essentially male.

Norrie's argument is basically this.[26] The dominant mode of attributing responsibility in criminal law constructs the subject of criminalisation as an abstract individual judged out with the broad parameters of his social context. The conditions of responsibility which legitimate the state's coercive response are essentially factual ones having to do with mental states contemporaneous with the commission of the offence. By decontextualising the judging process in this way, criminal law attempts to ensure its own legitimacy by insisting that it ascribes responsibility on fair terms, as is required by the punitive nature of its response, the general value ascribed to autonomy in liberal society, and the quasi-moral mode of judgment employed by criminalisation.[27] This decontextualised and formalised mode of attribution serves to keep out of the courtroom the muddying social and political issues which are in fact deeply implicated in a broader understanding of how behaviour comes to be defined as criminal: it keeps out of sight those facts which produce the embarrassing truth that criminalising power in fact disciplines a sector of the population vividly marked by socio-economic status, by race or ethnicity, and by sex. It constructs legal justice, in other words, in a way which keeps it relatively insulated from broader notions of social justice.

But the strategy is highly unstable. This is because the imperative for criminal law to legitimate itself within a liberal framework constantly leads to doctrinal concessions which in fact reveal the broader relevance of the subject's social context.[28] For example, the defences of necessity, provocation, self-defence or duress shift the time-frame of the law's inquiry away from the moment of the commission of the

---

[25] See for example Lacey et al. (1990), Chapter 1; Lacey (1985), p. 453; Wells (1982), p. 209.

[26] What follows is a schematic reconstruction of the argument of Norrie's Crime, Reason and History (1993).

[27] I leave aside here the fact that criminal law often operates more as a bureaucratic/administrative system than as a quasi-moral one. I think that the diversity of modes of criminalisation in fact adds strength to the argument which follows, but it complicates it in a way which reaches beyond the scope of the paper. For further discussion see Farmer (1992) Chapters 1 and 2. For further discussion of the analogy between legal and moral judgment, and of its limits, see Norrie (1995).

[28] *Cf.* the argument made by Naffine in the passage quoted above at note 18.

'actus reus' to encompass as relevant a wider set of antecedents.[29] Debates about 'reasonableness' inevitably raise ethical and political questions. And at the sentencing stage, the defendant's action is even more fully contextualised, with the production of social inquiry reports which, even within a just deserts approach to punishment, envisage a degree of discretionary individualisation-of particular rather than standardised justice—which is at odds with paradigm legal method.[30] Of course, within doctrine, criminal law has a number of strategies geared to containing these concessions within narrow limits-for example by constructing defences as excuses which go to 'factual' aspects of the defendant's responsibility rather than as justifications which embody a more 'at large' questioning of the actual standard being applied.[31] But the fluidity of the conceptual categories of legal doctrine which these 'exceptional' concessions reveal itself unsettles the common-sensical givenness of the 'normal' mode of attributing responsibility. The careful delineation of the departures of legal doctrine from its own standard method is therefore an effective critical strategy for exposing the politics of criminal law.

It should be fairly obvious even from this brief sketch that there are strong continuities between this critique of the contours of the subject of criminal law and the feminist argument about the masculinity of the legal subject.[32] A central aspect of the argument in both difference feminism and critical criminal law is a strategy of what we might call recontextualisation *as critique*. In Norrie's account, subjects of criminalisation are recontextualised within a political and socio-economic world whose conditions help to explain the substantively differential chances which differently situated subjects have to keep within the norms of criminal law as interpreted by enforcement agencies.[33] This argument is used in turn to undermine the supposed legitimacy of liberal systems of criminal law, and to reveal the ideological operations within doctrine which sustain that image of legitimacy. Feminist theory also recontextualises the subject-for example the woman who has killed her husband within the long-term context of his violence towards her, or within more general gendered imbalances of power. And this is used as a discursive strategy to reveal the substantive sexual injustice of the application of the criminal law's usually circumscribed focus. By seeing how criminal law excludes certain features of context which are extra-legally crucial to the shape of women's lives, we

[29] *Cf.* Kelman (1981), p. 181.

[30] *Cf.* the broader argument made by Daly (1989).

[31] See for example Lacey et al. (1990), pp. 38–40, 490–500; Norrie (1995).

[32] This is not to say, however, that critical criminal lawyers have been quick to make the connection. My own book on punishment (1988) which employs a similar argument about liberal individualism in a critical analysis of theories of punishment; is one whose pages are peopled by feminine pronouns but not by embodied women, whose substantive voices are perhaps all the more firmly silenced through the grammatical tokens which I used. In the index of Norrie's book, we find white collar crime but not women; serial murder, but not sex; jack the ripper, but not gender.

[33] These should be broadly understood to include not only official agencies such as police and courts but also, for example, news media and ordinary citizens, whose reports to the police are the main initiators of the criminal process.

can reveal how women (and indeed non-'normally' situated men) are silenced. For they are made to tell their stories within a framework which, by assuming a particular image of 'normal' subjecthood, systematically excludes certain features of experience and keeps difficult political issues about imbalances of power out of the courtroom. This is an argument which of course reveals law's method not so much as a decontextualisation but rather as itself a specific and politically problematic contextualisation: abstraction is an ideology as much as a fact, and what matters is what gets abstracted and how.

5.2 Contextualisation as Feminist Strategy

In some of its forms, however, the feminist argument builds on its critical recontextualisation to make a further and significantly different set of normative and strategic points. It asserts that the recognition and realisation of intersubjectivity and connection—what we might call the relational aspect of subjectivity-has itself been of greater importance in women's than in men's lives. Furthermore, it has been marked as feminine in our culture and correspondingly disvalued. One important source of this kind of argument is Carol Gilligan's book *In a Different Voice*,[34] which drew a distinction between an individualistic, rights or justice-based mode of constructing moral questions and a holistic, responsibility-based, relational or caring model. Debate has raged about how we should understand Gilligan's association of the caring voice with women: whether this is a replay of damaging gender essentialism; whether the caring voice is, rather than something to be valued and celebrated, in fact the voice of the oppressed; and what the implications are for the critique and reconstruction of law and legal method. Here I merely want to point out the way in which arguments like Gilligan's have sometimes been taken to provide an ethical mandate for a set of institutional strategies which seek to relocate the legal subject within a broader bodily, psychological and relational context. This has taken the well-known shape, for example, of arguments for specific defences such as that based on pre-menstrual syndrome or battered women's syndrome, or, perhaps less problematically, the reconstruction of existing defences such as provocation, diminished responsibility or self-defence in terms which take account of broader features of a woman's situation which are relevant to the behaviour in question.[35] I want to consider this feminist leaning towards strategies of contextualisation, which I think entails certain confusions and complexities which have sometimes gone unnoticed.

What are we to make of the idea that a legal method which contextualised subjects more broadly-attending to their bodies, their relationships and

[34] Gilligan (1982); for critical discussion, see Benhabib (1992), Chapters 5 and 6; Larrabee (1993); Frug (1992), Chapter 3.

[35] O'Donovan (1991), p. 219; McColgan (1993), p. 508.

responsibilities-would in itself be favourable to women?[36] Clearly, the question of how we recognise and accommodate all subjects' interdependence, how we recognise the relational, embodied and affective aspects of lived experience within institutions whose method is to judge, fix, categories (indeed whether these features of legal method could go unreconstructed) is crucially important. But the notion that we could make any progress to its solution by an introduction of increased 'contextualisation' of the conceptual framework of legal subjecthood strikes me as somewhat naive.[37] For the idea that contextualisation within a broader set of relationships could in itself be progressive seems to depend on the idea that the broader social relationships within which we might locate a reconceptualised legal subject (for example by modifying rules of evidence to encompass the subject's location within the practices of the family, of the labour market, of the political sphere) and the non-legal discourses of femininity and masculinity which might thereby be invoked, can be assumed, on average, to be less excluding of women, less limiting and less strongly marked by stereotyped assumptions about sex difference than legal discourse and legal practice themselves. It assumes, in other words, that these other social practices are less implicated in the cultural production of a particular masculinity and femininity than is law.

It may well be that local instances afford opportunities of progressive recontextualisation. The weakening of the immediacy requirement in self-defence cases strikes me as one possible example, although unless carefully handled it might well play into the interests of the stronger rather than the weaker party in any conflict. But other instances may rather reproduce and indeed institutionalise the assumptions about femininity and masculinity which we want to question. Is it appropriate, for example, to allow a man accused of rape to contextualise his misrecognition of the woman's 'no' as 'yes' within the cultural context of prevailing ideas about women's sexuality? Another troubling example is the development of the notion of 'battered women's syndrome', which contextualises the effects of violence to women within what amounts to a psychiatric pathology which can be comprehended by the diminished responsibility defence.[38] As an individual strategy for a defence lawyer concerned to protect to the best possible degree her or his client's interests, this is of course impeccable. But our diagnosis of the broader discursive implications of what is effectively a deepening construction of diminished responsibility as the feminine and of provocation as the masculine defence must be more ambiguous.

The politics of contextualisation, then, cannot be assumed to go in one direction only. Indeed, as experience with more radical changes such as those represented by institutions of informal justice and mediation has shown, dispute-resolving frameworks which seek to emphasise and build upon pre-existing relationships and responsibilities sometimes reproduce the power relationships with which the parties

[36] *Cf.* Minow (1987); Minow and Spelman (1989), p. 1597.

[37] I have discussed this point in more detail in 'Community in Legal Theory: Idea, Ideal or Ideology?' (1995) Studies in Law, Politics and Society.

[38] As argued for example in the case of *Ahluwalia* (1992) 4 All ER 889.

arrive at the decision-making forum even more starkly than do more formal arrangements.[39] Before we assert the value of contextualising the doctrinal subject in terms of her being and her relating rather than of her having certain powers or capacities, therefore, we need to think about the broader assumptions which will inform the ensuing judgments about who we are and how we live. For it is these assumptions which will determine how real people—with differently sexed bodies, of different races, ages, religions, nationalities, with different sexual orientations—will be inserted into the legal framework. We need to focus not just on the structure of legal doctrine but on criminalisation, understood as a broad social practice whose shape is determined in many places other than legislatures or indeed courtrooms.[40] For the patterns which mark the path of criminalising power are informed not just by assumptions about what capacities characterise a 'normal' subject but also about what kinds of characteristics and ways of life are acceptable, both at large, and in relation to people with particular kinds of bodies. As soon as we begin to think, for example, about how people are selected for prosecution, or what form of sentence is selected for particular types of offenders, we have to acknowledge that the sum effect of criminalisation, far from being to judge abstract legal subjects, is to target problem populations, to label suspect communities, to stigmatise certain forms of relationship, to disqualify certain ways of life. We have tended to lose sight of real ways in which criminal justice, among other legal practices, already contextualises its subjects and indeed instantiates something approaching a relational ethic-often in ways which are oppressive to women among others.[41] The strategy of recontextualisation, in other words, could only promise progress if it were preceded by a more differentiated and inclusive acceptance of varying ways of life.

This argument entails that the primary focus of feminist critique has to be not legal doctrine or law at all but rather the broader assumptions about masculinity and femininity which have marked the insertion of sexed bodies into the doctrinal framework. Focusing for a moment on those broader assumptions, it seems to me that there has been a tendency in feminist work to lose sight of the contradictions which we know to characterise prevailing views about women and men, and to narrate legal discourses of subjectivity as ones of seamless sexism which construe men as the active, rational, responsible subjects and women as passive, emotional and victimised. In other words, we have been too ready to map our argument about the gendered conceptualisation of legal subjectivity onto what is really a broader critical analysis of legal and social discourse.[42] Of course, these images are not

[39]For critical analysis of the contextualising aspects of institutions of informal justice, see Abel (1982); Matthews (1988); de Sousa Santos (1992).

[40]For examples of feminist research on broad practices of criminalisation, see Eaton (1986); Allen (1987); Carlen (1983).

[41]For a persuasive analysis along these lines, see Daly (1989).

[42]The movement between' these two levels of analysis is exemplified by the passage by Naffine quoted at note 18 above.

without their doctrinal confirmations.[43] I cannot resist the temptation to allude to my favourite legislative instance: the definition of incest, which penalises a man for 'having' sexual intercourse with one of his female relations and a woman for 'permitting' (graciously, one presumes) one of her male relations 'to have' intercourse with her.[44] But once we focus on the broader assumptions about femininity and masculinity which inform judicial discourse, it becomes apparent that one of our main critical tools is feminist rhetoric. And at a rhetorical level, the recapitulation of discourses of victimised and passive feminine identity is ultimately disempowering. It is a much more effective strategy to instance, with as much irreverent humour as possible, the extraordinary contradictions in the ways in which legal discourse constructs men and women, femininity and masculinity, in the process of 'applying the law to the facts'-placing real women and men within doctrinal categories which themselves turn out to be extraordinarily little constrained by the gendered assumptions which have been argued to shape them. We could recall, for example, that the powerful and sexually aggressive man who rapes a woman is also the vulnerable creature who is so susceptible to the influence of feminine wiles that he loses control of his volitional capacities at the mere sight of a woman out on her own at night, and who is so far from being in command of his cognitive capacities that he sometimes cannot tell the difference between that apparently rather straightforward dichotomy, yes and no. Conversely the passive female victim of men's sexual aggression is equally the calculating seductress, the deceptive woman; the pathologised 'single mother' whom we have heard so much about recently is equally that paragon of rationality who controls even her reproductive faculties so as to maximise her chances of council housing. One of the avoidable double binds that we have sometimes been caught in, then, is a reassertion of the very stereotypes we are challenging. By getting seduced by the explanatory power of our doctrinal critique, and in our enthusiasm to deconstruct the oppositions which it has exposed, we see them where they may already have been dislodged; we construct them as more seamless than they are. We confirm the stories we say legal doctrine has told, and even begin to believe that they are as powerful as the most sexist man could wish.

6 Reconceiving Feminist Politics

6.1 A Hierarchy of Differences?

I now want to consider the continuities between difference feminism and other critical positions which interpret the legal subject as marked not only by sex but also by other axes of social differentiation such as class and race.[45] Among these

[43] We can take many examples from Kennedy (1992).

[44] Sexual Offences Act 1956 ss.10 & 11.

[45] One way of reading Norrie's argument, of course, is as a construction of the criminal legal subject as marked by class.

various socially important and ethically problematic 'differences', should that based on sex be accorded any particular status? This may seem an old-fashioned question. After all, the association of non-standard subjects with the body, with affectivity. and with the private can easily be extended beyond the category of sex. For example, recent work on post-colonialism suggests that the role of the 'racial' other in giving back its identity to the white subject is structurally similar to that of woman in relation to man.[46] The most obvious way to construe the broad critical project is therefore as one which seeks to expose all the varied politically problematic axes of differentiation which mark the construction of the legal practices. It is a project which will raise many different questions and which may entail different sets of critical strategies. But it does not imply a need to accord priority to anyone among relevant differences.[47]

The idea that sex difference is *the* basic difference has, of course, played a role in what has been known as radical or cultural feminism, in much the same way as class difference has had theoretical and political primacy in Marxist thought.[48] But in recent feminist theory there has emerged a new set of arguments which appear to suggest a primacy-or at least a particular status-for sex difference. The arguments are based on a complex and sometimes unpalatable cocktail of psychoanalysis and deconstruction. I shall try to reconstruct this cocktail in a simplified way-something which I think can be done without much violence to its substance and with some improvement to its flavour. I want to give it some attention, because I think it re-presents us with the recurring dilemma about sexual essentialism which has plagued radical feminism and which continues, as I have argued, to trouble 'difference' feminism. This new development is of particular concern because it is voiced by some of the most intellectually sophisticated and rhetorically gifted exponents of contemporary legal feminism.

The argument finds its most vivid and articulate expression in the work of Drucilla Cornell.[49] It takes off from a standard psycho—analytic account of the early Oedipal drama, and in particular the child's separation from its mother, which structures the acquisition of its identity in a sexually differentiated way. In gaining its own identity, a child also experiences a loss of connection. The male child will react to his loss by taking comfort in his possession of the penis, which promises to 'bring the mother back' because it is the means of satisfying her desire. The female child, on the other hand, has no such strategy available to her.[50]

---

[46] In the legal sphere, see Fitzpatrick (1992).

[47] The identification of just what those 'other' differences are requires substantial argument. For the purposes of this paper, I shall simply assume that class, race or ethnicity and sexual orientation are obvious candidates for inclusion. For an excellent discussion of the challenge posed by this kind of integrated approach, see Harris (1990). For useful general discussion of problems of essentialism in social theory, see Fuss (1989).

[48] For further discussion see Jaggar (1983), Chapters 5 and 9.

[49] Cornell (1991, 1992b).

[50] Although, as feminist critics and psychoanalysts have pointed out, the moment of separation itself has a different configuration for the female child. Her acquisition of identity is in relation to a

This basic story is given a distinctive twist by Lacan's reinterpretation of Freud. In Lacanian thought, the subject's birth is marked by its acceptance of the Law of the Father through its entry into the symbolic order of language. Whilst the male child's desire for the mother is repressed and becomes part of the unspeakable Real, language becomes the medium through which he seeks symbols to express and fulfill that repressed desire. And because language attempts to fill the lack experienced on the birth of the subject, the sexual differentiation implicit in children's acquisition of identity becomes encoded in the role of the phallus as the 'transcendental signifier' which underpins the construction of meaning. It is the metaphor for what could bring the mother back, and hence the ultimate symbol for the power of the word. This is what is meant by the claim that language is phallogocentric.

Lacan insists that the penis and the phallus are not the same—the first belongs to the imaginary order, the second to the symbolic. But in the masculine imagination, the operative fantasy is that having the penis is the same as having the phallus: hence language itself is a symbolic order in which the possessor of the phallus is subject and she who does not possess the phallus is defined in terms of lack. Furthermore, this castrated other—Irigaray's 'sex which is not one'[51]—has a special relationship to the pre-linguistic fantasy world. For the realms of fantasy and desire which are repressed on the entry into language are associated with the feminine, which is not properly a subject of the symbolic order; conversely the symbolic order is associated with the masculine. As Cornell puts it,

'Woman is assimilated as the necessary basis for the illusion of the ego's self-sufficiency.[52]

Women can appropriate the phallus-and who better to know how this is done than a woman law professor-but the phallus remains the very symbol of potency and of power. Put simply, to enter into the masculine world, women must take up the masculine position.[53]'.

When I attempted—in a practical deconstruction of the public—private distinction-to sketch this theory over breakfast one morning, my husband, after listening patiently, replied: 'Only a man could have thought such a theory up (as it were)'. His wry turn of phrase, funnily enough, expresses exactly why Lacan has had

---

subject to whom she is in an important respect similar- thus the need for differentiation, and the trauma it entails, may well be less acute. In different veins, see Chodorow (1978), pp. 50–51 (whose object-relations theory is the subject of critique); Chodorow (1978); Mitchell (1974); Mitchell and Rose (1982). *Cf.* Irigaray (1994), p. 18: 'Woman's subjective identity is not at all the same as a man's. She does not have to distance herself from her mother as he does-by a yes but especially a no, a near or a far, an inside opposed to an outside-to discover her sex. She is faced with a different problem entirely. She must be able to identify with her mother as a woman to realise her own sexuality. But her mother is the same as she. She cannot reduce or manipulate her as an object in the way a little boy or a man does.' See also Irigaray (1992) pp. 167, 212–213.

[51] Irigaray (1987). Irigaray's title *This Sex Which is Not One* also plays on the idea that the feminine genre is less implicated in the illusion of unitary identity and self-sufficiency than is the masculine.

[52] Cornell (1992b), p. 177.

[53] Cornell (1992b), p. 175.

such a fascination for feminists. For Cornell's interpretation of Lacan fixes precisely upon the sense in which the phallus is *thought* up. Lacan's affirmation that the equation of the penis and the phallus is imaginary entails that it is merely a metaphor for what the mother desires. The masculine privilege which Lacan argues to be encoded in language is based on a fantasy-albeit a fantasy which has acquired a social 'reality'. As long as we recognise the susceptibility of language to reinterpretation, the possibility of its imaginative reconstruction, we can begin, linguistically, to change the metaphor, to displace the association, and to deflate the currency (or perhaps the erection) of the male subject of language. The specifically feminist deployment of this argument therefore locates feminist politics primarily at the level of linguistic reconstruction: political action may itself be constituted by rhetorical strategies.

Thus the argument is that even if linguistic structures are marked by sexually specific dynamics, those structures are not fixed, and their concepts can be re-imagined, reconstructed. Since linguistic signs always get their meaning by reference to and through differentiation from other signs, that meaning is never closed: language has an irreducibly performative aspect. In any linguistic utterance there is an implicit reference both to what is unspoken and to what might have been spoken, and this gives rise to what Cornell calls the 'utopian moment' in the deconstruction which she derives from the philosophy of Jacques Derrida.[54] Far from simply representing or reflecting the world in an unproblematic way, language can never completely capture lived (or psychic) experience: all linguistic usage is in a sense metaphorical, and meaning is constructed by means of a dynamic process of deferral and differentiation evoked by the term 'différance'. The feminist project, then, is the gradual construction or recovery in language of a specifically feminine imaginary which can end women's silence or exclusion from audible speech. In Cornell's words, this is a project of 'recollective imagination' geared to the writing of a 'new choreography of sexual difference': the recovery of repressed or unheard meanings within institutional speech such as legal discourse.[55] It is aimed at opening up our sense of the contingency of current legal arrangements: its intention is to locate gaps and spaces within which meanings sympathetic to currently subordinated ways of life can gain an institutional foothold.

I want to question Cornell's reliance on Lacanian psychoanalysis by tracing some of its implications for the effectiveness of the linguistic strategies for which she argues. Without feeling qualified to add much to the extensive feminist literature on the topic, I am unconvinced that Lacan can be rescued for feminist use. In his particular account of the sexual structure of the originary drama, it seems to me that the story of the dynamics of the acquisition of identity are told from a male point of view, in the sense that it is the boy's trauma which determines the way in which that trauma is fixed in language and psychically managed in the public world.[56] In a

[54] For Derrida's own reflections on law, see Derrida (1992) p. 3.

[55] For an instance of a similar method applied to the recovery of forgotten legal histories, see Goodrich (1993), p. 276.

[56] Similar points are made by many of the critics cited at footnote 50.

sense, Lacan's theory is simply a replay of the standard sexist account of the public-private distinction, of masculinity and femininity, of reason and emotion. Far from needing sophisticated psychoanalytic theories to explain to us how to think beyond the phallic framework, it seems to me that we already do so.[57] Indeed the phallus is a dangerous toy for contemporary feminism. We may take comfort, however, in the thought that this particular toy is much like a balloon: if we simply let it go, its power is lost; it is automatically deflated. If any feminist engagement with Lacan is called for, it is probably one of satire: a strategy of talking the phallus down, like a balloon, by sending it up.[58]

I want to make two specific points about the political implications of a feminist espousal of Lacanian thought. First, it is easily read (even if this is a misreading) as an alliance which entails the privileging of sexual differentiation over other axes of social oppression. It may therefore inhibit the development of our understanding of how those different 'othernesses' intersect and affect one another-the development, in other words, of an integrated critique which acknowledges the marginalisation of dialects other than the feminine in prevailing discursive practices. And in weakening those links, it may reinforce the hold of the double bind of essentialism. For this double bind is, I would argue, more threatening to feminism than to other critical positions, because the idea of sex difference as fixed or structural is still seen as more plausible than the analogous arguments in relation to class, race or even sexual orientation. Whilst the Lacanian account in principle interprets sex difference as a construct, it is a construct which is so basic, so deeply embedded in the structures of identity—acquisition and language, that it may well seem the functional equivalent of an 'essential' difference. Secondly, it seems to me that, at a rhetorical level, the assumption of the power of the phallus and the diagnosis of femininity as, in essence, a condition of pathology-of abnormality, abjection, and silence—echoes through and taints many of the arguments of and images deployed by this kind of feminist critique, as it is relentlessly mapped back on to women's speaking bodies. This is particularly so in the case of some of Irigaray's recent work, as I shall try to illustrate in the final section of this paper.

But is the psychoanalytic theory detachable from the rest of Cornell's account?[59] Her really important insight, it seems to me, is her location of a utopian moment

[57] One excellent example is provided by the strategies against rape canvassed by Marcus (2002). These include articulating the insight of 'the fragility of erections and the vulnerability of male genitalia' (p. 400). Feminist satire provides yet another instance.

[58] Cornell would certainly reject this interpretation of Lacan. She insists that we can read him historically, and that we should recognise that his account of sexual difference is specific to the 'era of the ego' - *i.e.*, modernity. This seems unconvincing, given that sexual difference also characterised the ancient societies whose dialogic philosophical method it is currently fashionable to celebrate as a style less implicated in the idea of self-identity.

[59] I am tempted to frame this question in terms of whether Cornell's argument can be detached from the phallus without being castrated in the process. But this, of course, would be to replay the very assumption which I am criticising: that lack of the phallus necessarily implies lack of power.

within deconstruction.[60] Certainly, this depends on the assumption that configurations of power become reflected in linguistic structures, thus depriving women (among others) of access to an authentic or audible means of expression in the public world. This would explain the experience vividly reproduced in female ethnographies of being silenced, of the marginalisation of women's speech in a myriad institutional context, including the legal. But we need hardly look to Lacan for the insight that language is gendered. We can find plenty of explications of and explanations for the power structures of language, in sociolinguistics for example, and in other disciplines which attempt to develop more concrete institutional accounts of how social practices—language among them—come to reflect and reproduce prevailing frameworks of power.[61] We should not turn our back on these broader intellectual resources, which may be less resonant with a closed and structural view of the gender of language—a view belied by a host of textual and oral manifestations challenging the gender hierarchy; feminist scholarship to name but one. Cornell's contribution is in suggesting how we may think beyond language marked by power. She has developed a persuasive critical analysis of law's mode of fixing meanings, categories, identities, and of the fragility and instability of this mode. But when, for example, she constructs an argument for encompassing discrimination against homosexuals within the concept of sex discrimination, she needs not the phallus but merely a simpler conceptual toy. This is the idea of gender—including sexual orientation-as social construct yet as powerful determinant of the realities of men's and women's lives.[62] What Cornell's account does lack, however, is an institutional theory capable of illuminating the circumstances in which particular rhetorical strategies are likely to be effective rather than ineffective or even dangerous. If rhetoric is a form of political action, then some assessment of the political implications of that rhetoric must form a part of the theory which underlies it.

I should conclude this section by emphasising that I do not mean to imply that no toys from the psychoanalytic playbox are relevant to feminism. For example, the notion of repression, particularly as applied to affectivity and the body, and the split subjectivity which this entails, strike me as important, as does the idea that the rhetorical power of language is sometimes to be explained in terms of its subliminal appeal to psychic needs which cannot directly be recovered in language.[63] But these ideas need not be based on a sexually invariant and primarily sexual originary

[60] I shall leave aside the further question of whether Cornell needs a specifically Derridean theoretical framework to affect the reconstructive projects which she recommends.

[61] See for example Cameron (1985, 1990).

[62] See Cornell (1992b). One way of explaining the appeal of psychoanalysis for feminism is precisely its promise to answer the question of why gender hierarchy has been so consistently mapped onto sexed bodies (see above note 23). I suggest that we are better theoretically employed in analysing how gender is constructed in social practices such as language and law.

[63] For an imaginative use of the idea of repression in critical legal analysis, see Goodrich (1994), p. 107. The subliminal power of 'political signifiers' is discussed in Lacey (1995); see also Salecl (1994) Chapter 2.

story—a story which threatens broader alliances which we have both intellectual and political reason for keeping intact.

7 Politics, Rhetoric and Misrecognition

I want, finally, to give a particular illustration of the pitfalls of versions of difference feminism which accord a priority to sexual difference. I argued earlier that the simple inference from theory to practice implicit in liberal feminism was rendered problematic by the transition to more complex, discourse-oriented inter- pretations; and, secondly, that the feminist commitment to translating theoretical analysis into political practice has sometimes led to unjustified inferences from theory to practice. Put simply, difference feminism has issued in a set of *rhetorical* strategies of critique which are themselves a form of political practice. Yet there is a constant danger they will be misrecognised and as prescribing an instrumental political practice[64]—and that feminist strategies may reinscribe discourses such as the legal and legally relevant with images of woman which perpetuate rather than challenge stereotyped and disempowering notions of the feminine. In some sense these difference feminisms are committed to reasserting the symmetry of male and female subjecthood-a 'strange' symmetry based upon the recognition of different but equally worthy forms of human subjectivity, and one in which the idea of neutrality can perhaps be resurrected in a sense which would not repress but respect difference.[65] Can they be any more successful in escaping conventional stereotypes than the policy of contextualisation which I have already criticised?

A particularly intriguing and imaginative example of the discursive politics intrinsic to difference feminism is Luce Irigaray's distinctive 'écriture féminine' which seeks to recover the repressed feminine, the unacknowledged body, and give them a place within language—albeit a language rather different from the analytic expressions of the symbolic order which generally characterise intellectual discourse. Irigaray's 'ecrirure feminine' is self-consciously poetic and elliptical, often dialogic in form, and evocative rather than analytic in style.[66] It was therefore something of a surprise to many of her readers when she formulated an apparently

---

[64] Or 'direct political action' as Cornell puts it (1992), p. 176.

[65] For example, Irigaray argues that ethical relations between persons must be premised on the existence of two different genres of human subjectivity-the masculine and the feminine: only once women as well as men have access to a recognised culture which underpins their subject status can relations between the sexes amount to genuine reciprocity or intersubjectivity as distinct from object-relations based on the notion of the other as property. See also the quotation with which this paper begins, Irigaray (1992).

[66] Irigaray's distinctive style is perhaps most vividly exemplified by *Marine Lover* (1991); see also *An Ethics of Sexual Difference* (1993a). It is interesting to draw an analogy with Rorty's argument (1989) that the crucial political project of extending human empathy is often best effected by novels and poetry rather than by political and moral philosophy.

institutional argument for special or sexuate rights. I want to focus on this aspect of Irigaray's work both because it is particularly susceptible of a very dangerous misreading and because it exemplifies the echoes of femininity as pathology which I identified as one of the dangers of the psychoanalytic framework which also informs her work.[67] I shall sketch her argument and then go on to ask two sets of questions about it: first, to what extent, judged as a rhetorical strategy of re-imagining the feminine, is it successful in evoking a powerful and different image of subjectivity? Second, how are we to interpret the fact that Irigaray's argument is couched in the language of institutional reform?

In *Thinking the Difference*—a set of essays originally written for meetings convened by the Italian Communist Party—Irigaray recapitulates a critique of the capacity-based and contractual notion of the subject as rights-bearer which we saw to be an important aspect of difference feminism:

'Redefining the right to civil identity is one of the urgent tasks of our time, not only for the sake of living women and men, bur for the sake of a possible future for the national and international community. Today, rights are increasing almost exclusively in the sphere of rights to ownership of property, benefits, various types of capital, etc. These new rights are greatly concerned with having (property) but little concerned with being(s)-women and men-and little with relationships amongst individuals based on this notion of free, responsible human identity.'[68]

As long as women have no civil identity of their own, it is to be expected, unfortunately, that they will conform to the only existing models, supposedly neutral, but in fact male. Hence the need to redefine the objective content of civil rights as they apply to men and women-since the neutral individual is nothing but a cultural fiction-and to attempt to establish the legal bases of possible reciprocity between the sexes.[69]

In imagining an ethical world which moves beyond liberal notions of neutrality, then, part of Irigaray's imaginative paintbox is a set of 'special rights'. These include the right to human dignity, which encompasses stopping the commercial use of womens' bodies and the right to valid representations of women in actions, words and images in all public places; and a right to human identity which encompasses the legal encodification of virginity as a component of female identity that is not reducible to money, and not cash—convertible by the family, the state or religious bodies.[70] They also include-less problematically, I think—the right to equivalence in

[67] This is not to imply that Irigaray is uncritical of Lacan: see above note 50.

[68] Irigaray (1994), p. xvii, Irigaray's original title was *Le Temps de la Difference*: *Pour une revolution pacifique*.

[69] Irigaray (1994), p. 75.

[70] Irigaray (1993b), pp. 86–87. It is interesting to note the resonance between Irigaray's specification of the right to dignity and Catharine MacKinnon's emphasis on pornography as a fundamental means of women's subordination: see MacKinnon (1989), Chapter 11. For critical comment see Frazer and Lacey (1993), pp. 92–95. Like MacKinnon's and Andrea Dworkin's anti-pornography ordinance, Irigaray's argument envisages the civil rather than the penal enforcement of rights in this area.

systems of exchange such as the linguistic, and representation in equal numbers in all civil and religious decision—making bodies.[71]

Irigaray's assertion of these special rights or women's laws moves between two very different voices or styles.[72] First is an evidently imaginary and speculative voice. Examples include her injunction to 'question the origins of the law currently in force, particularly in relation to the time when women really were civil persons, a time misleadingly termed Prehistory'.[73] It is also expressed in her depiction of a past female law as characterised by features such as respect for local places and divinities, a higher morality based upon love and peace, and 'a community of all members of humankind'.[74] At other moments she borrows the language of an institutional programme for legal and political reform. In response to an interviewer's question about her interest in law, she replies:

'Why deal with legal questions more concretely? Because. . . . I have regularly worked with women or groups of women who belong to liberation movements, and in these I've observed problems or impasses that can't be resolved except through the establishment of an equitable legal system for both sexes.'[75]

And speaking of one particular problem-that of incest-she argues:

'Faced by [this form] of men's lack of civility. . . . practising real incest within the family-legal recourse is necessary. I propose that the right to virginity as belonging to the girl, and not to her father, brother or future husband, should be enshrined in law. In other words, I think that the right to virginity should be part of girls' civil identity as a right to respect for their physical and moral integrity.'[76]

What should we make of Irigaray's argument as a feminist politics? It may be that her movement between speculative and institutional languages is itself a rhetorical strategy designed to underline the point that current constructions of the legal are contingent-could be otherwise than they are. And perhaps there is no real danger that her proposals will be read at their institutional face value. But even judged as a rhetorical strategy, it is worth noting that many of the images which she invokes-virginity, motherhood, peace, the integrity of the planet and women's special feeling for this- resonate with conventional stereotypes of femininity, and would, if institutionalised in public speech as much as in law, have the effect of fixing women within identities which it is surely Irigaray's political strategy to question

[71] Irigaray (1993b), p. 89.

[72] For a thoughtful meditation on Irigaray's apparently contrasting projects, see Pottage (1994), p. 131.

[73] Irigaray (1993b), p. 92.

[74] Irigaray (1993b), p. 90. The reference to community is problematic given the logic of identity built into many understandings of community: see Benhabib (1992), p. 68; Young (1990), Chapters 4 and 6.

[75] Irigaray (1994), p. 82.

[76] Irigaray (1994), p. 74. *Cf.* p. xvi; '. . . civil law must be changed to give both sexes their identities as citizens'; sec also p. 60. In somewhat more philosophical mode, see also Irigaray, (1992), pp. 18–19; 42–43; 90–100; 205–210.

and unsettle. Indeed, some of her comments are virtually indistinguishable from the images of femininity in the most sexist discourse:

'Men are uncivil as a result of too many rights and too few duties, and women as a result of too few rights and too many duties, for which they compensate by impulsiveness and subjectivity without social bounds, in the form of either persistent childish behaviour or maternal authoritarianism extending into the social sphere.'[77]

I am inclined to regard this as an almost compulsive repetition of the notion of femininity as a condition of disorder, abnormality and pathology which is embodied in Lacanian psychoanalysis. It is a condition which Irigaray's own lyrical meditations and evocations in her ecriture feminine serve practically and concretely to undermine.[78] Yet its reiteration in aspects of her argument for civil rights can hardly be doubted to have adverse rhetorical effects from a feminist point of view. Irigaray's defenders have been quick to assert that hers is 'no separatist politics'.[79] But as a woman who hates housework, has no nostalgia for virginity, is not a (biological) mother, and who would like to be able to behave impulsively without being accused of being 'a typical woman', I find it hard to identify with a politics whose central components include rights 'to virginity, motherhood by choice, preferential guardianship of children and caring for the home'.[80] Whilst it is true that Irigaray is most easily (mis)taken for an essentialist when her readers ignore the 'aggressive role of rhetoricity in her prose', her framing of that rhetoric within a language of institutional reform seems to come so close to rewriting woman as other as defined indominant discourse that one needs to be a highly qualified philosopher to see the difference. A rhetoric which calls for such close reading can hardly count as an effective contribution to feminist politics.

There is, however, a really important issue underlying Irigaray's argument for special rights. This is the claim that it is not merely the substance but rather the form of civil rights which needs to be reconstructed.[81] In Irigaray's view, the questions of form and substance are inextricably linked. The core of her argument is that rights need to be reconstructed so as to recognise not just object or property relations but also intransitive relations between different kinds of subjects—a genuine intersubjectivity which moves between, and which can only be premised on the mutual recognition of the existence of, (at least?) two irreducibly different genres. This point

[77] Irigaray (1994), p. 78. See also her comment on p. 82 about women's lack of public responsibilities leaving us (significantly, she says 'them') 'mired in instability, dissatisfaction, criticism'.

[78] Indeed, this discourse of Irigaray's tempts me to think that she has not learned the lesson she attributes, beautifully, to Nietzsche: 'when the other does not hear you it is better to be silent. By doing violence to the ear, one loses the music.' Irigaray (1991), p. 39.

[79] Spivak (1992) pp. 54, 74–75.

[80] Irigaray (1994), p. 81. Some aspects of Irigaray's argument-for example that on virginity-also suggest a lack of familiarity both with legal reforms already widely effected and with the socio-legal insight that legislative inscription is far from being the same as practical instantiation.

[81] This argument is most fully developed in Irigaray (1992), a book whose title evokes the intransitivity of genuinely ethical relations which are premised on the recognition of irreducibly different being(s).

appears to speak to the form of rights, but in the distinctive configuration of her argument it also entails a separation of the subject matter of rights according to the specificities of two sexually differentiated cultures or ways of life. Only if the substantive interests, concerns and values appropriate to feminine culture are instantiated juridically can the promise of relational and intersubjective as opposed to competitive and proprietary legal and ethical relations be realised.

Two interesting interpretive questions may be raised about Irigaray's argument. First, I have suggested that her delineation of the content of some of the special rights for women recapitulates stereotyped and disempowering visions of femininity, and fixes women within 'a feminine culture' as valued and defined by men in a heterosexist world. To the extent that this critique is persuasive, can Irigaray's argument about substance—about feminine culture—either be detached from the argument about the form of rights, or be re-imagined in a way which both is less stereotypical and avoids the obvious problem of fixing women and men within particular sexed identities? Second, is it possible to escape the essentialist resonance of Irigaray's argument, and all the problems which this entails, by re-reading her analysis of the role of sexual difference as a metaphor for difference more generally—for example, for difference based on race or sexual orientation? If the liberating power of her theory is its capacity to escape the imperialistic illusion of self-identity and to express the imperative of attention to difference—an insight encapsulated in the idea that '"Je suis sexué(e)" implique " je ne suis pas tout(e)"'—can it be re-read as entailing that, for example, 'I am white' also implies 'I am not everything'?[82] If the appeal of her ideas lies in their capacity to address the issue which I raised in my earlier discussion of criminalisation-that of how we should go about ensuring the acceptance of varying ways of life as a precondition for a meaningful politics of recontextualisation-then why should this accommodation of difference be confined to two distinctive cultures?

A number of difficulties immediately confront such an interpretation. The most obvious objections to it include the actual centrality of sexual difference to Irigaray's texts, and theoretical problems, given the structure of her argument, about the possibility of extending her analysis to differences which are not binary in the way in which she understands sexual difference to be. It is nonetheless, I would argue, in the possibility of such a re-interpretation that the full political potential of Irigaray's project might be imagined. Without such a re-reading, the expositional vividness of the particular content of her special rights overwhelms her subtler argument about their form. The composite argument therefore risks being read as an invitation to institutionalise stereotyped visions of the feminine within a conceptual form currently marked, as Irigaray herself recognises, by a property-based, competitive and individualistic view of the world. The having of rights is based on the having of capacities, and geared to entitlements to goods on a contractual model: the language of rights is quintessentially the masculine language of performance, measurement,

[82] Irigaray (1992), p. 91.

control.[83] Irigaray's comments on the need for rights to reflect 'being' rather than 'having', and on the relational aspects of rights 'entre nous', are suggestive: yet they become submerged in her discourses on the substance of special rights. A more radical project of conceptual reconstruction than she has so far attempted is implied by the broad framework of her argument.

In short, Irigaray is more persuasive in her poetic and speculative than in her political-institutional mode. In a sense her argument for special rights falls between two stools. Whereas Cornell, staying within the analytic mode, focuses to some extent on a concrete and detailed project of showing how the specificities of legal discourse can afford opportunities for questioning and reconstructing legal rules and categories along different lines, and whereas Irigaray's écriture féminine provides a powerful poetic source of the imagination of a differently configured world, Irigaray's argument for special rights provides neither a compelling image of difference nor a comprehensible political strategy.

8 In Conclusion

Appropriately enough to a paper which promised to glimpse the loosening of double binds, I must leave many threads untied. The main image with which I want to leave you is the positive one of the rich and varied colours and textures of the tapestry of which feminist legal scholarship is a part. Some threads can, however, be drawn together.

The 'difference feminism' which I have described is premised on a complicated and differentiated view of the power of law: it acknowledges what Santos has usefully distinguished as the violent or coercive, the bureaucratic or regulatory, and the rhetorical or persuasive aspects of law's power.[84] Each of these aspects calls for critical analysis. And each engenders a different relation between theory and practice-or perhaps I should say, a different conception of political practice. Strategies which seek to mitigate the injustice of particular instances of law's coercive power as it applies to women will always be an important part of the feminist project, particularly for practitioners. But there is a need for realism about just how much can be changed by legal means. Furthermore, I have argued that it is only if we conceptualise the legal or the legally relevant in an inclusive way that we can come to a sensible appreciation of the real role of law in underpinning gender hierarchy. Ultimately, it is only by understanding at an institutional level how legal and other practices interact and sustain each other that we can make any realistic assessment of the scope for change.

The critical projects of exposing the gendered nature of law's power and of trying to imagine how this might be differently configured are of equal importance to

[83] See references cited at note 21.

[84] de Sousa Santos (1980), p. 249.

feminist legal scholars. With the move in critical legal theory towards an understanding of law's discursive, rhetorical power, rhetorical counter-strategies have themselves been revealed as an important part of feminist politics. But they can only be effective if they are recognised as such, and not mistranslated directly into instrumental political and legal interventions which speak rather to the coercive or bureaucratic aspects of law's power.

Much work, practical and theoretical, analytical and imaginative, needs to be done if the notions of neutrality, rights, equality, justice are to be understood in their racially, sexually and otherwise oppressively patterned reality, and if they are to be reconstructed in a way which promises the genuine accommodation of different forms of life, different subjectivities. For feminism, there is always a deep pitfall to be avoided here. For without an elusive mix of courage and caution, of audacity and subtlety, it may be that in seeking to imagine difference, in pursuit of its ultimate inclusion or recognition, we may not so much make a difference, as reproduce, as it were, the same difference. In doing so, we inevitably lend weight to its misinterpretation as fixed. Only if we are constantly aware of this double pitfall will we have any hope of developing strategies for stepping around it.

The breadth of my frame has necessarily entailed a somewhat impressionistic tapestry. But I have taken my cue here from a very powerful female role model: George Eliot. In *The Mill on the Floss*, she explains how Mr. Tulliver's general sense of the 'complicated, puzzling nature of human affairs' meshes with his apparently contradictory 'tendency to act promptly under the influence of a strong feeling'—one of perhaps rather few composite dispositions which he might be taken to share with feminist legal theorists. George Eliot remarks: 'I have observed that for getting a strong impression that a skein is tangled, there is nothing like snatching hastily at a single thread'. Her observation tunes with a general point which I hope to have made: that in our diagnosis and analysis of double-binds supposedly facing feminist thought, our tendency to focus on single threads, or groups of threads, rather than on the larger practices of which they are part, has sometimes accentuated our sense of impasse. And our narrow focus can blind us to larger problems which we may be creating in trying to loose a single strand which is invariably connected to others. It is an irony, given my theme, that the social conditions of Victorian England dictated that George Eliot had to assume the nominal subject position of a man in order publicly to address her readers. Yet, notwithstanding the masculine veil with which she wrapped, or perhaps pretended to wrap herself, we—women and men—now read her as a woman. This is, I suggest, a nice metaphor for the possibility of recognising the sexually differentiated positions which we occupy as social subjects without denying the power of a woman's voice.

References

Abel R (ed) (1982) The politics of informal justice. Academic
Allen H (1987) Justice unbalanced. Open University Press
Atkins S, Hoggett B (1984) Women and the law. Blackwell

Benhabib S (1992) Situating the self. Polity Press
Butler J, Scott JW (eds) (1992) Feminists theorise the political. Routledge
Cameron D (1985) Feminism and linguistic theory. Macmillan
Cameron D (1990) The feminist critique of language: a reader. Routledge
Carlen P (1983) Women's imprisonment. Routledge
Chodorow N (1978) The reproduction of mothering. University of California Press
Collins H (1982) Marxism and law. Oxford University Press
Cornell D (1991) Beyond accommodation - ethical feminism, deconstruction, and the law. Routledge
Cornell D (1992a) Gender, sex and equivalent rights. In: Butler J, Scott JW (eds) Feminists theorise the political. Routledge
Cornell D (1992b) The philosophy of the limit. Routledge
Daly K (1989) Criminal justice ideologies and practices in different voices: some feminist questions about justice. Inter J Soc Law 17:1–18
De Sousa Santos B (1980) Law and community: the changing nature of power in state capitalism. Int J Soc Law 8:379–397
De Sousa Santos B (ed) (1992) State transformation, legal pluralism and community justice. Social and Legal Studies
Derrida J (1992) Force of law: the mystical foundation of authority. In: Cornell D, Rosenfeld M, Carlson DG (eds) Deconstruction and the possibility of justice. Routledge
Dworkin R (1977) Taking rights seriously. Harvard University Press, Massachusetts
Eaton M (1986) Justice for women? Open University Press
Farmer L (1992) The genius of our law. Cambridge University Press
Fitzpatrick P (1992) The mythology of modern law. Routledge
Frazer E, Lacey N (1993) The politics of community - a feminist critique of the Liberal-communitarian debate. University of Toronto Press
Frug MJ (1992) Postmodern legal feminism. Routledge
Fudge J (1989) The effect of entrenching a bill of rights upon political discourse: feminist demands and sexual violence in Canada. Int J Soc Law 17:445–463
Fuss D (1989) Essentially speaking. Routledge
Gilligan C (1982) In a different voice. Harvard University Press
Goodrich P (1993) Gynaetopia: feminine genealogies of common law. J Law Soc 20:276–308
Goodrich P (1994) Jani Anglorum. Signs, symptoms, slips and interpretation in law. In: Douzinas C, Goodrich P, Hachamovitch Y (eds) Politics, postmodernity and critical legal studies. Routledge
Graycar R and J Morgan (1990) The hidden gender of law. The Federation Press
Harris A (1990) Race and essentialism in feminist legal theory. Stanford Law Rev 16:581–616
Hart HLA (1968) Punishment and responsibility. Clarendon Press
Hunt A, Kerruish V (1992) Gender discrimination in law's empire. In: Hunt A (ed) Reading Dworkin critically. Berg Publishers
Irigaray L (1987) This sex which is not one. Cornell University Press
Irigaray L (1991) Marine Lover of Friedrich Nietzsche. Columbia University Press
Irigaray L (1992) J'Aime A Toi. Grasset
Irigaray L (1993a) An ethics of sexual difference. Arhlone Press
Irigaray L (1993b) Je, Tu, Nous: toward a culture of difference. Routledge
Irigaray L (1994) Thinking the difference. Athlone Press
Jaggar A (1983) Feminist politics and human nature. Rowman & Littlefield Pub Inc
Kelman M (1981) Interpretive construction in the substantive criminal law. Stanford Law Rev
Kennedy H (1992) Eve was framed. Chatto & Windus
Kingdom E (1991) What's wrong with rights?: problems for a feminist politics of law. Edinburgh University Press
Lacey N (1985) The territory of the criminal law. Oxford J Legal Stud 5:453–462
Lacey N (1986) Legislation against sex discrimination: questions from a feminist perspective. J Law Soc 14:411–421
Lacey N (1988) State punishment: political principles and community values. Routledge

Lacey N (1993) Theory into practice? Pornography and the public/private dichotomy. J Law Soc 20:93–113
Lacey N (1995) Community in legal theory: idea, ideal or ideology? Stud Law Polit Soc 15:105–146
Lacey N, Wells C, Meure D (1990) Reconstructing criminal law. Weidenfeld and Nicolson
Larrabee MJ (ed) (1993) An ethic of care. Routledge
Littleton CA (1987) Reconstructing sexual equality. Calif Law Rev 75:1279–1337
Lloyd G (1984) The man of reason: male and female in Western philosophy, Methuen Young Books
Lorde A (1984) Sister outsider. Crossing Press
MacKinnon, Catharine A (1989) Toward a feminist theory of the state. Harvard University Press
Marcus S (2002) Fighting bodies, fighting words: a theory and politics of rape prevention. In: Butler J, Scott J (eds) Feminists theorise the political. Routledge, pp 385–403
Matthews R (ed) (1988) Informal justice? Sage Publications
McColgan A (1993) In defence of battered women who kill. Oxford J Legal Stud 13:508–529
Minow M (1987) Justice engendered. Harv Law Rev 101:10–95
Minow M, Spelman E (1989) In context. Southern California Law Rev 63:1597–1652
Mitchell J (1974) Psychoanalysis and feminism. Allen Lane
Mitchell J, Rose J (1982) Feminine sexuality: Jacques Lacan and the Ecole Freudienne. W. W. Norton & Co
Naffine N (1990) Law and the sexes - explorations in feminist jurisprudence. Allen & Unwin
Naffine N (1994) Possession: erotic love in the law of rape. Mod Law Rev 57:10–37
Nedelsky J (1989) Reconceiving autonomy. Yale J Law Fem 1:7–36
Norrie A (1993) Crime, reason and history. Weidenfeld and Nicolson
Norrie A (1995) Legal and moral judgment. In: McVeigh S, Rush P, Young A (eds) Criminal legal practices. Oxford University Press
O'Donovan K (1985) Sexual divisions in law. Weidenfeld and Nicolson, London, London
O'Donovan K (1991) Defences for battered women who kill. J Law Soc 18:219–240
O'Donovan K, Szyszczak EM (1988) Equality and sex discrimination law. Blackwell Publishing
Olsen F (1983) The family and the market. Harv Law Rev 96:1497–1578
Olsen F (1990) Feminism and critical legal theory: an American perspective. Int J Soc Law 18:199–215
Pottage A (1994) Recreating difference. Law Critique 131:162–187
Rorty R (1989) Contingency, irony and solidarity. Cambridge University Press
Salecl R (1994) The spoils of freedom. Routledge
Smart C (1984) The ties that bind. Routledge
Smart C (1989) Feminism and the power of law. Routledge
Spivak GC (1992) French feminism revisited: ethics and politics. In: Butler J, Scott JW (eds) Feminists theorise the political. Routledge, pp 74–75
Taylor C (1985) Philosophy and the human sciences. Cambridge University Press
Wells C (1982) Swatting the subjectivist bug. Crim Law Rev:209–220
Williams JC (1989) Deconstructing gender. Mich Law Rev 87:797–843
Young IM (1990) Justice and the politics of difference. Princeton University Press

Nicola Lacey is School Professor of Law, Gender and Social Policy at the London School of Economics. She is a Fellow of the British Academy, served as a member of the British Academy's Policy Group on Prisons, which reported in 2014, and was from 2014–2019 the Academy's nominee on the Board of the British Museum. In 2011 she was awarded the Hans Sigrist Prize by the University of Bern, for scholarship on the rule of law in modern societies; and in 2022 she won the Law and Society Association's International Prize. Her publications include A Life of HLA Hart (OUP 2004); Women, Crime and Character: From Moll Flanders to Tess of the D'Urbervilles (2008); The Prisoners' Dilemma (2008), and In Search of Criminal Responsibility (2016).

Sexual Abuse, Sexy Dressing, and the Eroticization of Domination

Duncan Kennedy

Contents

Abstract A semiotic analysis of dress as the production of socially meaningful signs supports the feminist analysis that sees sexy costumes as loaded with allusions to abuse, and as a factor in eroticizing male domination of women. But the same analysis suggests the possibility of pleasure/resistance through sexy dress, and particularly the possibility of eroticizing female sexual autonomy. The reality of male abuse of women burdens or discourages the activities of fantasy, play, invention and experiment through which we have whatever hope we have of evolving or transcending our current modes of male and female sexuality. For this reason, men have at least a potential erotic interest in fighting against it.

1 Introduction

This article brings together two topics that may seem antipodal: male sexual abuse of women and sexy dressing.[1] Sexual abuse is a serious, indeed a terrifying thing, and we often dismiss fashion, sexy or not, as trivial, no matter how much of our time it

[1] This article is dedicated to the memory of Mary Joe Frug.

D. Kennedy (✉)
Harvard Law School, Cambridge, MA, USA
e-mail: kennedy@law.harvard.edu

N. Lacey et al. (eds.), *Reassessing Feminist Legal Theories*, Gender Perspectives in Law 5, https://doi.org/10.1007/978-3-031-75423-4_3

occupies. But the topics are linked, nonetheless, in two opposed discourses. One of these I will call the "conventional view," by which I mean the discourse of mainstream or traditional American culture about sexuality and sex. In this view, female sexy dress is linked to abuse because it sometimes causes it. The other discourse I will refer to as "radical feminism," meaning to distinguish it from liberal, socialist, cultural and post-modern feminisms. In this discourse, sexual abuse is a constitutive factor in the regime of patriarchy that is reflected and reproduced in fashion. Abuse causes sexy dress, rather than vice versa.

Although I respond in this article both to the conventional and to the radical feminist view, I don't see myself as neutral between them. Rather, I would describe myself as a straight white male middle class radical trying to come to terms with the radical feminist challenge to the sexual culture that has formed my own identity. The conventional view is a foil; the radical feminist view is a promise but also a threat.[2] It promises understanding, routes to change, and a possible political alliance toward transcending our gender regime. The threat is to the possibility of self-respect as a straight man.

Both promise and threat derive from the power of the radical feminist analysis of the eroticization of domination. This is the notion that the regime of patriarchy constructs male and female sexuality so that both men and women are turned on by experiences and images of male domination of women. I accept these radical feminist claims: Abuse plays a central rather than peripheral role in our mode of sexuality. Sexuality plays a central rather than peripheral role in male domination. "Merely personal" phenomena like sex and dress are forms of political participation in the regime of patriarchy. The question then is whether it is possible for straight men and women to be sexual, to experience pleasure within the regime, without collaborating in oppression.

In the longer article from which this paper is drawn, I approached this question circuitously. I first defined sexual abuse and described the legal regime that restricts and also tolerates it, presenting a tentative analysis of the way sexual abuse law functions in the distribution of power and welfare between men and women. I then took up the role of sexual abuse in the regulation of female behavior, and in the constitution of male and female identities.

These parts of the original article made two points. First, there is at least an apparent conflict of interests between men and women with regard to the legal prevention of sexual abuse. Men, and particularly men who do not abuse women, are affected in many ways by the social refusal to do more against it. It seems plausible that men count many of these effects as benefits. A serious effort to reduce abuse must address in one way or another the male interest in its perpetuation.

---

[2]The works that I particularly experienced this way, and to which I feel most indebted, are Dworkin (1987), Dworkin (1982), Firestone (1970), MacKinnon (1983), Olsen (1984), West (2000). See generally Linden (1982). For more references, see *infra* Part III. I also want to acknowledge the impact on my thinking of two articles by Schneider (1980, 1986).

Second, much sexual abuse is "disciplinary," in the sense that it functions to enforce patriarchal social norms. These norms cover a spectrum from the very specific (norms about sexy dressing) to the "characterological" (norms about what a man or a woman "should be like" rather than about particular behaviors). Appropriating the radical feminist analysis of how the formation of character through the sexualization of male domination functions to support the overall regime of patriarchy, I sketched a "minimalist" critique of that position, based on an analogy to the neo-Marxist critique of orthodox Marxism for overstating the internal coherence and homogenizing power of capitalism. I then suggest the possibility of "pleasure/resistance" in the belly of the beast.

The sections published here argue that women's dress practices are the site of conflicts within the regime, rather than simply a reflection of it. There are several loosely defined subcultures that contest the conventional view of sexy dress—that it is a form of female misbehavior that explains and indeed justifies abuse. These include the feminist community, with its own version of what is wrong with the practice and with the conventional response to it. But there is also a pop subculture of sexy dress with a quite different interpretation, and other ideological tendencies as well. Women, who have no choice but to dress somehow within this system of contending normativities, and their male and female audience, act neither as mere tools of patriarchy nor as the autonomous subjects of liberal theory. A semiotic analysis of dress as the production of socially meaningful signs supports the feminist analysis that sees sexy costumes as loaded with allusions to abuse, and as a factor in eroticizing male domination of women. But the same analysis suggests the possibility of pleasure/resistance through sexy dress, and particularly the possibility of eroticizing female sexual autonomy.

The conclusion returns to an earlier theme, arguing that the reality of male abuse of women burdens or discourages the activities of fantasy, play, invention and experiment through which we have whatever hope we have of evolving or transcending our current modes of male and female sexuality. For this reason, I argue that men have at least a potential erotic interest in fighting against it.

As this summary has already made clear, my view is powerfully conditioned by my straight white middle class male social position. It seems to me unnecessary to explain or apologize for my inability to write from elsewhere than where I am. But my willingness, indeed my desire to write about this topic from this position owes a lot to the emergence in the 1980s of what I will call pro-sex feminist postmodernism,[3] typified for me by the work of Jane Gallop,[4] Judith Butler[5] and Mary Joe Frug.[6] Like theirs, my approach is heavily influenced by structuralism[7] and

[3]See generally Vance (1983).

[4]Gallop (1988).

[5]Butler (1990).

[6]Frug (1992).

[7]See, e.g., de Saussure (1986); Levi-Strauss (1966); Piaget (1962).

post-structuralism,[8] but I do not think of myself as a feminist any more than I think of myself as a black nationalist.[9]

2 Sexual Abuse and Female Dress

In exploring the connection between the practice of sexual abuse and the production and reproduction of sexuality through female dress and men's responses to it, how should we understand the relationship between abuse and "sexy" or "provocative" dressing? I argue that this pairing plays a quite important role in the ideology of the patriarchal regime.

It is a part of the "conventional view" that women sometimes provoke abuse by their dress. This view is currently undergoing a serious challenge sometimes directly and sometimes indirectly inspired by feminist thinking. Within the challenge, there are ideological distinctions that correspond to the multiple possibilities of response to the norms and images of the regime.

2.1 The Production and Regulation of Sexy Dress

What I mean by sexy dressing is female dress-in-a-setting that large numbers of people label as "sexy" or "provocative." A person who disapproves of a particular sexy dress performance may call it "cheap," or "slutty," or "exhibitionist," or even "self-objectifying." In mainstream American culture today, costumes conventionally regarded as sexy in the sense of provocative generally choose exposure over covering, tightness over looseness, brightness (or black) over soft color, transparency over opaqueness, and symbolic shaping of breasts, waist, buttocks and feet over "natural" lines. (As put by a practitioner, "If you can't see up it, down it, or through it, I don't want to wear it.") There are similar complex dimensions for accessories, hair, make-up, and so forth.

The sexiness of a costume is a matter of degree. Women combine the elements to produce a spectrum with infinitely fine gradations from less to more. But which fashion performances people regard as sexy is also very much a matter of arbitrary convention. A revealing, tight, bright, transparent, shaped costume that doesn't follow the specific fashions of the moment is likely to be seen as weird or "gross" rather than sexy.

---

[8] Derrida (1976); Foucault (1980). I am following in the footsteps of Kennedy (1985).

[9] See Peller (1990). Some other works in this volume of the *New England Law Review* that seem to me quite similar in perspective to my own are Abu-Odeh (1992), Danielsen (1992), Engle (1992), Keller (1992) and Klare (1992).

Table 1 Norms and requirements of women's dress

Women's Dress:		
	More sexy	*Less sexy*
Family life Public space	In bedroom before sex Dinner party Nighttime Night club Beach Health club	In kitchen with kids Family picnic Daytime Airport Church Folk concert
The workplace	Sales work Street prostitutes Actresses & models enacting sexuality	Professional work High priced call girls Women script writers

Finally, whether a given costume counts as sexy dressing in the sense I will be using the term depends on the setting in which it is worn. Sexy dress is sexy in terms of the dress codes that regulate virtually all social space. These codes pervasively regulate the degree of sexiness permitted in each setting, but they do not operate to suppress female sexuality or impose a puritan morality.

Rather, we are talking about the spatial and temporal distribution of behavior that is itself socially produced. In American society today, there are norms, requirements of more or less sexy dressing (and sexy behavior generally) in some places at some times, as well as a variety of prohibitions of it in other times and places. A very tentative map might look something like Table 1.

2.1.1 Sexy Dressing as Deviation from the Norm of the Setting

Dress codes try to match the spectrum of costumes, from less to more sexy, to the spectrum of settings, from less to more sexually charged. Within a given setting, the code specifies some part of the costume spectrum as permissible. Dress is sexy for the setting when it is close to, or at, or over the line that separates dress for this setting from dress for a more sexually charged one. Office wear that suggests a nightclub is sexy because it deviates in a particular direction from the office norm. Dress is conservative for the setting when it is at the line in the other direction.

Within a setting, to put on a costume composed of the conventional elements of dress is to produce a sign, in the same way that to speak a word is to produce a sign. The particular costume, say a halter top, like a word, will have a different meaning, and convey different things about the speaker, according to the context. In this discussion, what counts is this meaning-in-the-setting. Sexy dressing is production of a sign that has the two meanings of "sex" and "deviance," because it is a sign that "belongs in" (is prescribed for) a more sexually charged setting than the one in which it is being worn. The halter top is likely to be sexy dressing when worn in the office but may be "modest" when worn at the beach.

Once we recognize the sign-in-context as "sexy dressing," with the meaning of deviance in a particular direction, the costume will have many other layers of meaning as well. The reading of the dresser's more complex message will vary according to all her socially significant characteristics, including, for example, race, age, and body type. Given the mainstream white stereotype of black women, a provocative costume is more likely to be interpreted as a uniform indicating actual employment as a prostitute, or at least as "slutty," rather than "sexy," if worn by a black woman, than it is if worn by a white woman.[10]

Old women and very large and very thin women are expected to accept the conventional social assessment that they are sexually unattractive, and dress so as to minimize their sexuality. If they dress sexily, that is, if they produce a costume-sign that is deviant in the direction of a more sexually charged setting, they are doubly provocative, and are likely to be interpreted as rebels or eccentrics or "desperate," and sanctioned accordingly. Since sexy dress calls attention to the body of the wearer, it is likely to prompt both the wearer and the audience to "apply" the conventional beauty standards of the moment. This means that sexy dressers who don't understand themselves as physically perfect will find themselves, as one practitioner put it, "trying to hide it and show it at the same time."

From what I have said so far, it should be clear that it is possible to engage in sexy dressing "by accident," that is, through ignorance or misapprehension of the dress code for a particular setting. But the dress code may also be contested or in transition, as for example when older people persist in interpreting a given costume as sexy dressing long after it has been "normalized" for a younger generation. Further, there is no necessary connection between the judgment that a particular woman has produced the sign of sexy dress and the judgment that she herself is "sexy," in the sense of sexually desirable. A woman dressed "conservatively" can be seen as "very sexy," and a woman dressed "provocatively" may be seen as "sexless."

There is, nonetheless, a conventional discourse about the sign system, things many people repeat about sexy dressing. In other words, there is a discourse about why women dress sexily (deviate), about what it is to experience dress as sexy (rather than just recognizing the sign), and about the consequences of acts of sexy dressing (production of the sign). This is the discourse that justifies the dress codes that establish and enforce norms for each setting.

In this discourse, a first basic idea is that sexy dressing is likely intended to and does likely arouse sexual feelings in some men. This is what keeps the sign system from "floating" completely free of reality. Indeed, speaking as a straight man I can testify that it—meaning deviation from the norm in the direction of the next more sexy setting—does often produce an experience of sexual interest, arousal, excitement in me and in some fraction of the men who see it. And also, that I often experience it as intended to do this by the woman who is doing it.[11]

[10] See generally Austin (1992).

[11] Anyone, man or woman, can recognize the sign as the sign of sexy dressing without experiencing sexual feelings in response, and without thinking it is "really" sexy, and regardless of whether they

It seems to me that this straight male reaction of excitement to sexy dressing (as conventionally defined sign) has something to do with both voyeurism and fetishism. The sexy dresser has modified her costume in a way that evokes or suggests looking at her in a setting that has a greater sexual charge than the one she is actually in. The associations of the more sexually charged setting are brought into the present one by the details of dress, which "represent" the costume of the other setting, and that costume in turn "represents" (as in fetishism) a part of or the whole sexualized female body.

Because sexy dressing violates the norm for the setting, the straight male reaction is complicated, indeed given a different "nature," by the addition of the particular man's reaction to the association of sexiness and deviance. Her dress is more than display. The woman who produces the sign seems to invite the watching straight man (cast as voyeur) to look at what, in that particular setting, she is supposed to hide.[12]

Only some men have this kind of reaction to the sign. Many men who recognize it do not respond to it at all, or react to it with panic or distaste. Many men "don't get it," in the sense of being oblivious. Others have voyeur-fetishist reactions that they

---

approve or disapprove of sexy dressing. At this level, all we are talking about is the existence of a conventional sign system. There is no necessary link, but only an indirect and complex one, between what is conventionally understood to be "it" and what men and women experience in response. Dress can be regarded as sexy for a long time without producing the experience, or produce the experience in one or many men without acquiring the social meaning.

It is not necessary for the moment to establish the exact process that connects (some) men's experience of dress as arousing and its categorization as sexy. I will proceed on the assumption that there are mechanisms, like the market and direct negotiation among men and women, that give specific forms this designation.

[12]The analysis of the last two paragraphs, which is crucial to the rest of this Part and the next, is heavily influenced by the work of Tracy Davis on the sexual meanings of Victorian actresses' clothing and by the general semiology of fashion of Roland Barthes:

> While clothing functioned [in the Victorian theater] as the sign of gender and sexuality was the referent of revealing clothing, certain articles of costume were more heavily weighted by the erotic lexicography of male culture. The clothing inextricably associated with a "guilty" body part became the indexical sign of the sexual part; in other words, it was fetishized. In the opinion of Anthony Storr, a sexologist, women use fetishized objects to attract men, so "a fetish may, as it were, be a flag hung out by the woman to proclaim her sexual availability.", Davis (1991), pp. 114–115 quoting Storr (1964).

Whether or not any particular item signifies a body part and also signifies "availability" depends on the vestimentary code of the particular culture. It might signify the "guilty" part, but not availability, or *vice versa*. Whether the wearer of a fetishized item of dress is using it as a "flag" to proclaim sexual availability is a matter of the intentions of the wearer, which cannot be conclusively inferred from either the production of the sign or the reaction to it. See generally Barthes (1983).

But Davis seems right to me that articles of clothing operate in our culture as signifiers of sexualized body parts. For instance, brassieres and underpants get an erotic charge (for some people) from what they signify. A costume that exposes neither bra nor breasts may, therefore, get a strong sexual charge by visually ***alluding to*** or ***evoking*** a bra and the breasts it signifies (supposing that some people in the culture in question eroticize female breasts). This will be true regardless of the intentions of the woman who produces the sign.

are aware of but feel guilty about or think are politically incorrect and fight hard against them.

Furthermore, men can have voyeur-fetishist reactions to any female self-presentation, without regard to the sign system, or in perverse reversal of its conventional meanings. Straight male sexuality, as we have constructed it, locks women into the role of performer no matter what they do to avoid it. Following the rules of sign-production does no more than increase the probability that a woman will produce the reaction or non-reaction she is looking for. But straight male voyeur-fetishist reaction to female dress, he notes defensively, is at worst a perversion, at best of a piece with all culture-appreciation, and not in itself abusive.

2.1.2 The Sexy Dress Subculture and Female Agency

Within the feminist theory that emphasizes the total power of men to shape gendered reality in their interests, it may seem obvious that what I have been describing is men's ideas about sexy dressing, which they impose on women who then enact them. In this model, men have (socially constructed) reactions of excitement, and they coerce women to produce them, period. The coercion may be direct (men penalize women for not being sexy for them), or work through the destruction of self-esteem so that women have no other means of feeling good, or through material deprivation that leaves them nothing else with which to bargain. In this view, there is little room for either female pleasure in sexual self-objectification or female agency in developing the repertoire of sexy dress ("why would any woman want to totter around on high heels?").

Both the conventional and the feminist view have a more sophisticated variant that emphasizes the production of sexuality through a subculture—a semi-organized group—of sexy dressers. The subculture has an ideology, its own media, and relationships with other groups, including particularly women who enforce the norms from which sexy dressers deviate and the men who are aroused by their practices. This view seems to me plainly better than the more individualist one.

The subculture exists within a situation of conflict about the eroticization of everyday life. Like others within the larger liberal capitalist system, its members only sometimes defend their practice with the argument that their way is best. More often, they play the liberal trump against majorities bent on enforcing compliance with their standards. "Women have come a long way, from burning bras to flaunting them. If a woman now chooses to look sexy, that is her right," says a Vogue editorial.[13]

As with other subcultures (beatniks, hippies, gangs, out gays), practices get their meanings through their relationships both to mainstream practice and mainstream ideology. In this case, sexy dress has an element of defiance, both of the

[13] Menkes (1992), pp. 103, 110.

conventional morality about dress[14] and of the feminist critique.[15] But at the same time that it defies it, the subculture influences the mainstream by providing an evolving vocabulary that can be incorporated piecemeal by sympathizers who don't want to "drop out" altogether.

It is possible to recognize the subculture but deny its autonomy. Its media—mail-order catalogues, women's magazines, soap operas, magazine and television advertising aimed at women, women's pulp fiction— are all heavily influenced by men. Men are dominant in their structures of ownership, and the male-oriented media that purvey arousal through sexy dressing (men's magazines, VHl, BET and Telemundo, movies, advertising aimed at men) obviously influence the women's media. The female subculture of sexy-dress may be best understood as an instance of women collaborating in their own oppression.

But given that sexiness is a matter not just of the setting but of the choice to move closer or further from the boundary of deviance within it, women as a group are not compelled to dress sexily for men. If all the women in a setting deviated toward the next sexier setting, what they did would not be deviance at all, but a redefinition of the norm. Some women deviate, but most don't. Vast numbers, traditionalist and feminist and in between, do no more than "follow" whatever the fashion may be, either not caring about sexual self-presentation or not daring it or feeling incapable of it or very consciously rejecting it.[16]

Why dismiss the vast amount of energy, imagination and work that women put into the constant evolution of the repertoire of dress? This happens at the micro level where there are an indefinite number of possible combinations of clothes and body, with distinguishable finely graded meanings in the language of sex. Women produce themselves as gendered artifacts using this vast repertoire—indeed they produce gender itself.[17] And it happens at the level of the media, where the repertoire itself develops.

This work seems to me driven by numerous forces, all of which involve both men and women, without it being possible to sort out the issue of control in any simple way. For example, because sexy dressing is a subculture that influences the mainstream, it has to keep evolving or risk being "normalized." Normalization threatens its existence as a subculture, which is dependent on deviance or defiance. It also deprives any particular sexy dress practice of its sexiness.

---

[14]de Nicolais (1992), pp. 174–175 ("Don't be shy—it's *fashion,* not lingerie! And you *want* to show some cleavage!").

[15]"At the Women in the Law Conference, I found myself in the ladies' room with a feminist friend, smoothing my bright red lipstick on more slowly than usual so I could enjoy her horror, as though I were shooting drugs right before her eyes." (Name of practitioner withheld).

[16]One might note in response that the very uniforms that define the norm in any given setting are powerfully shaped by men's eroticization of femininity. High heels are often given as an example. I agree with this point and discuss it at length infra Part V. But high heels are only sexy dress, the topic here, when they are at least close to out of place, or adopted for the specific purpose of signifying sexuality.

[17]See Butler (1990), pp. 134–141.

This is partly because sexually arousing objects have a tendency to lose their charge over time. Familiarity breeds indifference. It is also partly because moving a particular costume (or costume element) away from the margin back toward the norm for the setting undermines its suggestive power for the voyeur-fetishist. When all the women on the beach have been wearing bikinis for years, the two pieces connote "all the other women on the beach," rather than "bra and panties." There is a contradiction between the words "risque" and "respectable" in the view of the *Ladies' Home Journal*:

> Dressed To Thrill
>
> Victoria won't tell all her Secrets, but we can guess: Sales are skyrocketing. Her catalogues have made risque undies respectable for all.[18]

Men influence this constant evolution rather than controlling it. Women negotiate with them, trying out new ideas and responding to the response. This is not a random Mendelian evolutionary process, but one in which women conceptualize men's desires and react to them with choices of their own among possible variations, according to their own authorial impulses. Women as authors compete among themselves for male approval, but they also influence each other, stealing and modifying each other's ideas.

Some men negotiate back, influencing women with praise but also with all kinds of other rewards, ranging from marriage proposals to "unearned" job promotions. Other men negotiate in the opposite direction, discouraging or penalizing the very same innovations. Women negotiate with other women as well, encouraging or severely punishing any hint of deviance. They are the primary enforcers as well as the violators of the codes.

All of this occurs in settings that are loaded with their own sign systems unrelated to heterosex. Every move along the spectrum of sexi-ness-for-straight-men is heavily constrained by the need to produce messages in all these other codes about all these other subjects. For example, dress encodes status in the workplace.

Perhaps the most important constraining context is that women dress for one another, participating in a discourse that is much more complex than that of sexy dressing for straight men, and, for many or most women, involves a greater investment of interest and energy. It is impossible to separate out the contributions of producers and consumers in this intersubjective complex, just as it is with pop culture in general. (Straight male) consumer sovereignty is a myth, as is the idea of simple imposition of mass culture by (male) taste-makers.

This is not to say that everything is all right because women have a free choice about how to dress, so whatever they actually decide to do represents what they "want" to do. Without denying that the regime gives men vastly more power than women, or that, as I will argue later on, sexual abuse has an important constitutive role both in the definition of sexy dress and in its regulation, it seems wrong to

[18] Harris (1991), pp. 114, 119.

dismiss female agency in the social construction of male excitement, and the possibility of female pleasures in the construction.

2.2 *The Conventional View: Sexy Dress Provokes Sexual Abuse*

She is a constant distraction to the male employees, with her spiked heels, fishnet stockings and plunging neckline. Her makeup is more appropriate for a nightclub, and her skirt is so short and tight that her colleagues wonder how she ever sits down.

Bauer and others say that employees have a responsibility to ensure that their personal appearance—especially in the workplace—does not indirectly encourage sexual harassment.

Not everyone agrees with that position, but a recent survey of 1769 psychiatrists suggests that many of them do believe in a link between "provocative" clothing and sexual harassment and sex crimes.

The survey included these statements and responses:

Female attire that appears to the male to invite direct sex attention tends to increase the risk of sex crimes. Yes: 63 percent; No: 21 percent; the rest undecided.

When a female minor is involved in intercourse or molestation in the home, one factor may be informality as to nudity or revealing attire. Yes: 81 percent; No: 17 percent.[19]

2.2.1 The Conventional View as Narrative

This story represents, I think, a complex intersection in our unstable cultural moment. Julie Hatfield's initial description of the sexy dresser's costume might conceivably be interpreted as part of the feminist critique of the regime's coercion of women into self-objectification for men. The story refers to "a debate over sexual harassment," and purports to reflect the views of "consultants who counsel management on how to curb sexual harassment in the workplace."[20] But her endorsement of female responsibility for controlling dangerous male sexual desires is firmly in the conventional camp, and disregards 20 years of feminist critique of that allocation of images and roles.

Hatfield has updated the conventional view by substituting "empirical data" for a simple appeal to "human (that is, male) nature" to establish the link between dress and abuse. The study to which she refers is truly post-modern social science: instead of attempting to gather data about the effect of dress on abuse, its authors polled "psychiatrists" about their views, with no indication that any of them had ever done

[19] Hatfield (1992), p. 31.

[20] Hatfield (1992), p. 31.

or seen any empirical work on the subject. Their responses have the same kind of authority as those of the man who when asked for medical advice happily gives it on the ground that although he is not a doctor, he has played one on television.

What the story does is to restate, with a slight feminist and a slight social science patina, a narrative that is both reflective of and a constitutive element in the regime's ideology of sexual relations. In this narrative, a woman wears provocative clothing and suffers sexual abuse. She demands redress of some kind from the abuser. He is put on trial on the basis of her accusations, but he is exonerated or excused on the basis of what she did. From within the ideology of the regime, this narrative is highly intelligible—it makes sense, in spite of the enraged and seemingly uncomprehending reactions of critics—and it is also highly functional.

The affect involved goes beyond "blaming the victim," as she might be blamed for not "taking care of herself": she "got what she deserved." She is a bad person. In the conventional view, what she has done wrong is to produce a particular sign, the sign of sexy dress, knowing that the sign (a) has a meaning, and (b) will produce an effect. She is responsible because in the narrative of sexy dress she understands the meaning and anticipates the effect.

The meaning of the sign, in this view, is that the woman desires to have sex with men outside the context of domestic intimacy. This is understood both by the woman and by the men who apprehend the sign. A secondary meaning of the sign is performative: it is, in itself, consent to having sex with some man outside domesticity, and she does or should understand that if she denies all the men in the setting, she will be forced or otherwise abused.

In this view, a woman who behaves in a sexually provocative way has agreed in advance to be raped or harassed if she decides she doesn't want sex with any of the men to whom she has communicated her availability. She has to go through with it. If she didn't want to go through with it, all she had to do was not produce the sign in the first place.

Well, why would a woman produce the sign? To traditionalists, this seems like a very naive question. The woman is a sexual mercenary or a slut or a tease. A mercenary is a woman who intends to get something out of a man by offering him sex in return. A slut is a woman who wants sex indiscriminately, like a man. A tease is a woman who pursues her mercenary or slut proclivity by exciting men but does not intend to "deliver" on the promise that is the meaning of the sign of sexy dress. She may be uninterested in actual sex or get sadistic pleasure from arousing and then frustrating male desire.

In each of these cases, in the conventional view, the type of female sexuality deployed is evil. It invites sex without either social legitimacy or love; it is manipulative or indiscriminate or sadistic. But it may work. When it does, the woman uses her sexual power over men, the power she exercises when she produces the sign of sexy dress, to achieve an immoral success. Abuse occurs when the woman who has set out to tease is "caught" and forced to perform her part in the bargain, or when the woman changes her mind and decides that she wants to withdraw the offer/promise she made when she produced the sign.

The man's corresponding desire for illicit sex is also immoral, though "natural", and just as wrong in the abstract as the woman's; and the abuse is wrong in itself. But there is an asymmetry in the situation which explains why she is the one most at fault. The woman in this narrative has taken the initiative by producing the exciting sign, and the man's reaction is involuntary. His violence is the expression of desire aroused and then frustrated. Women produce these anti-social reactions through their conscious acts, so both the lust and the violence are their responsibility.

But there is more to it than this. The male abuse of the sexy dresser is not just contract-enforcement or an unfortunate consequence of involuntary male excitement; it fulfills a sadistic angry impulse on the part of the blaming public. She "got what she deserved," "it served her right," "she was asking for it." This punitive reaction of traditionalist men and women seems to be related to her apparently intentional violation of the patriarchal bargain of gender in which women will be madonnas (wives/mothers or virgins) or whores.

The sexy dresser threatens the interest of traditional men and women in the stable reproduction of the regime. She is toying with the explosive, "natural" forces of sexuality outside the framework. It's not only that she is giving in to temptation or getting caught when she changes her mind; her whole course of conduct, what got her there in the first place, was a form of cheating, free-riding, selfish subversion of the tenuous arrangements that provide women in general with security against abuse and men with protection against the destructive force of their own competitive desire for women.[21]

---

[21] The following is from a supermarket tabloid. It is data only about the conventional view, since it has clearly been re-written in tabloid style and may well be an outright invention of a (possibly male) staffer:

> CANDID CONFESSIONS: Extraordinary secrets of ordinary people.
>
> *Big itch was the best revenge on class witch:*
>
> Last summer, a bunch of us high school seniors went on a two-week camping trip. We were in couples except for this tramp, Nina.
>
> Nina was always trying to steal someone's boyfriend during the school year and she was no different on our little trip.
>
> On the first night, my friend Donna and I caught Nina rubbing up against Donna's boyfriend Mike out in a clearing in the woods.
>
> We read Nina the riot act, but she just laughed it off.
>
> She kept wearing these high-cut shorts with no panties and a skimpy tube top with no bra. And when it came time to change into bathing suits for a swim, she'd find a bush you could practically see through to change her clothes behind.
>
> After 3 day of this, the rest of us girls were getting edgy. Nina's sexy antics had our boyfriends steamed up and ready to pop. She was constantly rubbing up against the guys or dancing like a stripper to the radio. There wasn't one girl who wasn't afraid that her guy was going to sneak off into the woods with Nina.
>
> Then, I caught my steady Jeff standing on the river bank and drooling as Nina splashed around in front of him—naked as a jaybird.
>
> It was the last straw! That evening, while everyone was around the campfire, I crept into Nina's tent with an armful of poison oak. I opened her sleeping bag and rubbed the leaves all over the inside ...— Cherie, 18, college freshman, Wake Forest, N.C., Globe (1992), p. 29.

The expanded narrative—in which the woman accuses the man of rape or sexual harassment, society affirms that if he has done what she says he is an offender, the facts are investigated, it turns out that she acted provocatively, he is let off and she is disgraced—raises and resolves the questions of whether there are women like this and how they should be treated. It also raises and responds to other questions that come to mind every time a woman accuses an apparently sane man of abuse.

Is it really true that women benefit from a bargain—autonomy surrendered in exchange for protection from abuse? If men can freely abuse women who are blameless, then perhaps there is no bargain and women give up their autonomy for nothing. On the other hand, if women who refuse the bargain and insist on sexual autonomy can get protection in their free-agent negotiations with men, then women also give up their autonomy for nothing.

What are men really like? If men will deal with women as equal bargainers in sexual transactions, then there is not that much danger in renouncing the bargain. On the other hand, if men who are not insane rape and abuse just for the pleasure of it, then even the bargain won't keep women safe.

The narrative answers these questions as follows:

1. The norm of patriarchal protection of women is clear—men shouldn't rape or sexually harass women who perform their part of the bargain.
2. The norm that women should find sexual fulfillment with a single male protector is clear—women shouldn't present themselves as sexually available outside domesticity.
3. Bad women who refuse the bargain—mercenaries, sluts and teases—are punished, by abuse and then by disgrace, so there are real benefits to the bargain even for women who feel ambivalent or angry about giving up their autonomy.
4. Men are indeed dangerous and violent, especially in relation to women who are asserting themselves as sexual free agents, so the bargain has a lot to offer.
5. But sane men are not randomly abusive—women are safe so long as they comply with the terms.

The narrative has appeal because these answers restore the equilibrium, the status quo ante, that was threatened by the woman's initial accusation. It seems plausible to me that people who hold the conventional view are likely to want, consciously or unconsciously, particular accusations of abuse in the real world to fit the narrative. They are likely to work hard at interpreting the event to promote this fit. They are likely to make assumptions, place burdens of proof, and imagine context in ways that will do all this. In short, the narrative is a tool for the ideological task of legitimating the regime.

2.2.2 Responses to the Narrative

The enemies of the regime can't "disprove" the regime-narrative any more than a poll of psychiatrists can prove that "revealing attire" causes incest. The narrative is not a formal theory, but a way to understand a specific course of events in the world.

In any given case, everyone might agree that it "didn't apply," or wasn't what actually happened. But it is still there to facilitate the traditionalist ideological project in the next case. The responses are no less ideological than the narrative itself, in the sense that they, too, attempt to construct templates, exemplary stories, "models," that will ease but also subtly influence future interpretations.

One response is a counter-narrative of abuse in which dress is irrelevant, a story in which it made no difference what she was wearing. In this version, male conduct is reinterpreted so that it is no longer an uncontrollable reaction to the production of a sign well understood by all participants, but rather a combination of the arbitrary sexualization of female bodies and the will to power over the victim. When men later produce the regime-narrative to explain what happened, they are lying or rationalizing. According to a letter to the editor in response to the Julie Hatfield story[22] quoted above:

Hatfield claims that female employees should leave their transparent clothing at home. But what if the harasser happens to be excited by sweatshirts and jeans, or by men's suits? Sexual harassment is not caused by women's clothing. On the contrary, it is caused by a perpetrator's hunger for power. Rather than tell women how to assuage aggressors, Hatfield and her cohorts should educate those aggressors in respecting women's rights.[23]

The difficulty with this response seems to me to be that it ignores the existence of the sign system. It is certainly true that some men will eroticize any form of female dress, and that there is no uniform that categorically repels unwanted sexual attention.[24] It may even be true that producing the sign of sexy dress actually provides protection against some harassers in some settings, because it intimidates them. And a woman who wears extremely modest clothes in a setting where the norm says she should dress quite sexily is likely to find herself approached coercively by men who see her as signaling sexual vulnerability. Male entrepreneurs abuse women sex workers who aren't sexy enough to sell.

So, it is right to describe the regime's theory that "provocative female dress is a significant cause of sexual abuse" as a myth.[25] It is a myth in the sense that a

---

[22] See Hatfield (1992).

[23] White (1992), p. 22.

[24] Pollack (1990).

> What is provocative? . . . Whenever a woman walked through the cafeteria, especially a young woman, the place would go wild . . . One woman in particular was a favorite target for this behavior . . . She wore the same white painters' pants that all the other painters wore. There was nothing in her dress or manner that welcomed the men's behavior. The only possible cause of this attention that I could identify was that she had blond hair.
>
> . . . I asked my fellow carpenters . . . 'What is going on here?' Their response was, 'She's just asking for it. Look at the way she wears those pants.' I was dumbfounded. Needless to say, the apprentice painter avoided the cafeteria after that., Pollack (1990), p. 57.

[25] "Many people know little about the crime [of rape] except the myths pervasive in our crime. Some of the more common are: . . . Otherwise decent men are spurred to rape by the clothing or behavior of women", Gordon and Riger (1991).

narrative singling out dress from the complex context of abuse is patently ideological, and in the sense that making everyone dress "conservatively" wouldn't end and (my guess) probably wouldn't even reduce the amount of abuse.

But I don't think it is just mythological thinking that explains the responses to an interview questionnaire about rape that lists possible measures the respondent might have taken "to increase [her] safety." One question asked, "when you are out alone, how often do you try not to dress in a provocative or sexy manner?", 58 percent of women answered "always," 18 percent "never," the rest in between.[26] Short of rape, many women perceive violating the dress code in the direction of being "too sexy" as creating a particular risk of persistent propositions, unwanted touching, suggestive remarks, exhibitionism, obscene phone calls, and the like, from both "creeps" and macho harassers, on the street and in the office.

It is not that the dress "causes" the reaction the way a germ causes a cold.[27] But in a particular case it may be obvious that the abuser interpreted the costume as a sign, as an expression with a meaning about the woman and/or about women in general. He then reacted to— abused—the woman as he interpreted her through the sign. If she hadn't produced the sign, she wouldn't have gotten the reaction, though maybe the man would have found someone else who did produce it and abused her instead, or, failing that, taken to abusing on a different basis. Although I don't know what portion of all abuse happens this way, I have seen it happen this way.

This is not to say that the woman who produces the sign intends to invite sexual attention, let alone abuse. The meanings of dress signs are currently contested, and consequently highly uncertain. Another letter to the editor in response to the Hatfield story:

> Enjoying what one wears is one thing, but many misguided women dress provocatively to seek attention and approval from men, not necessarily their advances. Men are told that such outfits are a signal that advances are welcome. Why, after all, would any sane person dress that way for her own comfort or pleasure?[28]

The Hatfield story in the Boston Globe included the following:

> Dress is quite an insignificant factor in such attacks,; said Phillip Resnick, a forensic psychiatry professor at Case Western Reserve Medical School in Cleveland. Rapists say that they decide they're going to rape that night, and they select their victim largely based on opportunity: Is the woman alone? Is it a dark street?, Hatfield (1992), p. 31.

> *Myth*: The woman asks for it—she dresses in an inviting manner. This is a common conclusion drawn by the harasser. It is also a rationalization that promotes harassment and retards solutions. Although there are individual cases to the contrary, limited studies available do not support a woman's dress style as a promotion of she asked for it, Hart and Dalke (1983). Contra Meritor Sav. Bank (1986) FSB v. Vinson, 477U.S. 57, 69.

[26] Gordon and Riger (1991), p. 17.

[27] Working Woman is likely trying to identify "traditionalist" respondents when it includes the following question in its survey: "Sexual harassment in your office ... Here are some general statements about sexual harassment. Do you agree or disagree with the following? ... (b) Women bring harassment problems on themselves by dressing and acting provocatively." Sexual Harassment in Your Office: The Working Woman Survey (1992), p. 14.

[28] Zazinski (1992), p. 22.

If abuse sometimes occurs in this kind of interactive context, then the anti-abuse position is in part a demand for a revision of the conventional meanings of dress language, or a resolution in favor of women's freedom of action of the current contest about those meanings. Even though they are "misguided," men should allow women to produce this sign without it having the meaning that (some) men attribute to it— they should not interpret it as an invitation or as consent in advance to violence.

This position accepts that there is a sign—sexy dressing—that is mutually understood on one level (we know what it is) but whose meaning is contested at another level (is it or is it not invitation and consent?). What is proposed is that men should agree that women can produce the sign without thereby offering an excuse for any modification in "proper" male behavior. A man who responded to the sign with unwanted advances or abuse would be breaking the rules and inviting punishment, just as he would be if he claimed that a bank's advertised "friendliness" justified his robbing it at gunpoint.[29] Sexy dressing would no longer be (or at least everyone would agree that it shouldn't be) dangerous in the way it is now. Or, if you believe that there really is no connection between production of the sign and abusive reactions, imagine that this view was general, so that the imagined threat of abuse was no longer a factor in women's dress decisions.

2.2.3 Different Reactions to the Relaxation of Sanctions Against Sexy Dressing

If we imagine that such a change in our social system actually occurred, so that there was no longer a developed script for the disciplinary abuse of sexy dressers, it seems likely that there would be changes in women's behavior as well as in men's. It is not that women would now be "free to dress any way they want," because even in the absence of abuse there would be the whole complex of internal and external pressures for compliance with the various dress codes. But production of the sign of sexy dressing would be less dangerous than it now is. The rest of this section explores the hypothesis that there would be a consequent increase in violations of the dress code in the direction of sexiness. Such a change would be controversial, indeed would bring out deep ideological conflict within the camp of critics of the regime.

The cost/benefit analysis of disciplinary abuse suggests that doing away with abuse of sexy dressers would have positive consequences for women who already violate the norm, and for those who would begin to violate it once the penalties were reduced. There would be losses for those who approve of the norm, and don't want to see more sexy dressing, even though they disapprove of vigilante enforcement.

---

[29] "There may very well be a link between dress that is interpreted as provocative and sex crimes by men, as the surveys cited by Julie Hatfield suggest, but it occurs in the minds of the perpetrators, not with the victims. Why must women continue to take responsibility for men's actions?", Martinich (1992), p. 22.

The whole subculture of practitioners and advocates would gain, including those who are turned on, and like being turned on, and those who appreciate it without a turn on, and would like to see more of it in spite of the norm.

The trouble with this approach is that it simplemindedly assumes that women now violate the norm because they "want" to, and would violate it more, for the same "reason," if there were fewer sanctions. If we are to get at the real conflict of interests between and among men and women, we have to explore these "wants" rather than taking them at face value. To begin with, there is the problem that the behavior regulated is the production of a sign for other people, and not an activity like eating ice cream in private.

A similarity to eating ice cream in private might be that the sexy dresser is engaged in "consumption," and values her freedom from sanctions because she wants to be able to enjoy this activity at the least possible cost. But because we are dealing with symbol-production, this hypothesis is less plausible than it is with more conventional kinds of consumption. Female dress is also expression, and it may in any particular case be a misrepresentation of the speaker's inner state and a strategic one at that. Reducing disciplinary abuse of sexy dressers will affect women differently according to how they characteristically relate to this (constrained) set of opportunities.

Conventional liberal thinking about this kind of issue tends to assume a sharp and unproblematic contrast between choice and duress.[30] Thus we can say that if some women respond to a reduction in disciplinary abuse of sexy dressers in the workplace by dressing sexier, they benefit because they have chosen to change their behavior. If they are within their "rights" in doing so, the private benefit is also a social good. But it seems much more plausible to suppose a continuum (perhaps a loopified continuum) between choice and duress in this case.

When we put together the variation in women's experiences of freedom or duress with the possibilities of strategic rather than simply expressive use of the dress code, it is clear that a change in incentives might be experienced in many different ways.

(a) A woman might experience a reduction in sanctions as coercing her into sexier dressing. The coercion might come from a particular man who wants her to dress deviantly for him, or from an employer, or from a clique of women friends. Sanctions against sexy dressers might be welcomed by such a woman because they counteract the pressure by giving her a "good reason" for her preferences. When she responds to the relaxation of dress discipline by dressing more sexily, she is not moving to a higher but to a lower indifference curve.
(b) The change might be experienced as allowing her to make men happy, by reducing the dangers to her of doing what they want, or of appearing to express the feelings they want her to be having. In other words, it might be the occasion for the pleasure of consent to the desires of another. In economic language, the woman's utility function might not be discrete from that of her audience. As in

[30] West (1985); Kelman (1979).

the previous case, no sexual feelings of the type conventionally understood to be expressed by sexy dressing are involved. It is not a question of what the woman herself, autonomously, feels and then expresses, but a question of what she thinks men want her to feel. Compliance (submission) might be eroticized or might not be.[31]

(c) A woman might derive sexual pleasure from the combination of her agency in creating a representation of sexuality and the sexual reaction of her audience. In other words, she might be an exhibitionist. She might experience this as a compulsion that she would rather be rid of, or as a part of her sexual nature that she is happy with. She might regret a reduction in sanctions as putting her more at the mercy of her compulsion or welcome the reduced riskiness of pursuing her kink.

(d) Some women might experience reduced abuse as increasing their power by allowing them to exploit an asset, the ability to dress sexily successfully, at the expense of other women (not as good at it) and of men (putty in their hands). Again, the gain has nothing to do with the ability to express "true" sexual selves, but rather with greater freedom to exploit the asset of perceived sexiness. For other women, the choice to dress more sexily in the post-abuse workplace might be no more than a way to minimize the losses caused by the increase in bargaining power of the advantaged group.

(e) The conventional understanding of dress as expression might apply, so that some women experience a gain in welfare because they can now "say what they mean" in a way that would previously have been dangerous.

(f) A woman might experience an increase not in the ability to express herself, but in the ability to produce a complex sexual persona, reflecting in part her "true" feelings about her sexual being, but also in part her ideas about women, sex, fashion and everything else, and in part her desire for sexual and aesthetic reaction from others.[32] Here the pleasure is in self-objectification as

---

[31] West (1985), pp. 90–111.

[32] "The Poetics Colloquium signified the world in which as a graduate student I had longed to make it. I was the only feminist speaker at the colloquium.

> Writing this paper, I tried to make it possible to speak where the men were speaking, despite my body, but also in my body. Since I experienced my inability to transcend the body, where women were trapped, I had to think a way that the body was already 'poetic,' which is to say, belonged in the realm of high literary theory where I aspired to be.
>
> ... I dressed in a manner that bespoke the body as style, stylized sexuality. I wore spike heels, seamed hose, a fitted black forties dress and a large black hat. I was dressed as a woman, but as another woman. If my speech signaled an identification with a woman of another place, my clothes bespoke an identification with a woman of another time. I was in drag. My clothing drew attention to my body but at the same time stylized it, creating stylized body, what in the paper I called a poiesis of the body. The fit between the paper and the look, the text and the performance, was articulated unconsciously, and it worked", Gallop (1988), p. 92.

performance, the pleasure of cultural creation and relationship, rather than that of being able to translate the inner sexual self into the world by representing it.[33]

In assessing each of these six hypothetical reactions, we have to take into account that the pleasures of sex are connected with the pleasures of ideological contest and of transgression. Changing the norm might de-eroticize behavior that had the pleasures of defiance or deviance. This might be true for both the sexy dresser and her audience. When the "punk" teenage subculture adapted the working class butch lesbian look, it changed its erotic significance by switching its meaning from one form of defiance to another. When punk fashion crossed over into the mainstream, leather jackets with chains lost and gained erotic and other kinds of meaning once again.

An increase in sexy dressing in the workplace, brought about by reducing disciplinary sanctions, might end up "normalized." The sexy dress subculture and its opponents would adjust to it, as would everyone else, and the "action" would shift to the outer boundary of a new rule. Exhibitionists, whether or not compulsive, would have to test the new as they tested the old, or lose their voyeurs; self-expressers would have to defy it in order to convey their true feelings; gender artists would have to play its edges to convey their particular cultural messages.

This "semiotic" property of the norm means that there is less at stake than at first appears. Women and men will communicate and produce themselves as culturally laden objects and perform, using the opposition the norm establishes between the required and the forbidden, no matter where we choose to draw the line. But it does not mean that nothing is at stake.

First, the relaxation of sanctions might have no effect at all on the quantum of sexy dress in the sense of deviation from the norm but have a major effect in the long run conflict over the eroticization of media, workplaces and public space. The particular types of eroticism characteristic of the regime might flourish, through the actions of the different types described above and their male collaborators, at the expense of the current variety of de-eroticized modes of female self-presentation.[34]

---

[33] "Gender ought not to be construed as a stable identity or locus of agency from which various acts follow; rather gender is an identity tenuously constituted in time, instituted in exterior space through a *stylized repetition of acts*. The effect of gender is produced through the stylization of the body and, hence, must be understood as the mundane way in which bodily gestures, movements, and styles of various kinds constitute the illusion of an abiding gendered self.

> ...The distinction between expression and performativeness is crucial. If gender attributes and acts, the various ways in which a body shows or produces its cultural signification, are performative, then there is no preexisting identity by which an act or attribute might be measured; there would be no true or false, real or distorted acts of gender, and the postulation of a true gender identity would be revealed as a regulatory fiction", Butler (1990), pp. 140–141.

[34] The norm of not dressing too sexily is a norm about where and when, rather than a straight out prohibition of a type of dress. Sanctions against women who violate the norm keep the "spheres" separate. The relaxation of dress code sanctions might change from both sides, and perhaps reduce, the sexual charge now associated with the contrasts between the various settings (daytime and nighttime street, movie set and back office, kitchen and boudoir, and so on). The consequences for

Second, the bodies and the psyches of the abused are at stake. The stage for the play of signifiers is something a killing field. A reduction in the total amount of violence against women, or even its delegitimation by repudiation of the regime-narrative in which "she asked for it," would have consequences, direct or indirect, for millions of women. These two sets of effects, those on the erotic quality of life under the regime, and those on the women who are the object of different kinds of disciplinary violence, evoke passionate responses. They involve the general ideological contest over sexuality.

2.2.4 Ideological Conflict Over the Discipline of Sexy Dressers

The conflicts of interests over sexy dressing arise in large part from ideological differences about its meaning for the actors and watchers who are involved. There are deep conflicts among men and among women about how to interpret "women's hedonic lives,"[35] about how we should respond to coercion, or engulfment in male utility functions, or exhibitionism, and so on. Likewise, about how to interpret and respond to the reaction of the audience of (male and female) dominators, voyeurs, prudes, aesthetes, and so on.

A very tentative map of ideologies might look like Table 2.

We might lay the grid of positions across the grid of times and places for the production and expression of sexuality. In the straight workplace, for example, each ideological position has a valance, pushing for more or less permissive norms. People in different ideological positions are likely to have very different assessments of the costs and benefits of an increase in sexy dressing brought about by a reduction in disciplinary sexual abuse.

Pro-sex traditionalism endorses traditional women's roles in the home, on the job and, in public space, but rejects the neo-puritan connection of sex and sin. It is an accommodation of the reactionary position to the evolution of liberal patriarchy toward greater permissiveness. Marabelle Morgan's "total woman" is all in favor not just of physical pleasure but of the sexual gestures and paraphernalia that are current in the culture. Sexiness within marriage, in her view, is a component of the wife's power over her husband; it is fair play in the battle of the sexes and a basis of stability (along with religion) for family life.[36] The Ladies Home Journal represents a milder, more sophisticated version of this position, with a strong liberal feminist element.

Men and women with this view tend to accept the conventional script according to which workplace sexy dressers invite, even if they don't deserve, disciplinary abuse—they are disregarding the God-given distinction of realms according to

---

those who derive pleasure from the contrast, and for those who invest in it ideologically, would be complex and far reaching.

[35] West (1987), p. 90.

[36] Consider bars with male strippers, and lingerie parties on the model of Tupperware parties, Enrenreich et al. (1986), pp. 134–160.

Table 2 Ideological conflict over the discipline of sexy dressers

Reaction	Liberal patriarchy	Radicalism
Neo-puritan traditionalism (sex = danger of sin)	Clean and dirty sex naturally separate (home and house)	Neo-puritan feminism (sex = danger of abuse)
Pro-sex traditionalism (*The Total Woman*[a])	"Consensual" sex healthy not dirty (sex manuals and the "sexual revolution")	Pro-sex post-mod (*Pleasure and Danger*[b])

[a]Morgan (1975), pp. 13–37
[b]Vance (1983)

which a woman should be a whore only in the marital bedroom. A marginal increase in office sexy dressing in response to a relaxation of sanctions is likely to look like exhibitionism, commodification, or post-modern blasphemy. Moreover, it is a threat to marriage, to the wife's legitimate monopoly on her husband's sex life.

The neo-puritan strand in radical feminism takes a much more uncompromising attitude toward the "sexual revolution" and the liberal feminist emphasis on consent as the criterion of healthy sexuality. In this view, the relaxation of sexual prohibitions along with the general eroticization of the culture have disserved women because their "consent" takes place in a context of radical power inequality. There is inequality in the way society constructs sexuality to conform to the male model (the eroticization of domination). Men and women socialized in this way then confront each other in one-on-one encounters in which men pervasively are violent or threaten violence, deploy their superior economic status, and manipulate the discourse of consent to get what they want.[37]

In this perspective, the central reality of sexual relations is danger to women from men. Moreover, "under male supremacy, heterosexuality ensures that each woman is intimately colonized by the dominant class."[38] For neo-puritan feminists, a reduction in sexual abuse is likely to be an important good, while any concomitant increase in sexy dressing is likely to look like the evil of objectification. From this ideological perspective, the change in the marginal woman's behavior is likely to look coerced or compulsive or commodified.

The non-abusive regulation of sexy dress, through negotiation among women and the application of merely social sanctions to deviants, looks to me, as a male observer, to be a common feminist practice. Many feminists enforce dress codes among themselves and work for their more general acceptance because they think they express a healthier, better attitude toward sexuality than that of the sexy dress subculture. They see the particular conventions of sexy dress, the actual content of the sign system, as expressing patriarchal views about female attractiveness, and particularly the view that what makes women attractive is vulnerability to domination and accessibility to male sexual appropriation.

I would put myself in the pro-sex po-mo (post-modern) box in the diagram. This position affirms not just the possibility but the actual occurrence (sometimes) of

[37] See generally Linden (1982), Jefreys (1990).

[38] Hagan (1991), p. 31.

great pleasure in heterosex, and the (sometimes) liberatory, oppositionist character of that pleasure. But it doesn't privilege heterosexuality, affirming the same possibilities in the practices of sexual minorities, as well as in the day-to-day practices that are coded to permit erotic life to flourish in everything from cooking to teaching to dressing.

An important difference from the neo-puritan strand in feminism (and from much of the rest of left thought) is a post-modern take on the meaning of the phrase "social construction." The cliche version is: "Until we elect to take over the job, the dominant culture constructs our reality and forms our values."[39] But the "dominant culture" never has either the coherence or the power to construct us in the way suggested, and we never achieve the "outside" position vis a vis ourselves- in-the-culture that would allow us to "take over the job." We are positioned at any given moment by everything that has gone before so that we can only do and be some things, and not others. When we most folly experience ourselves as choosing, as improvising, we are ringing the changes on the limited scripts the culture makes available. But we nonetheless sometimes change those scripts.[40]

The pro-sex po-mo manifesto has already been written, by Marny Hall, under the rather mysterious name of "anti-sex":

> Anti-sex, despite its oppositional designation, is apposite, rather than opposite, patriarchal sex. Consequently, at the same time that anti-sex challenges old constructions, it contains elements of the old which may be teased and twisted into new pleasure scripts that are tailored to the histories, fantasies and neurophysiologies of intimates. In this scrambling process, old phallocentric practices, instead of serving as the invisible template of lovemaking, can be impelled into consciousness, rearranged, refurbished, and combined with elements from other dimensions of experience.[41]

People in the pro-sex po-mo position are no less attached to making moral and political judgements about social structures and individual conduct than anyone else. The pro-sex po-mo idea is not that "anything goes," but rather that "anything might go." Coercion, engulfment, compulsion and sexual abuse are real, there to hate. Pleasure and resistance relate to them (it seems) symbiotically, even parasitically, rather than through a permanent obliteration and replacement of the regime.

The language of dress simultaneously promotes eroticized male domination of women and permits its subversion. Items of clothing do more than signify, however, even in the simplest case of the signs on the men's and women's room doors. Dressing is one of the most important ways in which people reflect, reproduce, and change through time our particular social constructions of the differences between men and women, of the appropriate relations between men and women,

---

[39] Hagan (1991), p. 31. Another example: "If sexuality is socially constructed, it both changes and it can be changed . . . Of course, such processes take time, but the social-constructionist position opens us to the possibilities of transformation, including to the responsibility to account for our own sexuality", Kimmel (1990).

[40] Butler (1990), p. 147.

[41] Hall (1991), p. 91.

and of hetero- and homosexuality.[42] If you want to figure out the regime of gender, you will find it set forth, or reflected, coded, in dress. But to dress is more than to reflect an order located elsewhere: it is to produce a sign, willy-nilly, to act, to express something.

As an expression, it is double. On the one hand, it says something about or represents the dresser, fits the dresser into one of the available, intelligible categories of people. But this is only half of it. Dress is performative in the sense that it does something in the world, rather than just representing an "interior." When a man or a woman puts on a costume, he or she implicitly affirms the ideas coded into it, not just as ideas about the self, but as ideas about gender. Dress is both an operation carried out using the conventions, and a comment on them.[43]

It may express adherence to the regime, or it may express some form of disengagement or opposition. It is like voting. It puts the wearer on one side or the other. When a dress performance reflects the ideas of the regime, it also reproduces the regime, in the sense of extending it in time as "the same thing." Where the ideas are divergent, they may change the regime, though usually they don't. I'm not sure whether this has to be so, but it seems clear to me that it is an aspect of our particular cultural situation.

For example, sexy dress (deviation from the norm in the direction of a more sexy setting) may be read as a critique of the boring, utilitarian asexuality of the setting and the people in it. Conservative dress may seem to be a critique of the gender stereotypes coded into the female fashions conventions of the setting. It may also be read as a critique of the conventionally feminine behavior of the other women in the setting.

A dress or a picture of a dress functions quite unambiguously, when opposed to pants, as a signifier of the idea "woman," and a person who fails to correctly interpret the sign is likely to be thought stupid or weird. But the theory that there are ideas beyond "woman" that are reflected, reproduced or resisted by this particular sign is

---

[42] Everyday dress practices, particularly those of the subcultures discussed in Part IV, respond to, but also powerfully influence the "gender media images" described in the following:

> [T]here is an important way that gender media images have become an essential for heterosexual sexuality. Since the capitalist patriarchal nuclear family has given way to a raft of alternative family forms, another material base is required to perpetuate the hetero-sexual 'masquerade' of the innate attraction between men and women. Since the contents of heterosexual desire are socially learned and there is no longer a hegemonic patriarchal family to provide the content of masculinity and femininity, there must be some other social arena which teaches males and females what the opposite sex desire from them. Thus, fashion and media images, once merely the perpetuators of images generated by the patriarchal family, have become the semi-autonomous social arena in which sexist and heterosexist desire are constructed. Ferguson (1989), p. 118. This is the level of connotation of "rhetoric" in Barthes' semiology. See Barthes (1983).

[43] Dressing is analogous, in its impact on its "audience," to movie-making: "Thus, one's gendered subjectivity is not only implicated, such as it is, in the spectator's encounter with each film, but also constructed, reaffirmed or challenged, displaced or shifted, in each film-viewing process", de Lauretis (1987).

obviously contestable. The women in the above examples might deny that they meant any such thing by their dress ("it's personal, not political"). Among those (most people) who engage in the contested practice of interpreting dress "ideologically" at least some of the time, there is no consensus about what particular ideas particular items of dress affirm.

This means that any given act of dressing can have different meanings for different observers, and different effects on them. It can look like opposition to one person but like conformity to another. A particular act of dress interpreted as conformity can incite one person to disgusted resistance and persuade another that resistance is hopeless. What acts will change the culture rather than reproduce it can never be predicted with certainty, and the very definition of change is likely to be contested in its turn.[44]

3 Abuse and Resistance in the Language of Sexy Dress

In the final section of my original article, I drew on a range of examples from both fashion and popular culture to show how dress repertoires have allusions to abuse through their genealogical connections back to narratives, and to demonstrate that these allusions to abuse are part of what makes the situation of the sexy dresser equivocal. Here I summarise that argument, and the reasons for thinking that there is, nonetheless, space for resistance, and for the eroticization of female autonomy rather than abuse.

It is possible to catalogue in a rough and ready way some of the main sexual narratives to which female costumes and particular items of dress refer in order to achieve their exciting effects. The process of allusion operates in two dimensions, the synchronic (to current narratives) and the diachronic (to past narratives).

"Sexy dress" as I have been defining it means dress that diverges from the norm for the setting in which it is worn "in the direction" of the next sexier setting. This means that the dress alludes to that sexier setting, and then to the next after that, all in the direction of settings in which men and women actually engage in sex. The sexy dresser invites the straight male audience to imagine being with her in the setting her dress alludes to. This is the synchronic dimension.

[44] If gender is a representation subject to social and ideological coding, there can be no simple one-to-one relationship between the image of woman inscribed in a film and its female spectator. On the contrary, the spectator's reading of the film (including interpretive and affective responses, cognitive and emotional strategies) is mediated by her existence in, and experience of, a particular universe of social discourse and practices in daily life. Thus, for instance, feminist criticism has shown that readings emerging out of a politically radical or oppositional consciousness can significantly alter the interpretation and the effects of filmic representation, as well as the spectator's self-representation, and may contribute to changing the social meanings and finally the codes of representation themselves. de Lauretis (1987).

The diachronic dimension is more complicated. One can arrange narratives in "genealogies," meaning sequences in which clothing and text in the present refer to an earlier combination which in turn refers to another still further back in time. Starting points are not "origins," but merely where we get to when we reconstruct backward as far as we can.[45]

One costume genealogy "begins" with Frederick's of Hollywood, moves on to the Cosmopolitan girl, and culminates in Victoria's Secret. Frederick's was the mail order catalogue associated with middle class stereotypes of "animal" working class sexuality, with "girlie magazines," strip joints and street prostitution.[46] Cosmopolitan was originally a complex attempt to formulate a sexual style for lower middle class pink collar employees that would combine elements from the world of Frederick's with the sex-positive ideology of the liberal intelligentsia and the "youth culture" of the 1960s.

The mass success of the lingerie section of the Victoria's Secret catalogue represents the gentrification of this cultural terrain—its simultaneous appropriation and transformation by the middle class. However, its name suggests the catalogue's aspiration to a position in a second genealogy. This one begins, perhaps, with *The Memoirs of Jacques Casanova*,[47] and continues in the sexualization of actresses through their representational association with middle and upper middle-class pornography and prostitution during the nineteenth century.[48]

Here the allusion is to aristocratic decadence and kinky sexuality, rather than to the "animality" of the working class. Queen Victoria's secret was that beneath the repressed exterior of nineteenth century life there was "rampant" illicit sex. The late twentieth century Victoria's secret is that she is a middle class professional woman dressed in a conservative business suit with "naughty" underwear underneath.

Some intermediate terms in this genteel progression include the upper-class institution of expensive "French lingerie" and the 1960s reception of *My Secret Life*,[49] *Fanny Hill*[50] and *The Story of O*[51] as "erotic classics" rather than "hard core." The mass success of *Victoria's Secret* lingerie is a comedown in this sequence, an appropriation of upper-class sexual culture from below.

[45] Foucault (1977).

[46] "Trashy or Sexy? Men, salesclerks report, gravitate toward black things, red things, sheer things, garter belts, and push-up bras ... These are articles women seldom buy for themselves as most of them don't care to look like prostitutes when undressing in the gym. There is a time and a place for them, but if you are worried about sending the wrong message, stick to pastels, anything silk and simple, or robes", Wolfensberger (1992), pp. 40, 72.

[47] Casanova (1929).

[48] Davis (1991), pp. 78–86.

[49] Harris (1963).

[50] Cleland (1963).

[51] Reage (1965).

A third "outlaw" genealogy, androgynous and sadomasochistic, begins with Elvis Presley, Marlon Brando, James Dean, Scorpio Rising,[52] Last Exit to Brooklyn[53] (the '60s book, not the '80s movie) and the iconic Hell's Angel "biker girl." It passes through groupies and plaster-casters[54] into lesbian s/m,[55] punk, Mapplethorpe, and the "metallica" subculture. The women in the *Rolling Stone* photos of the "heavy metal societies of New York and L.A.," by Mark Seliger,[56] look strikingly like the Vogue photos accompanying the Declaration of the Right to Sexy Dressing. According to Elle:

> Hell's Angels and Hollywood starlets have one thing in common this year—Harley hunger. Brando started it, of course, when he straddled his gleaming road hog in "The Wild One". But what used to be a symbol of in-your-face rebellion is fast becoming the ultimate fashion accessory. Whether it's the '92 Sportster 1200 or the latest model Softail Custom, a Harley-Davidson looks both classic and sexy, even standing still. That's not to say it isn't a serious machine.[57]

This genealogy reaches the present, momentarily enters high fashion, and momentarily fuses with the other genealogies in Madonna's Blond Ambition tour costumes designed by Gaultier and in the current work of Karl Lagerfeld.[58]

It should be clear from my examples that the genealogies of sexy dress involve a double movement—backward through time and outward toward the social margins as defined by the straight white middle class. There is the upper margin of Victorian aristocracy, the lower margin of proletarian sexuality, and the horizontal margin of outlaw culture. There are also geographic margins—the France of "Oo-la-la," the South Seas (the sarong), and the "Latin Firecracker" (Flamenco skirt, fan, head-dress). In the United States there is a racial margin—the locus of white fantasy representations of black male sexual athleticism (for example, the movie *Mandingo*[59]) and black female promiscuity.[60]

Genealogies connect sexy dressing to abuse through a four-step process. The first step is an item of dress. The Ladies' Home Journal article that credits Victoria's

---

[52] Movie from 1964.

[53] Novel by Selby (1964).

[54] Des Barres (1987).

[55] *E.g.* Califia (1990).

[56] Seliger (1991), pp. 51–52.

[57] Great Style (1992), pp. 18, 20.

[58] Orth (1992), p. 116. "That's how Lagerfeld answers the critics who say his recent work for Chanel—which borrows liberally from downtown hookers and hustlers as well as from uptown debs on drugs, in tank tops and tulle ballerina skirts - is vulgar. Maybe you are longing for those chic-of-the-week $1000 Chanel motorcycle boots? - exact replicas, except for the trade- mark *C*'s, of the $70 variety he appropriated from the look of S&M boys in leather bars fifteen years ago. But in Lagerfeld's head they are already gone, out". Orth (1992), p. 157.

[59] Mandingo (Paramount Pictures Corp. 1979).

[60] See generally Collins (1991), pp. 77–78, 166–79; Hooks (1992), pp. 61–77. Why isn't there the close connection between white sexual stereotypes of black women and dress that exists for the others?

Secret with making "risque undies respectable" lists the "biggest undercover best-sellers":

Lacy pushup bras
Teddies/camisoles
Slinky slip gowns
Bikini panties in hot colors
Bustiers[61]

The costume item in the setting evokes, perhaps only by a minor detail, the costume worn by women in another setting in a different period. A hint in the shape of the bodice of an otherwise "conservative" dress might evoke a Victorian bustier. Second, the bustier might evoke an image of a woman wearing a bustier in an upper-class boudoir in a Victorian "naughty" postcard. Third, the image of the Victorian woman in the postcard wearing a bustier in an upper-class boudoir might evoke a female character in a narrative, specifically a narrative from Victorian pornography. The woman in the bustier is a maid, or a young woman of good family. Fourth, the image of that character might evoke what happened to her in the narrative: she was seduced, devirginized, looked at, bound, whipped, shared, enslaved—against her will until she lost control and loved it. Across cultural genres—books, music videos, films, lingerie catalogues, magazines—we can trace recurring tropes: the reference to masturbation; the reference to the social margins; the reference to women's sexual power over men; the reference to the female defiance of patriarchy. In short, sexy dressing can reasonably be read as reflecting and reproducing (some) men's, and the regime's, "celebration of the rape, abuse and humiliation of women."[62]

There is, however, considerable nuance here. According to the regime, women are allowed (or required) to call attention to their sexuality only in some contexts—for example, within marital privacy, when they are single women looking for men in bars or clubs or at parties, when they are prostitutes, and when they are producing images of sexuality in movies or advertisements or the like. In other settings—the street, the workplace, the classroom, the supermarket—they are to desexualize themselves.

Dress that deviates toward sexiness in a desexualized setting carries with it the message of the setting: that the woman is not sexually available. She is wearing a costume. It may say a lot about her, and about what her attitude might be in a different setting, but it most definitely does not have the meaning in this one that it would have there. Indeed, the meaning of sexy dress out of place sometimes seems to be that the woman claims the right to present herself as sexual without the permission, which she can have only at the cost of being available, that goes with being a wife alone with her husband, a single person on the make, a prostitute, or an actress acting. And then she claims the further right to deny sex to the men she has aroused.

[61] Harris (1963), p. 119.

[62] Bordo (1991), p. 128.

Of course, this is not *the* meaning of sexy dress. It might mean something entirely different. Moreover, women are not equally free to signify in this way. Bell Hooks claims that since black women "are coded always as 'fallen' women in the racist cultural iconography we can never, as can Madonna, publicly 'work' the image of ourselves as innocent female daring to be bad."[63] But sexy dressers do sometimes put men in the position of picking up an allusion to settings in which women are available, while having to obey the norms of the actual setting, which make them unavailable. And there are many possible male reactions to this kind of female resistance that conveys sexuality, and at the same time, defiantly, autonomy.

It seems to me that many men react to this apparent message not with fantasies of dominating or abusing women, or even with hostility, but with disquiet or fear. It is not fear of the particular sexy dresser, but fear for their investment in women particularly conceived—as beings whose sexuality is open to their appropriation, as beings whose love for particular men abolishes their autonomy, or who are the common property of all men. The sexually autonomous woman disrupts the madonna/whore diad by advertising her refusal to be either one.

It is easy to dismiss the negative male reaction as the consequence of patriarchal indoctrination. The regime does indeed demand that men be "proprietors" for whom their women's "morals are always in question and decency always invoked: 'Why did you look at that guy like that?' 'You're really going out in that short skirt?' "[64] But anyone, man or woman, who has experienced intense sexual jealousy knows better than to be patronizing about it. The sexually autonomous woman is potentially threatening to all men because her defiant existence suggests that no woman is "true" in the way patriarchy promises that the madonna type will be true.

In some men, the reference to defiance of patriarchy evokes not only fear and anger, but also a set of positive reactions. I think these are rooted in a paradoxical combination of connection and disconnection. The woman whose dress defies patriarchy conveys the comforting message that women are more like men in their sexuality than either patriarchy or feminism have much acknowledged. No woman will be true in the way the culture promises that the madonna type will be true. But neither are women the aliens they would be if they *could* be like that.

Second, there is the allusion to sex without either the whole range of domesticating, regularizing, defining roles and rules of the regime, or the context of prostitution. By this I don't mean sex without responsibility or intimacy; sex without either is widely available within the regime, both in and outside of marriage. The (straight white middle class) male fantasy of the female free agent is of a woman who doesn't owe you sex under the terms of the patriarchal bargain (not "a wife") and isn't looking to get something out of you (not "a whore"). The reference is to sex in which the man doesn't have to worry whether the woman "really" "wants it."

Third, the sexy dresser is doing something the man would do if he could. His stereotypical feminine traits—forbidden by the regime—get projected onto the

[63] Hooks (1992), p. 160.

[64] Heyn (1992), pp. 46, 48.

woman who enacts femininity against the norm of the setting. Whatever she may actually be feeling, the sign of sexy dress is the sign of narcissism, exhibitionism and desire, body power. We (men) can have it through identification with women, if only women will "take it on." Most (straight white middle class) women don't seem to want to. And why should they?

But wanting women to enact body power, and enjoying—being sexually excited by—their performances when they do, is not the same thing as wanting to dominate or abuse them. Indeed, sexy dressing sometimes affirms the possibility of this kind of female power brought home from the temporal, spatial and racial margins; in other words as a possibility within straight white middle class life in the present, rather than located necessarily, only and forever in the abusive narratives of the red light district, the Victorian boudoir and the motorcycle gang.

As with all pleasure and all interstitial resistance, there is a "dark side" to this collaboration. There is the problem that the male fantasy of the female free agent is only apparently disentangled from the madonna/whore duality. She is defined only negatively. The minute the woman is a real person, we are caught again, inevitably, in the web of roles. People do owe each other and want things from each other as soon as they know each other even a little. This stuff has to be negotiated, and the fantasy of free agency on either side can make this harder rather than easier.

The web of roles is given (at least for the time); the reality of inequality between men and women within the regime is given (at least for the time); inequality between particular men and women (with women sometimes advantaged) is given; and that a sign is not a signified is given. Given all this, even the most purely pleasurable, purely oppositional reference of sexy dress is shadowed, for the male audience, by the possibility that the signifier (dress) is a lie about the signified (the woman). She is "really" coerced or a commodifier or engulfed or compulsive, rather than the self-expresser or gender artist we let ourselves hope she was. It turns out she was only masquerading as a masquerader.[65]

I think this is often the case for the woman herself; she does not know whether or not she's lying, or whether it is possible either to lie or to tell the truth.[66] I also think that any particular woman's pleasure in her defiant sexy dress is often shadowed by the possibility that no one, not one single person, experiences it as she would want.

I think nonetheless that some of the time, some sexy dressers and some of their audience are engaged in pleasure/resistance in the interstices of the regime. They are eroticizing female autonomy. In so doing they undermine not only the structure that opposes madonna and whore but also that which opposes straight white bourgeois vanilla sexuality to the (imagined) kinky, animal, androgynous sexuality of the margins.[67]

[65] On the different interpretations of femininity as masquerade, see Doane (1991), pp. 25–26, 37–39; Butler (1990), pp. 46–54.

[66] "If the inner truth of gender is a fabrication and if a true gender is a fantasy instituted and inscribed on the surface of bodies, then it seems that genders can be neither true nor false but are only produced as the truth effects of a discourse of primary and stable identity", Butler (1990), p. 136.

[67] I argued above that this can happen because the woman wears clothing whose message of erotic availability is contradicted by the well-understood norms of the setting, so that she is neither

This must be always an uncertain form of politics because the signifying woman may be doing more harm than good, feeding the conventional view in which the tease deserves what she gets and men get off on woman-wanting mixed with woman-hating. For both men and women, it seems to me, the experience is compromised because it occurs within, is indeed dependent for its meaning on, the larger web of references to male sexual abuse of women and to male degradation in relation to them. It is never just "the truth" (something to be relied on) that the experience is indeed pleasure/resistance rather than something else, something bad, instead.

Doing and appreciating sexy dress is flawed as pleasure/resistance in another way. It is asymmetrical. The (straight white middle class) men (or man) watch and the woman performs. It seems plausible to me that this pattern reenforces, helps reproduce one of the bad aspects of patriarchy: its construction of woman as the object of the attentive, adoring, excited male gaze, the actress active by being-for-the-men, while the men dispose of her fate, and the fate of the world, on the side.[68]

What is wrong with this politically is that it contributes to disempowering women as actors within the "male sphere." What seems to me wrong with it erotically, as a (straight white middle class) man, is that it requires each party to give up a possible pleasure—that which might be found in the activity the regime allocates to the opposite sex. To say this is to make a choice between two plausible routes beyond asymmetry.

One is to try to get rid of sexual objectification and to de-eroticize power in sex. Getting rid of objectification on the male side means avoiding experiencing the woman as the involuntary bearer of multiple sexual significations hooked up to multiple sexual narratives, and trying to experience her as a "real person." From the woman's side, it means sacrificing the possible pleasure, avoiding the possible degradation, and renouncing the possible power that are to be had by playing the sexual fantasy object.

---

available nor unavailable, but autonomous (male) and simultaneously the repository of body-power (female). This might be an example of what Judith Butler is talking about in the following passage:

> In the place of a "male-identified" sexuality in which "male" serves as the cause and irreducible meaning of that sexuality, we might develop a notion of sexuality constructed in terms of phallic relations of power that replay and redistribute the possibilities of that phallicism precisely through the subversive operation of "identifications" that are, within the power field of sexuality, inevitable ... If there is no radical repudiation of a culturally constructed sexuality, what is left is the question of how to acknowledge and "do" the construction one is invariably in. Are there forms of repetition that do not constitute a simple imitation, reproduction, and, hence consolidation of the law ...?", Butler (1990), pp. 30–31. "If the regulatory fictions of sex and gender are themselves multiply contested sites of meaning, then the very multiplicity of their construction holds out the possibility of a disruption of their univocal posturing. Butler (1990), p. 32.

[68] "Both visually and narratively, cinema defines woman as image: as spectacle to be looked at and object to be desired, investigated, pursued, controlled and ultimately possessed by a subject who is masculine, that is, symbolically male". de Lauretis (1987), p. 99.

De-eroticizing power in sex means looking for the sexual charge, the excitement, that is sometimes present when the other is "just the same" while at the same time "different," without difference implying hierarchy. It also means trying to "deprogram" one's own excitement at images of domination and submission. Though this is unmistakably the liberal humanist sexual program, it seems to me what is often behind cultural and socialist feminist theorizing about sex as well.[69]

But there is another way to imagine getting beyond asymmetry, be ginning with Judith Butler's[70] point that:

> The pro-sexuality movement within feminist theory and practice has effectively argued that sexuality is always constructed within the terms of discourse and power, where power is partially understood in terms of heterosexual and phallic cultural conventions. ... If sexuality is culturally constructed within existing power relations, then the postulation of a normative sexuality that is "before," "outside," or "beyond" power is a cultural impossibility and a politically impracticable dream, one that postpones the concrete and contemporary task of rethinking the subversive possibilities for sexuality and identity within the terms of power itself.

4 Conclusion: An Erotic Interest in Ending Abuse

As consumers, men and women operate on the cultural map by picking and choosing among the kinds of arousal the culture offers them. In this mode they do more than simply register their personal relationship to the social field they are born into. They participate willy-nilly. But they are more passive than in the modes of self-creation, such as fantasy, play, experiment, and invention. In our active being on the map, whether in public or in private, we seek sexual excitement and also moral value, and produce them, or flee them, rather than merely registering them in ourselves or choosing among pre-set alternatives. Like it or not, we find ourselves changed by the experiences that ensue, and sometimes we change our surroundings.

We fantasize, play, experiment and invent using the repertoire our culture makes available. Fantasy and play involve the reversal of expectations and of social valuations, and entering imaginatively into situations that one might flee in real life. Experiment and invention are not either unless they contravene a norm of some

---

[69] See Linden (1982); See also Bartky (1990):

> The right, staunchly defended by liberals, to desire what and whom we please and, under certain circumstances, to act on our desire, is not an issue here; the point is that women would be better off if we learned when to refrain from the exercise of this right. A thorough overhaul of desire is clearly on the feminist agenda: the fantasy that we are overwhelmed by Rhett Butler should be traded in for one in which we seize state power and reeducate him... Samois in effect advises P. to ignore in her own life a general principle to which, as a feminist, she is committed and which she is therefore bound to represent to all other women: the principle that we struggle to decolonize our sexuality by removing from our minds the internalized forms of oppression that make us easier to control. Bartky (1990), p. 51.

[70] Judith Butler, Gender Trouble, p. 30 (supra note 5).

kind. It is part of the dark side that the connected repertoires of stereotypical gender identities, archetypical narratives, and costumes associated with the identities and the narratives, all allude to the real life practice of abuse. Because there is no way to operate without these tainted repertoires, there is always the risk that what we think is escape or daring resistance in the interstices is turning us into victims or victimizers.

It seems to me that for many people, myself included, the relationship between what it is exciting to produce or consume and what is "good" is profoundly complex, and problematic. The relationship is not as simple as a perennial conflict between an internal moral code and a set of internal propensities to excitement. It is always hard to tell whether the code that says "no" or "yes" is "really" inside us or an imposition from outside, from an authority that is open to question. The same is true for the charges we find associated with things we want or equally passionately don't want to do. Our turn-ons are conditioned, always open to the critique of external imposition, just as codes are sometimes mere indoctrination.

Moreover, even what we "really" believe is open to our own interpretation and reinterpretation. This can be, as in legal opinion writing, ex post rationalization, or casuistry, or "evolution of timeless principles to meet new circumstances," or what we ourselves regard as our own moral growth. The same is true of erotic charges. We learn them and unlearn them. Abuse, tangled into the cultural images through which we produce and interpret our own and other people's sexuality, seems to me to weigh heavily on this tricky, risky enterprise.

I think that men and women might fantasize, play, experiment and innovate more, and perhaps more happily, if there was less of this danger. By this I mean specifically if there were less incest and rape and sexual harassment. I don't mean that there would be fewer fantasies involving these things. Rather, I mean that the positive uses of such fantasies, for both men and women, would be less impeded by guilt and fear. Sexual abuse is, as the radical feminists have rightly, rightly insisted, an instrument of male disciplinary terror against women, and, as the radical feminists have rightly insisted, our culture inculcates erotic pleasure in male domination of women in every aspect of life.

These fantasies, and play, experiment and innovation that use them as elements, including the practice of sexy dress, sometimes reflect and reproduce the most hateful aspects of the way men treat women under the regime. But they are not just, or essentially, or always, politically incorrect. According to Ann Ferguson, there are two ways to interpret the recent increase in the male pornography industry:

> Either one can see it as a relatively benign male fantasy "backlash" to the increased sexual autonomy of women or else as a determined attempt by male chauvinists to sexually objectify women so as to legitimize sado-masochistic gender roles in heterosexual sex.
>
> Though it cannot presently be proved which of these two analyses is correct, the sexual symbolic code as presented in the public media is clearly a site of contestation ....[71]

---

[71] Ferguson (1989), p. 116.

On the other side, the choice is just as stark:

> Is it true that persons who get off on masochism in bed are by that practice perpetuating a vulnerable ego in other areas of their social life? Or is that person merely venting an unconscious (and possibly unchangeable) aspect of her emotional life thus expurgating its influence from the rest of her life? . . .
>
> Despite the heated claims by both proponents and opponents of S/M that it is empowering *vs* disempowering to the women who engage in it, there is no clear proof either way . . .[72]

There is more wrong with this than the insistence that fantasy *must be* one thing or the other, and that someone might prove which one it is. It might be one *or* the other for a particular person in a particular context. It might be other things as well. Here are three others, from the straight white male side, the first from Scott MacDonald. He starts from the idea that "the same cultural history which has defined women as Beautiful has had . . . as its inevitable corollary, the Ugliness of men; women have been defined as beautiful precisely in contrast to men."[73]

> To me, the nature and function of pornography have always seemed understandable as a way for men to periodically deal with the cultural context which mitigates against their full acceptance of themselves as sexual beings. The fantasies men pay to experience in porn arcade booths and movie houses may ostensibly appear to be predicated on the brutalization of women. But from a male point of view, the desire is not to see women harmed, but to momentarily identify with men who—despite their personal unattractiveness by conventional cultural definitions, despite the unwieldy size of their erections, and despite their aggressiveness with their semen—are adored by the women they encounter sexually.[74]

Second, what of the theory that upper middle class white male masochism boomed in the 1980s, along with the New York dominatrix business, in response to the social insistence that these men behave in a super-macho way while working as Michael Douglas in Wall Street?[75] The inverse of this theory is that *sometimes* male fantasies of dominating women represent not backlash, but symbolic compensation for male efforts to comply with the feminist ethical demand that they renounce their super-

---

[72] Ferguson (1989), p. 215.

[73] MacDonald (1983), p. 40.

[74] He adds:

> In [some] instances the fantasy is in punishing resistant women for their revulsion. Of course, the punishments—usually one form of rape or another—often end with the fantasy woman's discovery of an insatiable hunger for whatever has been done to her. This frequent turnabout appears to be nothing more than a reconfirmation of the stupid, brutal myth that women ask to be raped or enjoy being raped, but—as sadly ironic as this seems—it could also be seen as evidence that, in the final analysis, men don't mean harm to women, or don't wish to mean harm to women: their fantasy is the acceptance of their own biological nature by women. I've always assumed that porn and rape ***are*** part of the same general problem, though I've always felt it more likely that porn offers an outlet for some of the anger engendered by men's feelings of sensual aesthetic inferiority, than that it serves as a fuel for further anger. But I'm only speaking from my own experience. I've rarely spoken frankly about such matters with men who use porn. MacDonald (1983), p. 42.

[75] Wall Street (Twentieth-Century Fox 1987).

macho stance in relation to women. Signe Hammer suggested, 15 years ago, a parallel theory about women: "Our basic rape fantasy reflects our anxiety about asserting ourselves in all areas - in work, sex, and relationships."[76]

Third, many written pornographic narratives of male humiliation, domination and abuse of women are told relentlessly from the female point of view (*The Story of O*).[77] They invite the male reader to participate in the consciousness of the victim, and particularly in her experience of overwhelming, ego-obliterating pleasure when she surrenders to the will of the male abuser.

It seems obvious to me that sometimes the goal is to permit the male reader vicarious access—access safely distanced by the combination of the gender and the helplessness of the victim—to the pleasure he might derive from giving up the fight to dominate other men. This might be pleasure/resistance, however distorted, in a regime that tells him competition with men is his reason for being and greatest role-appropriate pleasure. In this interpretation, it is men, rather than women, who can fantasize their own pleasure in self-surrender only when they fantasize it as forced, and only when they can pretend that it is they themselves who are doing the forcing.[78]

I don't mean to suggest that a given fantasy (or a given costume) has one or another of these meanings for its audience because that is the meaning that is "in" it. Quite the contrary, my point is that men and women *use* fantasies (and costumes), constrained by the elusive requirement of some minimal "fit," on the way toward these diverse imaginary pleasures. In the extreme case, abolishing real life male sexual abuse of women would reduce the dangerousness of this enterprise, for both men and women, by cutting the connection between rape fantasies and real life rape, between incest fantasies and incest.

In such a world, some people would stick fast to what turns them on, and others would "stretch the envelope". I would feel freer to fantasize the boy hooker in myself if I weren't so scared of pimps—but also freer to fantasize the john in me. Whichever way one chose to go, Susan Keller's image of the process of gender change would be easier to accept:

> I suggest that there is no pure gender culture. Instead, I think of all cultural artifacts as being like the Watts Towers in Los Angeles, a structure/sculpture in the middle of Watts that was decorated over many years with various throwaways—pieces of plastic medicine bottles, pottery shards, used tile, Seven-Up bottles. Everything, like the Watts Towers, is a re-creation from stuff that was already created, which itself was recreated from stuff that

---

[76]Hammer (1976), p. 11 as quoted in Morgan (1977), pp. 227, 230. Morgan comments: "It. . .provokes the startling thought that assertive women in general and feminists in particular might be especially prey to such culturally implanted self-punishing devices." But it seems to me wrong to see the "devices" as "self-punishing." The self-punishment is in guilt about one's fantasy, which is pleasure, whether it involves punishing or being punished.

[77]Reage (1965).

[78]The work that seems to be most clearly inspired by some such idea is the 1985 trilogy by A.N. Roquelaure [Ann Rice], The Claiming of Sleeping Beauty, Beauty's Punishment, and Beauty's Release. For yet another take, see Benjamin (1988), pp. 51–84.

> was already created. Every possibility that exists, and that we will be transformed into, will be, like the Watts Towers, composed of the leftovers, scavenged treasures of the dominant culture.[79]

The argument for a male erotic interest in reducing the sexual abuse of women is thus quite complex. Abuse screws women up sexually, and that's bad for men. It discourages women from risking, disciplines them not to risk the forms of pleasure/resistance through which we might eroticize autonomy and soften the contrast between the straight white middle class cultural center and the imagery of exciting but dangerous margins that are often real-life sites of oppression. And it burdens both men's and women's fantasy, play, experiment and innovation with questions, risks, fears, and guilt that trap us in the reproduction of patriarchal sex. Being against abuse is not, for men, just a matter of human rights, empathy, protecting "our" women, romantic paternalism or political correctness, however valid and important each of those may be.

Both the idea of reducing the violence so we can get on with playing within while evolving the repertoire, and the idea of overthrowing the repertoire altogether, are open to the critique that people would end up worse off in fact with more freedom and less repression. We would still have our inner demons, and lots of outer ones as well. There is no hors-repertoire. Power to the imagination all the same. When Madonna hurries down the hall at the end of the *Justify My Love* video, smiling to herself, it would be better on balance that she not end up . . . dead.

Cases

US Supreme Court (1986) *Meritor Savings Bank v. Vinson* 477 U.S. 57

References

Abu-Odeh L (1992) Post-colonial feminism and the veil: considering the differences. New Eng Law Rev 26:1527–1537

Austin R (1992) Black women, sisterhood, and the difference/deviance divide. New Eng Law Rev 26:877–887

Barthes R (1983) The fashion system. Hill and Wang

Bartky SL (1990) Feminity and domination: studies in the phenomenology of oppression. Routledge

Benjamin J (1988) The bonds of love: psychoanalysis, feminism, and the problem of domination. Pantheon

Big Itch was the Best Revenge on Class Witch (1992) Globe

Bordo S (1991) Material girl. In: Goldstein L (ed) The female body: figures, styles, speculations. University of Michigan Press, pp 106–128

[79] Keller (1990), p. 468.

Butler J (1990) Gender trouble: feminism and the subversion of identity. Routledge, New York
Califia P (1990) Doc and fluff: the dystopian tale of a girl and her biker. Alyson Books
Casanova G (1929) The memoirs of Jacques Casanova. Random House for The Modern Library
Cleland J (1963) Memoirs of a woman of pleasure. Putnam
Collins PH (1991) Black feminist thought - knowledge, consciousness, and the politics of empowerment. Routledge
Danielsen D (1992) Representing identities: legal treatment of pregnancy and homosexuality. New Eng Law Rev 26:1453–1508
Davis T (1991) Actresses as working women: their social identity in Victorian culture. Routledge
de Lauretis T (1987) Technologies of gender: essays on theory, film and fiction. Indiana University Press
de Nicolais S (1992) The Bra. . .Meant to be Seen!, Cosmopolitan 174–75 (D" on't be shy—it's fashion, not lingerie! And you want to show some cleavage!")
de Saussure F (1986) Course in general linguistics. Open Court, La Salle, Illinois
Derrida J (1976) Of grammatology. The John Hopkins University Press, Baltimore
Des Barres P (1987) I'm with the band: confessions of a groupie. Chicago Review Press
Doane MA (1991) Femmes fatales: feminism, film theory, psychoanalysis. Psychology Press
Dworkin A (1982) Right-wing women. TarcherPerigee
Dworkin A (1987) Intercourse. Free Press
Engle K (1992) Female subjects of public international law: human rights and the exotic other female. New Eng Law Rev 26:1509–1526
Enrenreich B et al (1986) Re-making love: the feminization of sex. Doubleday
Ferguson A (1989) Blood at the root: motherhood, sexuality and male dominance. Pandora Pr
Firestone S (1970) The dialectic of sex: the case for feminist revolution. William Morrow and Company
Foucault M (1977) Language, counter-memory, practice. Cornell University Press, Ithaca
Foucault M (1980) The history of sexuality – Volume 1: an introduction. Pantheon Books, New York
Frug MJ (1992) Postmodern legal feminism. Routledge, New York
Gallop J (1988) Thinking through the body. Columbia University Press
Gordon MT, Riger S (1991) The female fear: the social cost of rape. Free Press
Great Style (1992) Elle
Hagan KL (1991) Orchids in the Arctic: the predicament of heterosexual feminism. Escapadia Press
Hall M (1991) Ex-therapy to sex therapy: notes from the margins. In: Silverstein C (ed) Gays, lesbians, and their therapists. Norton, New York, pp 84–97
Harris F (1963) My life and loves. Grove Press
Harris L (1991) Behind the bedroom door, Ladies' Home J 114:119
Hart LB, Dalke D (1983) The sexes at work: improving work relationships between men and women. Prentice Hall
Hatfield J (1992) Defining appropriate dress in the workplace. Boston Globe
Heyn D (1992) The intelligent Woman's guide to sex: sex is not enough. Mademoiselle
Hook B (1992) Black looks: race and representation. South End Press, Boston
Keller S (1992) Powerless to please: Candida Royalle's pornography for women. New Eng Law Rev 26:1297–1308
Keller SE (1990) Review essay: justify my love. W St Univ Law Rev 18:463–468
Kelman (1979) Choice and utility. Wis Law Rev 3:769–797
Kennedy D (1985) Spring Break Tex Law Rev 63:1377–1423
Kimmel MS (1990) Introduction: guilty pleasures—pornography in Men's lives. In: Kimmel MS (ed) Men confront pornography. Crown, New York, pp 1–24
Klare KE (1992) Power/dressing: regulation of employee appearance. New Eng Law Rev 26:1395–1508
Levi-Strauss C (1966) The savage ming. Weidenfeld and Nicolson, London
Linden R (ed) (1982) Against sadomasochism: a radical feminist analysis. Frog in the Well

MacDonald S (1983) Confessions of a feminist porn watcher. In: Kimmel MS (ed) Men confront pornography. Crown, New York, pp 34–43
MacKinnon C (1983) Feminism, Marxism, method and the stale: toward feminist jurisprudence. Signs 8:635–658
Martinich L (1992) Link between dress and harassment? No, Boston Globe 22
Menkes S (1992) Vogue point of view: the cutting edge. Vogue
Morgan M (1975) The total woman. Revell
Morgan R (1977) Going too far: the personal Chronicle of a Feminist. Random House
Olsen F (1984) Statutory rape: a feminist critique of rights analysis. Tex Law Rev 63:387–432
Orth M (1992) Kaiser Karl: behind the mask. Vanity Fair
Peller G (1990) Race consciousness. Duke Law J 1990:758–847
Piaget J (1962) Play, dreams and imitation in childhood, Norton
Pollack W (1990) Sexual harassment: women's experience v. legal definitions. Harv Women's Law J 13:35–48
Reage P (1965) Story of O. Groves Press
Schneider EM (1980) Equal rights to trial/or women: sex bias in the law of self-defence. Harv Civil Rights Civil Liber Law Rev 15:623–647
Schneider EM (1986) Describing and changing: Women's self-Defense work and the problem of expert testimony on battering. Women's Rights Law Rep 9:195–220
Selby H Jr (1964) Last exit to Brooklyn. Marion Boyars
Seliger M (1991) Heavy metal nation. Rolling Stone
Sexual Harassment in Your Office: The Working Woman Survey (1992) Working Woman
Storr A (1964) Sexual deviation. Penguin Book, Harmondsworth
Vance C (ed) (1983) Pleasure and danger: exploring female sexuality. Pandora Pr
West R (1985) Authority, autonomy and choice: the role of consent in the moral and political visions of Franz. Kafka and Richard Posner. Harv Law Rev 99:384–428
West R (1987) The Difference in Womens' hedonic lives: a phenomenological critique of feminist legal theory. Wis Women's Law J 81
West R (2000) The difference in Women's hedonic lives: a phenomenological critique of feminist legal theory. Wis Women's Law J 15:149–215
White B (1992) More guidelines from the school of should. Boston Globe
Wolfensberger B (1992) Destination romance. Boston Globe
Zazinski J (1992) On the clothes women wear at work. Boston Globe

Duncan Kennedy is Carter Professor of General Jurisprudence Emeritus at the Harvard Law School. He is considered to be one of the founders of the Critical Legal Studies movement. He has received several honorary degrees, most recently the *Doctor Honoris Causa* from the University in Buenos Aires. Among his prominent works are "The Rise and Fall of Classical Legal Thought", "A Critique of Adjudication [fin de siècle]", "Sexy Dressing, etc.", "Thoughts on Coherence, Social Values and National Tradition in Private Law," and the monograph "Legal Education and the Reproduction of Hierarchy: A Polemic Against the System". Kennedy has been a member of the American Civil Liberties Union since 1967.

Gender Justice: Reassessing Theories of Justice from Feminist Perspectives

Dragica Vujadinović and Adriana Zaharijević

Contents

Abstract Justice is one of the central concepts of both traditional and contemporary political philosophy, always aiming to articulate the best political order/s, those devoted to the common good, the well-being of the community, and a fair share of the community's goods among citizens. Within the mainstream theoretical tradition, discourse on justice is linked to the public sphere of law and politics, with the public/private dichotomy in the background. Feminist critical reconsideration of justice points to the crucial importance of introducing family and gender justice into the justice discourse. This chapter aims to demonstrate how family justice and gender justice are essential for a proper conception of justice within an inclusive understanding of equality in constitutional democracies and the context of global justice.

The chapter also demonstrates how contestable the mainstream division between the public and private spheres is, as well as the consequential reduction of justice to the public sphere. The chapter begins by problematizing the figure of justice as a

D. Vujadinović (✉) · A. Zaharijević
University of Belgrade, Belgrade, Serbia
e-mail: dragicav@ius.bg.ac.rs

N. Lacey et al. (eds.), *Reassessing Feminist Legal Theories*, Gender Perspectives in Law 5, https://doi.org/10.1007/978-3-031-75423-4_4

woman, which is further developed in the first section. The second section considers the meaning and genesis of the concept of justice, with particular stress on family justice and gender justice. The third section explores the position of gender justice in contemporary theories of justice, with a particular focus on John Rawls's conception of justice. We also consider two other mainstream theories of justice, Michael Walzer's communitarian and Philip Green's social-democratic theories, both of which contain elements of family and gender justice. Relevant examples of liberal feminist thought on justice of Susan Moller Okin, the feminist socialist thought on justice of Nancy Fraser, and the social justice conception of Iris Marion Young are considered in the final section.

1 Introduction

The symbols of justice—toga, scales, and sword—look the same all around the globe. The bearer of these recognisable insignia—seated or standing, calm or enraged, overdressed or fully naked, blindfolded or gazing piercingly—is a woman. Iustitia, as we know her today, is only one of many names for the ancient goddesses who held justice in their hands. Justice—wise, balanced, and mercilessly swift—has always been figured in the female form.

What is justice? In the *Institutes of Justinian*, justice is defined as "the constant and perpetual will to render each his due".[1] In Cicero's *De Natura Deorum* variant of the same definition—*iustitia suum cuique distribuit*—justice is akin to the ancient goddess who decides, in an impartial and equitable way, who deserves what and how much. The decision befalls individuals ("*to each* his due"): it is a just portion of what is deserved—and no one deserves everything, no one is allowed to abstract all others who may as well demand what is their *due*. The ancient goddess appears in the guise of "the constant and perpetual will", a will no human can ever possess, being mortal and forever doomed to partiality.

Although portrayed as a woman, historically, justice seems to have been of concern solely to men. Not only does justice render each *his* due, but it most often takes place in the realm from which women had been barred, the public domain. Until the twentieth century, justices, the human bearers of justice, were exclusively men, and family—the space where women "reign"—was most often understood as a realm where principles of justice do not apply. The private sphere was (to be) protected from public encroachments, and part of its "protection" consisted in its being regulated by markedly different rules. Thus, the perpetual plastering of justice

[1]The definitions of justice are many and this particular one, despite its representability, is not exhaustive. For example, for Aristotle justice is more clearly and directly articulated in terms of political power distribution. "To each his due" refers primarily to a just share in political decision-making depending on what each social strata deserves in political terms.

in the shape of a woman helped to disguise the deep systemic injustice towards women.

How does one explain the fact that justice has always been portrayed as a woman, and that women only recently became "proper" subjects of justice? For Aristotle who gave us one of the first definitions of justice, it is the *place* one occupies throughout life that makes them a political being. Not everyone, however, has a place to represent, and not everyone is a member of a community to which justice applies. Thus, instead of being full members of the community, women are merely representable creatures who appear under the heading of a household, *oikos*, represented by its head—one who in ancient polis was never a woman. The moderns would understand this multiple representation in terms of *persona ficta*, the person-agglomeration of all *his* possessions that represents them as if they were part of *himself*, be those possessions material or human.[2] In the private domain, men, women, slaves, and children appeared as plural, but in the public, they were singularized, represented by the one who had an assigned place in the community to which justice applied. This idea had a long practical life. In nineteenth-century England, women were tried in court only for committing the crime of murder. For all lesser crimes, justice was assumed to be the responsibility of their "baron" or "lord",[3] under whose wing and cover all their actions were performed.[4] Only as murderers were women considered legal persons. Moral, political, and legal meanings of the concept of justice did not include women, because women were not seen as human beings in full capacity.

Things have changed. Women have been individualized as legal persons and are hence subjects of justice. However, the very concepts of person, of individual, *and* of justice, have been derived from a time when women did not conform to them.[5] These concepts claim to have universal reach and validity on the basis of which they now extend to women. The question, however, is whether they can be applied to women if they were created in and for a world in which women were either subsumed under the person of *their baron*, or seen as unfit for self-sufficiency, rational reasoning, or property-owning. Not only were women excluded from a variety of political pillar-notions such as *zoon politikon*, a contracting individual, a member of the civil society, etc., but once they were included, they were seen as continuously deficient—lacking in superegos, consciences, cognitive capacities, and moral

[2] Zaharijević (2014).

[3] Blackstone (1765), p. 430.

[4] "The doctrine obtained that the husband and wife were but one person possessing but one will and that that will resided in the mind of the husband as the person "fittest and ablest to provide for and govern the family". It was a doctrine of elegant simplicity and one capable of remarkable results. It was a doctrine that removed, in theory, the burdens of responsibility and the sanctions of morality from any woman that entered the holy state of matrimony. Logically considered, all her crimes and all her sins emanated from the duplicated brain of her husband and her lord. Not only did she convey to him her person and her worldly goods, but she added the entire responsibility to the weight of his own". JEG de Montmorency (1897), p. 197.

[5] Naffine (2004).

reasoning based on universal ethical principles and abstract thinking. If justice is "the constant and perpetual will to render each his due", how do we add a *she* and how do we measure *her* due?

Feminist theory "in all its diversity begins from the conviction that the social, political, and cultural arrangements that shape women's lives are unjust".[6] As a practical theory, feminist theory aims to make the world a more just place for everyone. Feminists, however, stumble upon inherited obstacles. Now that women are made equal in law, how does one achieve their equality in humanity? How does one patch the lacks that were for millennia seen as inherent to the nature of their sex, or to women as sex? How does one extract women from their assumed *naturalness* to conceive them as *abstract* and *artificial* beings—as persons or individuals? Ultimately, do we need more abstract concepts—cleansed of all historical sediments, belonging to a time when persons and individuals referred only to the male property-owning heads of families—or do we instead need to turn to more particularized universals? Feminist philosophers have little agreement on this point. One of the major issues is how to approach the history of thinking about philosophical concepts devised thus far: should we retain them and simply go on with them in a world that has changed, or should we strive to reform them? Revolutionize them? Drop them altogether and search for more capacious conceptual schemes to accommodate a changed world? Ultimately, can we ever do that?

The model of feminist justice developed in the early stages of the second wave was grounded in traditional liberal political theory. Liberal feminists understood justice as the fair and equitable distribution of resources among discrete individuals equal among themselves. If women were discriminated against on the basis of their sex, they were unequal and treated unjustly. "Thus justice requires equal opportunity and rights for women as the means to ending this discrimination."[7] In many parts of the world, this is still a dominant way of understanding justice, if not in theory, then certainly in practice. However, justice requires much more than that. Injustice has many faces—five, according to Iris Marion Young: exploitation, marginalization, powerlessness, cultural imperialism, and violence.[8] In the complex world we live in, feminists seem to suggest, our experiences cannot be individualized and equalized in a merely abstract manner.

In the framework of what is called *gender justice*, the bodies of individuals are important. Bodies are our social reservoirs of experiences. Gender justice strives towards allowing everyone to thrive, regardless of their gender, gender expression, or sexual orientation. In this framework, it is assumed that for some of us, there are more or more solid barriers, and that some of us lack protection and require more of it. Those barriers removed and that protection provided—at home, in school, in healthcare, at work—would ensure that we appear as subjects of justice in the public. In that sense, gender justice strives for equity, equal rights, and equal distribution of

[6]Kiss (1998), p. 487.

[7]Villanueva Gardner (2006), p. 122.

[8]Marion Young (1990).

resources, access, and opportunities, *and* equality, equal outcomes for all. Gender justice is understood as a precondition for an ideal of a just society in which everyone has equal status. In the world as it is now, we are not equal even when we are equal in law—and what is *her* and *his due*, let alone *their* due, differs. Gender justice thus functions as a constant and perpetual empowering of those who need empowerment in order to appear as proper subjects of justice.

2 Justice as a Woman: Paradox of Worshipping and Devaluating Women

In patriarchy, especially in its pre-modern version, the public and private spheres were sharply divided, with women primarily, if not exclusively, confined to the private domain of reproduction, care, and domesticity.[9] In the public sphere, women were viewed as persons without legal and political subjectivity, or as second-class persons. In modern and contemporary times, patriarchy has still not been overcome. It persists within the dialectic of patriarchy and emancipation,[10] or the constant struggle between deeply rooted patriarchal tendencies and the counter-tendencies of emancipation.

Given this, there is a vast discrepancy between Iustitia, the iconic image of the woman as the representative of the highest virtue, and the factual devaluation of women in social, legal, and political life in both pre-modern and contemporary societies. Emma Stafford[11] notes this paradox: Ancient Greek and Roman, as well as much older Egyptian and Indian religious traditions, related justice to women. The female personification of the virtue of justice such as Dike, along with the fact that "Olympos has just as many goddesses as gods", were in stark contrast with the devaluation and subordination of women in real life.[12]

May Wood attempted to explain this paradox by relating justice to care as the traditional domain of women: "To be concerned about justice is to exhibit care. Perhaps this is why the concept of justice is personified as a woman. Whether reviled or revered for it, patriarchal societies have historically associated women with caring. To care is, among other things, to pay specific and diligent attention. Justice demands care. Without it, disorder, inequality, and suffering become normal."[13] Donna Marie Giancola illuminated the said paradox through recourse to "matriarchal religions", which preceded the patriarchal culture and were not based on the public/private dichotomy and the structural devaluation of women.[14] In "matriarchal

---

[9]Walby (1989), pp. 213–234.

[10]Vujadinovic (2023b), pp. 16–18.

[11]Stafford (2020).

[12]The author remarks: "Given the inferiority of mortal women in Greek thought this might seem surprising, but denigration of female deities is rare", Stafford (2020).

[13]May Wood (2022), p. 7.

[14]Giancola (1998), p. 47.

religions", according to Giancola, goddesses were the emanation of the Mother Earth, Great Mother; they were the source of unity of earth and humanity and of the all-encompassing order. "The older view (the one that we have almost forgotten) was rooted in the early Goddess religions where Justice was seen as the avenging/ mediating force of the Great Mother. The other view developed later in the dominant patriarchal Aryan culture of norms and laws, and provides the basis for our modern-day conception of justice as an abstract principle."[15] As Giancola states, the earliest religion of the ancient Greeks was centred on the worship of Mother Earth, an embodiment of fecundity, the fertile giver of life to plants, animals, and humans. She bases her argument on the Neolithic agricultural civilization characterized by a matriarchal religion, a "gylanic" (emphasizing fertility) and peaceful culture. This civilization was subjected to a series of invasions, beginning at c. 3500 BC, by the herding peoples whose culture was basically androcratic: patriarchal, patrilineal, and militaristic.[16] The gradual transition from indigenous people's matriarchal culture of worshiping Mother Earth led to the establishment of a patriarchal culture that operated with an abstract notion of Justice related to law and order. However, elements of the earlier matriarchal culture centred on Mother Earth were preserved through the goddesses Dike and Themis as representatives of justice, as well as through the role of Moira/Fate.[17] The genesis of the goddess Athena born from Zeus's head also speaks in favour of this transition. Though at first portrayed as an "unadorned woman whose peaceful character, wisdom and nurturing heart were symbolized by the olive branch and the owl", Athena would later become a paradigmatic warrior rather than a protectress.[18]

Giancola provides a similar analysis of Indian culture and early Buddhism, as well as Tibetan Buddhism and Buddhism "after patriarch".[19] According to her, the

[15] Giancola (1998), p. 47.

[16] Giancola (1998), pp. 48–49.

[17] Homer preserves the tradition of the primal Mother-Goddess under the guise of "Fate". "It is she who rules the universe and whose power binds both humans and gods." In Hesiod, Dike executed the law of judgments and sentencing in accordance with the new emerging culture, but together with her mother Themis, carried out the final decisions of Moira, what implies the link with the Mother Earth Goddess. In Hesiod, "Moira, Themis and Dike are the divine descendants of the Great Mother-Goddess. This personification of Dike will stand in contrast to justice viewed as custom or law, and as retribution or sentence." Giancola (1998), p. 40.

[18] Giancola (1998), p. 40.

[19] "The early pre-history of India corresponds in many ways with that of ancient Greece, where, again, the Aryans ('the people of sky') invaded the early matriarchal gynocentric culture of the Dravidians which can be traced back as early as 3000 B.C. Here we can see the similarities in terms of their matriarchal beliefs and rituals in their Paleolithic caves and mounds. The earliest Great Mother cults of Asia were earth-centered, focusing on fertility and life-giving energy. Their rituals included celebrations of nature and the offering of plants and herbs to the source of creation. With the conquest of the Aryans, the religious focus shifted from that which was immanent in nature to the transcendent sky gods with rituals involving fire and smoke. The early Goddess religions attempted to assimilate the patriarchal gods into their culture and, for some time after the initial invasion, the Goddess was worshipped as one of the primary deities. Yet, as was the situation in ancient Greece, this adaptation soon gave way to the superimposition of patriarchal gods and

similarities between the early West and East are to be found in the "matriarchal" roots of Western and Eastern mythical and philosophical traditions grouped around the ideas of the Great Mother as the main creative energy, the divine creator, and the final judge of all reality. Only later do we witness a gradual transition to the universal, abstract concepts of justice, coloured by patriarchal principles.[20]

3 What Is Justice?

In legal terms, justice refers to the universal character of legal norms and universal formal equality (equity). In order to be understood as substantive equality, it needs significant expansions, entailing the right to differences and recognition of equal opportunities and equal results for those unequal (due to gender, class, race, sexual orientation), as well as justifiable/legitimate/unbiased judging in accordance with the laws. In political terms, justice refers to a proportional distribution of power, honour, and goods. Put differently, justice is a fair share of resources—the redistribution of economic, political, and social well-being for the sake of treating each human equally. For all these reasons, justice is often referred to as the highest political virtue.

Distributive justice in particular is always related to equality, which presupposes formal equality/equity, and which further articulates proportional equality—the one related to merits, i.e. certain relevant values that determine criteria of substantive equality and inequality, equal distribution to equals and simultaneous unequal distribution to un-equals. The old Aristotelian understanding of justice as equality for equals and inequality for un-equals, i.e. the proportional distribution of political power[21] due to merit, underwent significant historical changes. In modern political

conception of Brahman as ultimate reality. With the conquest of the Aryans, Rta as the way of nature became subsumed under the law of karma." Giancola (1998), p. 50.

[20]The gynocentric pre-patriarchal nature of justice leads this author to a fruitful conclusion that the feminist deconstruction of justice necessarily leads to fusing gender justice and eco-justice: "The pre-patriarchal nature of justice, we find in the Great Mother (Triple Goddess), is not androcentric, not universal, not abstract. Her judgment is not so much about principle, but about concrete relations, relations of humans to each other, to animals, to plants to the reality of nature. Today, feminist philosophers are attempting to reconstruct a new vision of global community, global ethics and eco-justice." Giancola (1998), p. 52.

[21]Aristotle, *Nicomachean Ethics*, pp. 2536–2787), p. 2637; cf. Aristotle—*Politics*, pp. 2788–3049. In *Politics,* Aristotle most strikingly elaborates the conception of distributive justice as the proper share of power in the rightful state, i.e. the state which serves the common good. Equality of all free citizens is one premise, another is equal participation in the highest levels of government of those most excellent (monarchical element), then equal participation of those characterized with prudence and knowledge (aristocratic element) in less important and lower levels of government and, finally, equal participation of *demos* in the least important levels of government (members of offices, calling magistrates to accountability). In short, justice for Aristotle means that all participants in political decision-making are equal before the law as free citizens, but mutually unequal due to the merit which belongs to their social strata, and equal within their own social strata from the point of

philosophy, distributive justice is not about the proportional manifestation of *zoon politikon* within different social strata. In Rawls's and Dworkin's egalitarian liberalism, for example, it refers to equal human beings, individuals, who do not have equal starting positions. Justice understood as fairness (Rawls) or as sovereign virtue (Dworkin) should lead to equalization of opportunities and produce equality among un-equals.

Does justice, conceived thus, apply to women? The history of the concept of justice (as well as of its putting into practice) has been characterized by male dominance in law and politics, and by the invisibility of women in the public domain. In the traditional understanding of politics, women are either subsumed under the heading of men or perceived as non-political actors. Equally so, in the traditional, as well as modern, understanding of politics, issues pertaining to the sphere to which women "belong" have been understood as allegedly non-political. Justice was gender-neutral or gender-insensitive: it should have been applied to all, but most often it was applied only to and by those who were understood as political beings.

Gender justice is absent from traditional conceptions and most contemporary conceptions of justice. Moreover, gender *in*justice is rooted in certain key theories of justice, such as Aristotle's. The necessary mutual link between political and gender justice has thus not been established as a matter of course. Instead, gender justice within the private sphere has been either ignored or, worse, considered acceptable, as something that does not interfere with justice in its true sense—justice in the public sphere.

Throughout the history of political philosophy, discussions about justice have persistently been accompanied by the assumption that in the private sphere, the domination of men over women is natural and thus necessary, *and* that this has no bearing on justice as a matter of the public sphere. This applies to traditional political philosophy, with Plato[22] being the most extraordinary exception.[23] The major

participation in levels of decision-making and power distribution proposed for their own social strata (pp. 2782–2783).

[22] Plato (1997).

[23] In book V of the *Republic*, in which the common good as the major aim of the city has been secured by abolishing private property and private interests for the guardians, in order that their rule be fully focused on the welfare of other citizens, the consequence was abolishing the family. Plato assumes that communalization of the property leads directly to the abolition of the family. Abolishing the family (in which women were in men's possession) results in separating biological femaleness—palpable and inevitable biological differences between sexes related to procreation (pregnancy, lactation, and a degree of difference in physical strength) from the conventional female sex roles, and enables that women equally as men can be the rulers. Within the ideal state, Plato considered guardians as one family, and bonds of fraternal love among the rulers held the ideal society of the Republic as the political community. There is no more private marriage and own children, communal childrearing leads to eliminating maternity as a full-time occupation, and women can no longer be defined by their traditional role. The guardian class as a whole must share the governing function. Therefore, the difference in procreative function between the sexes has no more relevance and does not present any obstacle for women to play equal role in the ruling

difference between traditional and contemporary theories of justice is that the former, if attention is paid to women at all, emphatically differentiated women from men and devalued women politically based on their sex. Newer theories attempt to avoid this by, for example, using gender-neutral language, implying that their assumptions apply to all indiscriminately. This terminological witticism—in which "she" now stands for "person" instead of the age-old "he"—obscures the fact that the sedimented histories of the "person" cannot be flattened out by a mere change of pronoun. Likewise, adding women to men—where women seem to function as a particular extension of the universal—is another sleight of hand that cannot solve the issue of women's former emphatic exclusion from the universal.

The strategy "add women and stir" does take into account the legal reality of equality between women and men. Women are no longer politically invisible as they were only a century ago, and it is a matter of justice that they have been acknowledged as subjects of justice—even if previously that had not been the case. Nevertheless, the mere fact that the sphere of the universal can be expanded, invites us to revisit earlier philosophical assumptions on what constitutes universality, humanity, and justice. This does not occur in the largest part of contemporary political philosophy. Rather, it either continues to ignore who the embodied subject of justice is, or it paints a picture of variously-bodied individuals who all receive justice in the same way. However, as long as the gender of the subject of justice remains outside the scope of the theories of justice—justice will be partial and non-universal despite its claims to universality.

There is another side to this story. A person may indeed become a "she". Also, where there were previously solely "men" there may now be "men and women". However, if family is omitted from the conversation about "men and women" as

---

class. Women are weaker physically, but individual members of both sexes are capable of performing all functions needed in the city, and so "philosopher- monarchs" can be women equally as men. Revolutionary in Plato's statement is that women are relieved from the traditional role and are considered as equally capable of filling many roles outside the traditional domestic sphere. Even more, they are capable to be the highest rank rulers, philosopher-monarchs/queens.

Plato maintained his awareness of women's capacities even in his other relevant book, *Laws*. Here he assumes that only different rearing and education between the two sexes practically lead to differences in their subsequent abilities and achievements, and that the legislator should proclaim the same education, training, civic duties for both sexes. However, his general statements could not persist in the face of the reintroduction of private property (and of marriage and the family, consequently), that led automatically to the identification of women and children with the other's possession/private property. Women are private wives and are treated as property rather than as persons. Marriage is compulsory for both sexes, but the male person decides whom he will marry, while the female person is "given" in marriage. Plato preserves to a certain degree a high estimation of women in *Laws*, although the highest offices are reserved for men and women are legal minors to a great extent like as in the real Athenian polis. On the other hand, the education of children does not belong to mothers, meals are communal for women, extramarital intercourse is equally punished for both sexes, divorce laws are more equal than in real life. In short, Plato cannot affirm equal capacities of women in *Laws* like in the *Republic*, because returning private property leads to the revival of traditional family and conventional female roles to a more or less extent. (See Moller Okin (1997), pp. 11–31).

subjects of justice, then their experiences continue to be measured by the same measure as before. As Susan Moller Okin claims, "The judgement that the family is 'non-political' is implicit in the fact that it is simply not discussed in most works of political theory today."[24]

3.1 Gender Justice as Family Justice

Gender justice is of equal concern for all human beings, regardless of their gender, sexual orientation, colour, ability, class background, and within both the private and public spheres. Gender justice encompasses family justice in the sense of overcoming traditional patriarchal male/female roles within a patriarchal family. Within this framework, care, solidarity, empathy, love, and respect are disjointed from the traditional patriarchal model of family, the constitutive elements of which are hierarchy, subordination, the power imbalance between men and women, and the possibility of the use of violence against weaker family members (women, children), as well as its social acceptance. If each human being is to be given equal consideration, the families in which we are raised must be democratic/non-patriarchal, non-binarized, and lived in a plurality of ways. Such an environment fosters relationships of mutual respect, autonomy, solidarity, and empathy instead of subordination, discrimination, oppression, and violence. For that reason, gender justice also encompasses family justice in terms of a fair share of the work in the household, child care, and care for elderly family members.

Gender justice, however, emphasizes connecting injustice in the private sphere/ the family with injustice in the public sphere. Public injustice is merely one dimension of injustice as a whole, which is always deeply rooted in family injustice, in the sense that power imbalances and the need for a fair share within power relations relate not only to the public sphere but also to the private sphere and the family. The family, which is defined today by the dialectics of patriarchy and emancipation, is the first political arena in which the struggle between patriarchy and emancipation takes place. The family is the "battlefield" where two tendencies collide: one to maintain gender heteronormative relations, and the other to establish a more or less fair share of obligations and responsibilities and overcome relationships burdened with power imbalance, hierarchy, and subordination. As the place of primary socialization, the family plays a more or less decisive part in the patriarchy/emancipation battlefield for creating individuals progressively capable of autonomous behaviour that is respectful of others in both the family and the public life; or, on the other hand, for creating individuals more in line with the embedded patriarchal legacy, i.e. with heteronomous features, ready to accept hierarchy and dominance over weaker family members and subordination to stronger family members, and accepting and reproducing social roles based on hierarchy, obedience, and use of

[24] Moller Okin (1989), p. 9.

violence. As Moller Okin puts it, "The injustice that results from the division of labor between the sexes . . .inflicts increasingly serious damage on children as well as women, and it destroys the family's potential to be the crucial first school where children develop a sense of fairness."[25] There must be justice in the family in order to have a just society. To reiterate Walzer,[26] social justice is impossible as long as gender inequalities persist, that is—as long as justice within families is absent.

Family justice must become an integral part of every theory of justice. Family justice and gender justice are important *per se*, and they have been inextricably connected to justice in the public sphere. The private/public dichotomy must be overcome because reproductive rights and gender-based violence have become a public matter, a state responsibility. Moreover, the state and international community must ensure the right to privacy in the proper sense to all women through welfare policies that are intersectionally sensitive to gender-based discrimination of various groups of women in various parts of the world: in the Global South and Global North, and at the individual, local, national, and transnational levels. Power relations, relations of domination and subordination based on gender, sex, and sexual orientation must all be overcome not only in the public domain but also in the private one.

4 Contemporary Political Philosophy and the Issue of Gender Justice

Revived in the 1970s with an emphatic focus on justice, Western political philosophy was a response to the legitimacy crisis of the liberal democratic order. At the same time, international law rooted itself in the philosophy of human rights. Theories of justice, especially liberal egalitarian ones—those of Rawls and Dworkin—tended to affirm universal human rights, the interconnection of principles of liberty and equality, and the central category of human dignity,[27] linking them with social and economic rights and the common good through the notion of distributive justice. Samuel Moyn explains this growing interest in human rights as a response to the collapse of the universalistic schemes of post-war liberalism and socialism, the search for European identity outside of Cold War terms, the American liberal shift in foreign policy in moralized terms after the Vietnam catastrophe, and the end of

[25] Moller Okin (1989), p. vii.

[26] M. Walzer, Review of the book of Susan Moller Okin, Moller Okin (1989).

[27] Habermas argues that the changing post-World War II conditions and the enactment the Universal Declaration of Human Rights (UDHR) put human dignity and the worth of each human being into the centre of international law and national constitutions. He also specifies a modern meaning of human dignity as very different from the pre-modern status-dependent human dignity. The modern one becomes universal human dignity, and universalization is accompanied by individualization. See: Habermas (2012), pp. 63–81.

formal colonialism: the construction of human rights exploded as a "persuasive moral alternative" and the "last utopia".[28]

In contemporary theories of justice, the meaning of legal equality is shaped by the standards of constitutional democracy; the fair share of political power is determined by principles of parliamentary democracy; and the universal idea of human rights and human dignity necessitates the inclusion of elements of economic and social equality in conceptions of distributive justice. In addition, the last decades of the twentieth century saw important conceptual moves towards a more inclusive understanding of substantive equality—equality of opportunities and equality of results—for all social groups and individuals who are in formal terms equal, but are still exposed to one or more forms of discrimination in their private and public life.

Procedural justice presupposes lawfulness and universal equality, but also requires a striking balance between universal formal equality and non-discrimination, and so demands expanding equality beyond abstract, universally valid civil rights towards the recognition of differences/particular collective and individual rights, and balancing between treating equal situations equally and unequal ones unequally. Special norms are necessary to guarantee equality for minorities, as well as for all vulnerable groups and individuals belonging to them, who are most often exposed to multiple discrimination/systemic oppression based on gender, race, class, and sexual orientation.

The deconstruction of abstract universal terms such as white-metropolitan-male-dominated began under the impact of the theories and practices of multiculturalism, critical legal and critical race theories, anti-colonial critique, and feminist political philosophy. White-Western-middle-and-upper-classes mainstream (male-stream) concepts and categories that had long been assumed to be universal have slowly been unmasked as white, Western, middle-class, and male.[29] Although it may appear that all of these diverse and multifaceted attempts (could have) worked together to produce a more thorough and more profound understanding of equality and justice, particularly one that would right the wrongs of the "world's largest minority", this was not the case.[30] Egalitarian liberalism, as well as theories of constitutional democracy, civil society, human rights, multiculturalism, and critical race, too often put gender issues aside and lack awareness of the importance of gender equality and gender justice. In most respects, the mentioned theories bear

---

[28]Moyn (2010). See also: Charles Beitz also insists on the novelty of contemporary human rights, and says that what distinguishes contemporary human rights from earlier conceptions of rights is the idea that "each person is a subject of global concern". Beitz (2011), p. 1.

[29]Bryson (1982). pp. 263–267; Crenshaw (1989), pp. 139–167; See also, Fraser (1997).

[30]Kymlicka's neglect of these wrongs may be taken as exemplary, although similar examples abound. According to him, the post-World War II human rights revolution consisted of *three* movements, which strived to vanquish the remnants and enduring effects of these older hierarchies: "(1) the struggle for decolonization, concentrated in the period 1948-65; (2) the struggle against racial segregation and discrimination, initiated and exemplified by the African-American civil rights movements from 1955 to 1965; and (3) the struggle for multiculturalism and minority rights, which emerged in the late 1960s". Kymlicka (2017), p. 2.

emancipatory, civilizational potential but their male writers and/or their male-dominated articulation most often result in their falling short of the requirements of gender equality, gender justice, and a fully consistent standpoint of inclusiveness. Feminist critical theories have been calling into question traditional political philosophy while also challenging the gender blindness of the mentioned contemporary progressive theories.[31]

The theories of justice developed from the 1970s onwards also exposed a lack of awareness of gender justice in the general framing of justice. Gender justice is almost entirely absent from the liberal takes on justice, such as Bruce Ackerman's *Social Justice in the Liberal State*,[32] Ronald Dworkin's *Taking Rights Seriously* and *Sovereign Virtue*,[33] William Galstone's *Justice and the Human Good*,[34] equally so from the communitarian theory of Alasdair McIntyre's elaborated in *After Virtue* and *Whose Justice? Which Rationality?*,[35] as well as from the libertarian theory, exemplified in Robert Nozick's *Anarchy, State and Utopia*[36] and Roberto Unger's *Knowledge and Politics* and *The Critical Legal Studies Movement*.[37] Probably the most renowned theory of justice, John Rawls's, does take family into consideration,

[31] See for example Bryson (1982), Moller Okin (1989).

[32] Ackerman (1980).

[33] Dworkin (1977, 1997) and Dworkin (2000). In chapter VI of *Law's Empire* (1986), Dworkin explains that the political virtues of justice and fairness do not suffice for political legitimacy, and that integrity is also needed. Integrity is more personal than justice in its various demands on various communities (as justice is conceptually universalistic). Integrity is closely related to fraternity, or true community (fraternity meaning community, sense of belonging based on values and principles). A political society that accepts integrity becomes a special form of community, special in that it promotes its moral authority to assume and deploy a monopoly of coercive force. In that context Dworkin uses family as an example (normatively speaking, even metaphorically speaking, so to say, for purposes of introducing a communal element into the liberal thought) of the fraternal associations/true community (besides friendship and neighbourhood). Fraternal associations must meet four conditions in order not to be only bare communities (based on the given state of affairs, on the context) but also the true ones: special obligation, personal obligation, concern, and equal concern for other members of the given fraternal association (fraternal associations are egalitarian). He considers family from the point of the egalitarian conception of fraternal associations, and assumes "interpretative attitude" or "critical interpretation" for existent families. From the mentioned justice standpoint, the patriarchal kind of family is not just, and does not represent a true community (fraternal association). Family members can use justice in "its normal interpretative role" for deciding what their associative responsibilities, properly understood, really are. This critical approach to the patriarchal family structure relieves daughters or other members of the patriarchal family from associative obligation. If "special parental power over daughters" is based on devaluation and discrimination (based on the assumption that they are less valuable than sons), there is no genuine association, and thus no associative responsibilities arise from it.

Dworkin, like Rawls, keeps the mainstream/malestream conception of justice as related to the public sphere. However, he also includes in a specific implied manner and in a limited scope the issue of family justice into his justice discourse.

[34] Gallstone (1980).

[35] McIntyre (1981) and McIntyre (1988).

[36] Nozick (1974).

[37] Unger (1975) and Unger (2015).

but it neglects the prevalent gendered division of labour within the family, along with the associated imbalances in the distribution of power, responsibility, and privileges. However, Rawls's theory of justice allows for a reconstruction from the critical feminist perspective, which we will show below. In addition, we will offer an analysis of two other, essentially different mainstream contemporary approaches to justice—the communitarian one, represented by Michael Walzer's *Spheres of Justice*,[38] and the social-democratic one of Philip Green, laid down in his *Retrieving Democracy*.[39] The feminist theory of justice, exposed in the liberal thought of Susanne Moller Okin and socialist thought of Nancy Fraser's *Justice Interruptus*[40] will be taken as a counterpoint, and also as examples of the rising converging trends across feminist theories of different political orientation, especially from the 1990s and further on, towards more inclusive, intersectionally articulated (less West-centric and white middle-class) thought.

4.1 Controversies in Rawls's A Theory of Justice

Many would still hail Marshall Cohen's early review of Rawls's major book as the "magisterial" and "most formidable" defence of the social contract tradition, providing a bold and rigorous account of "the principles to which our public life is committed".[41] Indeed, Rawls's version of the social contract seems to be the first to accommodate all social actors. The subjects of Rawls's theory of justice are emphatically "persons", "human beings", "parties". For example, "It seems reasonable to suppose that *the parties* in the original position are equal. That is, *all* have the same rights in the procedure for choosing principles; *each* can make proposals, submit reasons for their acceptance, and so on. Obviously the purpose of these conditions is to represent equality between *human beings* as moral *persons*, as creatures having a conception of their good and capable of a sense of justice."[42] The terms used are allegedly neutral, abstract, universally applicable. In addition to that, justice as fairness, as defined by Rawls, is based on the principles of equal citizenship, equal basic political rights, and the difference principle related to social and economic rights.[43] All of these rights—at the time when Rawls offered his theory of justice—

---

[38] Walzer (1983).

Moller Okin says: "Michael Walzer *Spheres of Justice*, too, is exceptional in this regard, but… the conclusion that can be inferred from his discussion of the family – that its gender structure is unjust – does not sit at all easily with his emphasis on the shared understandings of a culture as the foundation of justice." (1989), p. 9.

[39] Green (1985).

[40] Fraser (1997).

[41] Cohen (1972).

[42] Rawls (1971, 1999 rev. ed.) p. 17 (italics added).

[43] "Social and economic inequalities are to be arranged so that they are both (a) to the greatest expected benefit of the least advantaged and (b) attached to offices and positions open to all under conditions of fair equality of opportunity." Rawls (1999 rev. ed.), p. 72.

refer to women as well. Crucially, Rawls's difference principle aims to take existent differences into account within the frame of just redistribution.

It is, however, precisely some of the elaborations of the difference principle that reveal a surprisingly simplified understanding of social disadvantages based on sex, race, and culture as fixed natural characteristics. Rawls argues: "If, for example, there are unequal basic rights founded on fixed natural characteristics, these inequalities will single out relevant positions. Since these characteristics cannot be changed, the positions they define count as starting places in the basic structure."[44] He explicitly claims that distinctions based on sex belong to this type, as well as those defined by "race" and "culture". "Thus if, say, men are favored in the assignment of basic rights, this inequality is justified by the difference principle (in the general interpretation) only if it is so to the advantage of women and acceptable from their standpoint."[45]

A stereotypically gendered perspective is particularly striking when Rawls speaks about the issue of the motivation of the parties in the original position to care about the wellbeing of their descendants, where he uses the concept of "heads of families".[46] The "parties", "persons", and "humans" are thus unmasked as men—which is unmistakably implied by the use of the strong and historically burdensome notion of the "head of the family".[47] Furthermore, if such an equation is plausible, it seems that *these* "parties" and "persons" are not fixed by their natural characteristics, while others are. To be the head of the family[48] in the "original position" introduces other issues as well. Namely, the constituents of the original position are obviously not only equal individuals, "persons" and "human beings". The "parties" are also *families* headed by fathers and succeeded by sons. This composite entity, the family headed by a man, in which the equal (original) autonomy of its individual members has to become suspect, sits strangely with the assumption that "the parties in the original position are equal".[49] There seems to be a tacit smuggling of men *as* human beings, separate and individuated from other men. This does not preclude them from being individuated from the entity they are heading, in which no proper separation and autonomous individuation is possible—the entity simply appears as the "family" he is the "head of". Thus children and wives are not represented in the original position, and we may assume that this inequality—in the originally equal state!—is

[44] Rawls (1999 rev. ed.), p. 85.

[45] Rawls (1999 rev. ed.), p. 85.

[46] "We can adopt a motivation assumption and think of the parties as representing a continuing line of claims. For example, we can assume that they are heads of families and therefore have a desire to further the well-being of at least their more immediate descendants." Rawls (1999 rev. ed.), p. 11.

[47] Moller Okin remarks critically: "Although the 'heads of families' assumption is made in order to address the issue of intergenerational justice, and is presumably not intended to be sexist, Rawls is effectively trapped by it into the traditional mode of thinking that life within the family and relations between the sexes are not properly to be regarded as part of the subject matter of social justice." Moller Okin (1997), p. 183.

[48] Rawls (1999), p. 126.

[49] Rawls (1999 rev. ed.), p. 17.

already "justified by the difference principle", presumably because it "is so to the advantage of women and acceptable from their standpoint".[50]

Liberal feminists contend, however, that if interpreted more radically and broadly, Rawls's conception of the meaning and purpose of the original position could be useful for feminists, because it "forces one to question and consider traditions, customs, and institutions from all points of view, and ensures that the principles of justice are acceptable to everyone, regardless of what position 'he' ends up in".[51] In addition, Moller Okin insists that it is precisely Rawls's second principle of justice that opens the doors to a feminist reconstruction of his theory of justice.[52]

4.2 *Walzer's Theory of Justice and Gender Justice*

Let us see if a thought that does not belong to the liberal-egalitarian frame but is still mainstream makes room for gender justice. The so-called communitarian theorists were particularly prominent in questioning Rawls's theory of justice, because it disengages from the moral and political thinking rooted in the actual conditions of life at a specific time and in particular communities, or what Moller Okin terms traditions, customs, and institutions. The communitarians attempt to construct theories of justice based on particular traditions and values deeply embedded in *our* communities, founded on meanings or understandings that are shared by *us*. As a matter of fact, Walzer's[53] theory of justice is communitarian only partly, given his reliance on "shared meanings" or "understandings" which he interprets in ways that lead to far more egalitarian conclusions. However, the communitarian aspect of his thought retains certain deficiencies of the communitarian theories of justice writ large, not being capacious enough for critical insights about social domination and leaving insufficient space for gender justice.[54] Walzer does not refer to the "shared understandings" inherited from the past but to the shared understandings within the current given culture/s, considered as fundamentally egalitarian ones. Although he leaves space for dissenting opinions, even for radical criticism based on inner contradictions between the declared principles and the way they are materialized through social practices and institutions, Walzer's proposed space for critique does not allow for critical reconsiderations of power imbalances linked to different forms of oppression, and he fails to account for the fundamental disagreements between the oppressors and the oppressed. Accordingly, his theory is not open to a critical feminist standpoint, because his conception of shared understandings cannot encompass gender-based power imbalances.

[50] Rawls (1999 rev. ed.), p. 85.

[51] Rawls (1999 rev. ed.), p. 150.

[52] Moller Okin (1997), p. 183.

[53] Walzer (1983).

[54] Moller Okin (1989), p. 43.

However, Walzer's idea of the "separate spheres" criterion for justice bears a certain capacity for a productive feminist reinterpretation. Specifically, he states that it is wrong to see contemporary family as separate from the sphere of distributive justice. "Kinship ties and sexual relations are commonly thought to constitute a domain beyond the reach of distributive justice. They are judged in other terms... It would, nevertheless, be a mistake to think of kinship and love as a sphere different from all the others... In fact, it is closely connected to other distributive spheres, highly vulnerable to their interventions and itself pervasively influential".[55] The rules of distribution in this domain depend on cultural understandings that change over time and are context-related. An elaborate system of rules constitutes concrete distributive justice, and since the rules of kinship are distributive in nature, they need to be consulted when we try to make sense of "who can sleep with whom? Who can marry whom? Who lives with whom? Who must show respect to whom? Who is responsible for whom?"[56]

The separation of spheres is also questionable with regard to other aspects. Oppression of women is only partly situated in the family[57] because there is also "a kind of political and economic misogyny": "Thus the denial to women of the right to vote, or to hold office, or to own property, or to sue in court, and so on. In each case, the reasons given, when anyone bothers to give reasons, have to do with women's place within the family. So kinship patterns are dominant outside their sphere. And liberation begins outside, with a succession of claims that this or that social good should be distributed for its own, not for familial reasons".[58] The radical change in the family will happen when women's life stops being placed in the private sphere and when the private/public dichotomy, here captured by the old trope of separate spheres, is overcome. Personal relations, domestic life, reproduction, and child-rearing will continue, the protection of children and taking pride in their achievements and protecting them will also continue, but children will forge their own path, while "bearing the unequal burdens of parental expectations and the unequal grace of parental love. These last inequalities cannot be eliminated; the family exists, and will continue to exist, precisely in order to make place for them".[59] However, the family will or has already changed. The independent family will be equally a place for men and women, a place of freely chosen love, love of siblings, while still being a dominant affective and moral force.

Therefore, Walzer recognizes the structural inequalities within the family, he assigns them to the private/public dichotomy, he envisions changes towards more just and equal family relations, but he does not clearly recognize patriarchal power

---

[55] Walzer (1983), p. 227.

[56] Walzer (1983), p. 228.

[57] Walzer (1983), p. 239.

[58] Walzer mentions that anti-suffragists had been against large-scale political participation of women in politics while it would introduce new forms of conflict, new calculation of interests in to the kinship system. Walzer (1983), pp. 240–241.

[59] Walzer (1983), p. 242.

relations as the basic source of family injustice. According to him, the family can only be perceived as a separate sphere if equality between the sexes reigns within it. He specifies the sharing of family obligations within his separate sphere criterion. The problem is however in the fact that Walzer expects this kind of change to happen *per se*, beyond the range of state intervention, although legal, political, and social changes are necessary for enhancing equality between the sexes, whether in the family or in general.[60]

4.3 Green's Theory of Justice and Gender Justice

Philip Green offers yet another take on separate spheres, linking it strongly to capitalist social relations. Green argues that social equality, a prerequisite for real democracy, is incompatible with the existent division of labour between the sexes. For him, any radical version of democracy must be based on liberal political and constitutional institutions and successful in improving them.[61] On the other hand, the normative stance of an egalitarian democracy, of a society of truly equal citizens, means also "a critique of contemporary inegalitarianisms of race, gender and class",[62] and the voice in favour of those "who now are excluded from authority, from power, and from the springs of social well-being".[63] Central to his theory of social equality/justice is a democratic division of labour. Change in the structure of power and authority must be fundamental "to have more than a cosmetic or symbolic impact".[64]

The existence of free elections and a formally neutral state apparatus is one among several necessary preconditions for a successful campaign for political equality. But political reform without structural economic reform has only limited potential, because "capitalism and political equality are incompatible".[65] For that reason, the rule of "private capital" has to be abolished, as it represents the core of the mutual link of political and social equality.[66]

Within the proposed model of egalitarian democracy, similar to the social-democratic welfare model of social redistribution or distributive justice which is political and social at the same time, Green elaborates ideas about overcoming gender inequality as the constitutive element of egalitarian democracy. He interconnects unequal division of labour in both production and reproduction as sources of gender inequality/gender gap and gender injustice. Reproduction, as well as

[60] Walzer (1983), p. 117.
[61] Green (1985), p. viii.
[62] Green (1985), p. vii.
[63] Green (1985), p. viii.
[64] Green (1985), p. 9.
[65] Green (1985), p. 23.
[66] Green (1985), p. 24.

differences based on sex and biology, are taken as the specific source of gender inequality: "... Democratic division of labor makes possible the bridging of the gender gap, but that will not happen automatically. Gender discriminations, unlike those which confront racial and other, similar minorities, have their origin neither in the division of labor in production, nor in invidious, exclusionary social practices; at least, not in those alone. Gender distinctions, rather, to some very significant extent, and most especially in contemporary capitalist societies, also have their root in the division of labor in reproduction."[67]

Green does not accept the argument of public/private dichotomy, because he believes that hierarchy within the sphere of reproduction and hierarchy within the sphere of production replicate each other.[68] He clarifies that even if there are no longer separate spheres for women and men in work, education, homemaking, and civic participation, if the division of labour in the sphere of reproduction is not overcome, women will still have one more obligation, which is always the source of their stereotyping by men and even by themselves. Women who accept the extant division of labour in the reproductive sphere are left with either being "superwomen" or choosing not to have children. As Green says: "We are led to the conclusion, therefore, that democratization of the division of labor in production requires, concomitantly, democratization of the division of labor in reproduction. This does not mean the abolition of the family... Rather, democratization must mean at minimum the transformation of the family: not that biological parents do not... remain responsible for the care of their children and the organization of housework, but rather that more people are engaged in the process. It takes place in more locations, and the time allocated to it is divided differently, than in the case in the contemporary nuclear family. A democratic division of labor in reproduction requires that as a matter of course, that is of mutual expectation, men share parenting in some rough equality with women, regardless of how much time off from external employments this may require."[69] The point is that both parents should be able to participate in the democratic division of labour in both production and reproduction at the same time. "Just as shared parenting is necessary to make possible the equality of men and women, so communal responsibility for childcare, in some form, is required to make possible the equality of parents and nonparents, within the division of labor."[70]

Besides the mentioned extraordinarily relevant ideas about sharing parental and child-care responsibilities and its implications for the restructuring of the family in many respects, Green points to violence as an inherent component of the patriarchal family, which should be eliminated by the proposed family restructuring: "... within the structure of our civilization, the sexual division of labor seems to encourage in men a tendency toward aggression, misogyny, and violence. Conversely, however

[67] Green (1985), p. 96.
[68] Green (1985), p. 97.
[69] Green (1985), p. 99.
[70] Green (1985), p. 100.

much we strive to avoid a dualism in which 'male' and 'female' become morally polar terms. At the same time we must acknowledge that there is recognizably such a thing as a distinctively female discourse less oriented toward norms of aggression and destruction."[71]

Green pledges for the feminization of the public discourse as essential for democratic equality, but also for any good life. He underlines that the feminization of the public order must be accompanied by the overcoming of female virtue, which has been reduced to the private sphere of domestic work.[72] In short, it is necessary to overcome patriarchy with its confining social roles and generation of devaluation of women, hatred toward women, and consequential violence against women. Green concludes that feminism must be the motor force (though not the sole one) of the parent/child relationship transformation within the wider process of complementary or cumulative transformation of society.[73] This gives Philip Green a special position in the long line of mainstream political philosophers. Although not primarily feminist, Green's theory provides us with a fine example of how gender justice needs to be incorporated for a comprehensive, and internally consistent, understanding of justice.

5 Feminist Theories of Justice: Moller Okin and Nancy Fraser

Let us now consider two very different, yet prototypical feminist elaborations of justice. Susan Moller Okin[74] is a liberal feminist thinker who, as a feminist, is deeply critical of the private/public as well as individual/community dichotomy found in classical liberalism. She follows egalitarian liberalism and its mainstream considerations of justice, but aims to make it more inclusive and more consistent from the point of universal human rights by widening its scope through gender and family justice.

Because justice within the family is central to her, she had to reject the main pillar of liberalism: the division between public and private. Moller Okin is clear about the detrimental effects of injustice in the family: "The injustice that results from the division of labor between the sexes affects virtually all women in our society, though not in all the same way. ... (It) inflicts increasingly serious damage on children as well as women, and it destroys the family's potential to be the crucial first school where children develop a sense of fairness".[75] For her, public injustice is only one

---

[71] Green does not mention patriarchy but his explanations of the power relations in the contemporary nuclear family necessarily implies it. See, Green (1985), p. 101.

[72] Green (1985).

[73] Green (1985).

[74] Moller Okin (1989).

[75] Moller Okin (1989), p. vii.

dimension of injustice, which is always deeply rooted in family injustice. Family is the first political arena where one practices (or not) a fair share of social obligations and responsibilities, where one practices (or not) social relations free from power imbalance, hierarchy, and subordination.

For Moller Okin, patriarchy is the common root of women's suffering injustice.[76] The patriarchal nature of the family and the ideology that surrounds it affects all women, regardless of whether they live in traditional families themselves. It still profoundly conditions the dialectical dynamics of patriarchy and emancipation,[77] with strong implications for the gendered nature of public life. Susan Moller Okin made a crucial philosophical breakthrough in the justice discourse; however, her critical reconsidering of family justice is still limited within the binary heteronormative form of the family.

Nancy Fraser, on the other hand, is a socialist feminist philosopher whose entire work revolves around issues of justice. However, Fraser develops her ideas in a completely different frame than Moller Okin.[78] According to her, these ideas need to be situated within the framework of the decline of the Left and social democracy after 1989 and the rise of neoliberal capitalism,[79] as well as the rising trend of communitarianism and multiculturalism. The central tenet of her thought is the division between redistribution and recognition, the latter being related to so-called identity politics. Fraser remarks that with the shift from social redistribution to recognition, "the most salient social movements are no longer economically defined 'classes' who are struggling to defend their 'interests', end 'exploitation' and win 'redistribution'".[80] Focus instead moves to *culturally* defined groups or *communities of value* who are struggling to defend their *identities*, end cultural domination, and win recognition.

Many vulnerable groups engaged in the struggle for recognition in the spirit of the human rights revolution. These struggles, however, take place in the context of neoliberal capitalist globalization (which violates previously achieved human rights and results of the class struggle, weakens trade unions and working class solidarity, obliterates the importance of the class struggle, exploitation, and oppression based on class and relevance of distributive justice), and are often in line with the

[76] However, the recognition of this common axis "is not to deny or de-emphasize the fact that gender may affect different subgroups of women to a different extent and in different ways", Moller Okin (1989), p. 7.

[77] Vujadinovic (2023b).

[78] Fraser (1997).

[79] Fraser calls it economic liberalism and considers it the third relevant factor of the "postsocialist condition" related to the weakening of the theory and practice of distributive justice: "The context for these developments, and the third defining feature of the 'postsocialist' condition, is a resurgent economic liberalism. At the center of political gravity seems to shift from redistribution to recognition, and egalitarian commitments appear to recede, a globalizing wall-to-wall capitalism is increasingly marketizing social relations, eroding social protections, and worsening the life chances of billions." Fraser (1997), p. 3.

[80] Fraser (1997), p. 2.

communitarian (collectivist/traditionalist/conservative) or liberal multiculturalist ideas (struggle for difference within the framework of universally equal human rights, but with class struggle put aside). In their extreme forms, struggles for recognition deny any relevance to distributive justice.

Fraser herself refuses to pit distribution against recognition. It is not a matter of deciding between "class politics or identity politics? Social politics or cultural politics? Equality or difference? Redistribution or recognition?"[81] Her aim is to develop a critical theory of recognition in order to distinguish the claims for recognition that advance the cause of social equality from the claims for recognition that undermine it.[82] Developing the discourse on intersectionality in a nuanced way, Fraser analyses the so-called bivalent (combined) modes of differentiation based on class and gender, and class and race. Bivalent collectivities are those oppressed collectivities that suffer injustice based on reasons related to both political economy and culture simultaneously. According to Fraser, gender- and class-based discriminations[83] require different remedies that are nonetheless interlinked: "they intertwine to reinforce each other dialectically because sexist and androcentric cultural norms are institutionalized in the state and the economy, and women's economic disadvantage restricts women's 'voice', impending equal participation in the making of culture, in public spheres and in everyday life. The result is a vicious circle of cultural and economic subordination. Redressing gender injustice, therefore, requires changing both political economy and culture."[84]

Intersections of class, race, gender, and sexuality make it more difficult to come up with affirmative remedies, but they also intensify the need for transformative solutions and calls for coalition building, as well as the fissuring of social movements for the programmatic purposes of transforming deep structures of both political economy and culture/identities and doing justice in the context of all current struggles against injustice.[85] In this context, gender-based injustice combined with racial discrimination encompasses both redistribution injustice and racial divisions of labour into exploitable and superfluous labour as well as divisions within paid

[81] Fraser (1997), p. 3.

[82] Fraser (1997), p. 5.

[83] Political-economic dimensions of gender-based discrimination or redistribution injustices are those related to the fundamental division between paid productive labour and unpaid reproductive labour, as well as the disparity within paid labour between higher-paid, male-dominated and lower-paid female dominated public and domestic service occupations. The cultural-valuation dimension of gender-based discrimination or recognition injustices are related to sexuality, subjection to androcentrism, masculinity, cultural sexism, devaluation of the feminine expressed in sexual harm, assault, sexual exploitation, domestic violence, stereotypical representation in the media, harassment and disparagement in all spheres of everyday life, attitudinal discrimination, exclusion or marginalization in public spheres and deliberative bodies, and denial of full legal rights and equal protection. Fraser (1997), p. 20.

[84] Fraser (1997), p. 21.

[85] Fraser (1997), p. 32.

labour, and recognition injustice related to Eurocentrism and privileging whiteness, accompanied by cultural racism, which is the pervasive devaluation and disparagement of people of colour, particularly women of colour.[86]

The most proper conception of (gender) justice is one that combines the best from the logic of redistribution and the logic of recognition and fuses socialism and culture in search of injustice remedies. However, it should be critically noted that the axis of patriarchy and the issue of family justice and power relations based on manifestations of patriarchy in private and public life[87] have not been clearly articulated within this otherwise rich and productive fusion of redistributive and recognition discourse (with relevant implications for the intersectionality approach) related to gender justice and justice in general.

5.1 Iris Marion Young: Five Stages of Oppression and Gender Injustice

Iris Marion Young is a socialist political scientist who created crucial bridges between feminist theory of justice, mainstream political philosophy, and post-Marxist traditions. In her works, Young developed ideas that frame a feminist understanding of justice. Justice does not refer only to individuals, but essentially to social groups.[88] Giving each what is their due is not an abstract action in which individuals get stripped of their qualities or social attributes. We always belong—willingly or not—to groups (and Young is careful to avoid the notion of class, strata, or identity here), and it is through our belonging to them that we are judged as individuals. This calls for an embodied approach[89] to the individuals to whom justice belongs, and for a politics of difference, which needs to be taken into account while assessing difference in distribution of justice.

Based on this understanding, Young develops a variegated approach to justice, refusing to define the primary or the fundamental cause of all types of injustices. In other words, she goes beyond Moller Okin's conflation of all forms of oppression with patriarchy, or Fraser's bivalent model of recognition and redistribution. For her, there are at least five different faces of oppression that are irreducible to one another: exploitation, marginalization, powerlessness, cultural domination, and violence.[90] Her conception of social justice does not have an exclusive focus on gender but encompasses gender-based oppression in an all-encompassing manner. Concerning exploitation, like Fraser, Marion Young points to the division between paid and unpaid work within production/reproduction, and to gender pay gaps within

[86] Fraser (1997), p. 22.
[87] See Vujadinovic (2023b).
[88] Young (2001).
[89] Young (1980).
[90] Young (1990).

production work. Concerning marginalization, she tackles all groups of individuals who are "useless" from the viewpoint of a work-oriented society, like the elderly, unemployed, single mothers, the disabled, young unemployed members of minority groups, and native people.[91] Of course, all of these groups—not just single mothers—face significant gender-based marginalization. Powerlessness refers to all those who do not truly participate in decision-making, as well as all those who are invisible, silenced, and unaware of their suppressed capacities and their vulnerability to manipulation and indoctrination. Powerlessness in the case of gender-based social injustice has all of the mentioned features, shaped by patriarchal heredity. Cultural imperialism, in the sense of taking the culture of the ruling class as the norm, affects women of different races across the globe. Thus, the fight against cultural imperialism encompasses issues of redistribution and recognition, combining social justice and gender justice. As such, it has become a hot topic in critical feminist race theory, Global South feminism, and anti-colonial feminist theory, but also in self-reflexive Western feminist theories, which attempt to overcome the West-centric, white, and middle-class oriented mindsets. The fifth source of oppression, violence, is the most obvious and visible form of oppression; it affects women and vulnerable/marginalized groups everywhere, even in the most democratic societies (Blacks, Asians, Arabs, gay men and lesbians) in a crucial way, with hate crimes and sexual violence as prevalent examples of violent oppression.

Marion Young extends the liberal background of considering social justice beyond material redistribution and public/private dichotomy, advancing feminist thought on justice beyond liberalism, socialism, and multiculturalism.

5.2 *Feminisms and Justice*

Although different schools of feminist thought communicate what seems like conflicting ideas,[92] there are also significant areas of agreement achieved through a reflective accumulation of feminist knowledge. The first such idea points to an expanded conception of politics, coming from the insight that "power relations between men and women are not confined to the public world of law, the state and economics, but that they pervade all areas of life".[93] This means putting aside the private/public dichotomy and introducing family relations, care, reproduction, body and sexuality, interpersonal relations, and privacy into the realm of politics.[94] It means introducing gender justice and family justice into justice discourse among liberal feminists, as is the case of Susan Moller Okin, but also among socialist feminists like Nancy Fraser, or among those who move beyond liberalism and

[91] Young (1990), p. 53.
[92] Bryson (1982).
[93] Bryson (1982), p. 262.
[94] Hisrchmann and Di Stefano (1996), p. 6.

communitarianism in considering group differentiation which retains the idea of individual autonomy, as is the case of Iris Marion Young.

As Bryson assumes, the proposal that personal is political cannot be ignored anymore by any stream of feminist political thought which attempts to take women's needs seriously. Moreover, both Marxist and liberal feminists look for ways to bring the issue of personal life into consideration. Marxist feminists offer the framework for the analysis of unpaid domestic work as a means of exploitation, while liberal thought points ever more to the importance of changes in the family, besides changes in legislation and public life, for justice and equality to take place.[95] Ultimately, all streams of feminism question the absence of the private sphere and family issues from the political, thereby changing the content of the political.[96] For example, the Marxist concept of productive work is expanded to include unpaid family work, while the liberal stream emphasizes the importance of difference for the concept of equality, the importance of interdependence for autonomy, and the relationship between reason and emotion, intuition and physicality.[97] Liberal thinkers move forward from the original position related to legal reforms towards subversive implications related to changing the family structure and economic framework of thought and practice. Marxist feminists no longer ignore the importance of law, and also focus on certain legal reforms, such as legal abortion and family allowances.[98] Liberal feminists do not challenge capitalism/free market; however, certain public-policies-oriented demands of some liberal feminists for equal pay legislation, and elimination of sexism in education and employment, lead to an increase of state intervention into the free market logic and strategic change within public policies.[99]

Black feminism introduced the intersectional approach to considerations of gender issues. Feminists of all streams started to converge in the assumption that gender inequality is not the only significant source of inequality, and that for many women there can be even more important race or class inequalities.[100] Simplified ideas about the universal women's experience, of women as a unified group, have been abandoned. There is also a rising awareness about the shortcomings of West-centric feminist thought; Western feminisms are now expected to be more open to the experiences of different cultures and non-white women, as well as to reevaluate their own ideas in the way that Western feminists demand from the malestream political tradition.[101] Third World, anti-colonial, and Global South feminisms open

---

[95] Bryson (1982), p. 262.

[96] Vujadinovic (2023).

[97] Bryson (1982), p. 263.

[98] Bryson (1982), p. 264.

[99] "...[I]t seems unlikely that an economic system based purely upon the pursuit of profit would provide good quality childcare and the kind of flexible working arrangement that would allow men and women to combine full participation in child-rearing with the pursuit of a career." Bryson (1982), p. 265.

[100] Crenshaw (1989).

[101] Crenshaw (1989).

up new perspectives for critical insights into the concrete multi-layered forms of oppression in the historical/political/cultural context combined with the neoliberal economic context.[102]

Theoretical-methodological feminist approaches point to the dialectic of patriarchy and emancipation in all modern and contemporary societies, expressed differently at individual, local, national, and global levels in each concrete-historical case.[103] On a global scale, there are both underlying patterns of gender inequality as well as tendencies of emancipation, and there is an enormous diversity of needs and experiences that divide as well as unify women.[104] The intersectional approach, which connects gender inequality with other sources of inequality, has become an overarching idea for understanding the different layers of power relations within different sources of the multiple discrimination and oppression of women belonging to lower classes, non-white races, living under authoritarian political, cultural, religious regimes, etc.[105] In addition, there is a more or less growing openness to acknowledge the issue of multiple gender identities, as well as a willingness to abandon or enrich the binary conception of gender.[106]

All of the above-said contribute to feminist theories of justice, which necessarily encompass family justice, deconstructing power imbalances in both the private and public spheres, deconstructing the patriarchal binary understanding of gender and family, and including non-binary agents into gender justice discourse as well as in an intersectional approach to vulnerable groups of women oppressed based on their class, race, sexual, religious, and/or cultural affiliations.

6 Conclusion: From Gender-Blind Justice Towards Gender Justice

This chapter aimed to consider what gender justice may be. Clearly, there is no single answer to this. It is, however, apparent that answers have begun to be formulated in the last several decades. The feminist theorization of justice sought to reveal the blind spots in what traditional or more contemporary takes on justice had to offer, producing fruitful expansions and rich re-articulations along the way. Some mainstream attempts at conscious inclusion of gender aspects of justice have also been noted as fine examples that should be followed in the complex, changing world in which we live. Our main conclusion is that today no theory of justice that disregards gender justice can be described as complete.

[102] Wing (2023); Campbell (2013).

[103] Vujadinovic (2023b).

[104] Bryson (1982), p. 266.

[105] Vujadinovic (2023b).

[106] Butler (1990); Butler (2004); Saeidzadeh (2022); Baer (2023); Verdu (2023); Banovic (2023).

This is a demanding claim because gender justice is never reducible to the credo "add women and stir". It thoroughly questions some of the basic tenets of our societies that have long-standing, if troubling histories. Such are, first and foremost, the dichotomy of private and public and the binary patriarchal understanding of the family. If substantive justice is to be willed, one cannot stop here. Intersectional recognition and fairer redistribution, together with ending all forms of oppression, are a prerequisite for a just world in which we all live, as individuals and representatives of social groups. Ending exploitation entails a profound transformation of capitalism; ending violence presupposes a halt to unending wars all around the planet and a halt to the structural devaluation of women (some faces of which are sexual harassment, sex trafficking, femicide, rape as a war crime and a crime within family and private life). Ending cultural imperialism, in its own right, demands that the previous two have been taken into account—since capitalism functions especially cruelly in the regions where wars have also been waged more recently and more ferociously. Gender justice conceptions thus also tend to overcome West-centrism, and to open up in a self-reflexive manner a space for understanding discrepancies between the "Global North" and "Global South".[107] Eco-justice is also very much part of this debate.

Clearly, gender justice is about changing the world in which justice is possible, which of necessity demands that our acquired concepts of justice also be remade.

References

Ackerman B (1980) Social justice in the Liberal state. Yale University Press

Aristotle (2015) Works (Translated under the editorship of W. D. Ross) Nichomach Ethics. Oxford University Press. pp 2536–2787

Aristotle (2017) Works (Translated under the editorship of W. D. Ross) Politics (Translated by Benjamin Jowett)

Baer S (2023) Constitutional law and gender. In: Davinic M, Kostic S (eds) Gender competent public law and politics. Springer

[107] The Global North vs. Global South division should not be reduced to geographic and economic meaning, because the Global South exists in the most developed Western countries among subordinated classes, races, cultures, sexual orientations, and also because there are individuals and social strata within Global South countries that belong to the top of the global pyramid (the wealth at the top belongs to a small percentage of the world's richest individuals, while rising poverty among lower classes and "surplus people" is expressed in the lower and wider parts of the global pyramid). See Ruppert et al. (2020).

The mentioned extension and enrichment of gender justice discourse with eco-justice stems from the fact that eco-justice requires the overcoming of neoliberalism, which undermines many of the already achieved emancipatory elements of gender equality (see Campbell, 2013), as well as the fact that eco-justice demands an essentially different treatment of nature, and revives elements of the pre-patriarchal understanding of Mother Earth, of care, creation, and sustainability of the planet and humans (see Giancola (1998)).

Banovic D (2023) Queer legal theory. In: Vujadinovic D, Alvarez del Cuvillo A, Strand S (eds) Feminist approaches to law. Springer
Beitz CR (2011) The idea of human rights. Oxford University Press
Blackstone W (1765) Commentaries on the laws of England (book the first). Clarendon Press, Oxford
Bryson V (1982) Feminist political theory, an introduction. Macmillan Press, London
Butler J (1990) Gender trouble. Feminism and the subversion of identity. Routledge, New York
Butler J (2004) Undoing gender. Routledge, New York
Campbell B (2013) End of equality. Seagull Books
Cohen M (1972) The social contract explained and defended. The New York Times. https://www.nytimes.com/1972/07/16/archives/a-theory-of-justice-by-john-rawls-607-pp-cambridge-mass-the-belknap.html?_r=0
Crenshaw K (1989) Demarginalizing the intersection of race and sex: a black feminist critique of antidiscrimination doctrine, feminist theory and antiracist politics. University of Chicago Legal Forum, p 39
Dworkin R (1977, 1997) Taking rights seriously. G. Duckworth&Co Ltd.
Dworkin R (1986) Law's empire. Belknap Press
Dworkin R (2000) Sovereign virtue. Harvard University Press
Fraser N (1997) Justice interruptus—critical reflections on the "Postsocialist" condition. Routledge
Gallstone W (1980) Justice and the human good. University of Chicago Press
Giancola M D (1998) Justice and the face of the Great Mother (East and West). Paideia—ComparativePhilosophy.https://www.pdcnet.org/collection/fshow?id=wcp20-paideia_1998_0005_0047_0056&pdfname=wcp20. Assessed 28 Aug 2023
Green P (1985) Retrieving democracy—in search of civic equality. Rowman & Allanheld
Habermas J (2012) The concept of human dignity and the realistic utopia of human rights. In: Corradetti C (ed) Philosophical dimensions of human rights. Springer, pp 63–79
Hisrchmann N, di Stefano C (1996) Revisioning the political. Westview Press, Oxford
Kiss E (1998) Justice. In: Jaggar AM, Young IM (eds) A companion to feminist philosophy. Blackwell
Kymlicka W (2017) Multiculturalism: Success, Failure, and the Future, Migration Policy Institute, Europe", http://www.migrationpolicy.org/research/TCMmulticulturalism-success-failure
McIntyre A (1981) After virtue. University of Notre Dame Press
McIntyre A (1988) Whose justice? Which rationality? Ducksworth
Moller Okin S (1989) Gender, justice, the family. Basic Books
Moller Okin S (1997) Philosopher Queens and private wives: Plato on women and the family. In: Shankley ML, Pateman C (eds) Feminist interpretations and political theory. The Pennsylvania State University Press
Montmorency d JEG (1897) The changing status of a married woman. Law Quart Rev 13
Moyn S (2010) The last Utopia: human rights in history. The Belknap Press of Harvard University Press, Cambridge and London
Naffine N (2004) Our legal lives as men, women and persons. Fem Leg Stud 24:621–642
Nozick R (1974) Anarchy, State and Utopia. Wiley
Plato (1997) Republic and laws. In: Cooper J, Hutchinson DS (eds) Plato complete works. Hackett Pub Co
Rawls J (1971, 1999) Theory of Justice, rev. edn. Oxford University Press
Ruppert U, Scheiterbauer T, Lutz H (2020) Feminisms of the global south: critical thinking and collective struggles: an introduction. Eur J Women's Stud 27:329–332
Saeidzadeh Z (2022) Feminist methodologies and gender research. In: Vujadinović D, Froehlich M, Giegerich T (eds) Gender competent legal knowledge. Springer
Stafford E (2020) Worshipping virtues—personification and the divine in ancient Greece. Duckworth and The Classical Press of Wales
Unger R (1975) Knowledge and politics. Simon&Schuster
Unger R (2015) The critical legal studies movement. Verso
Verdu SA (2023) The concept of gender in law. In: Vujadinovic D, Alvarez del Cuvillo A, Strand S (eds) Feminist approaches to law. Springer

Villanueva Gardner C (2006) Historical dictionary of feminist philosophy. Scarecrow Press
Vujadinovic D (2023) Feminist reconsideration of political theories. In: Vujadinovic D, Alvarez del Cuvillo A, Strand S (eds) Feminist approaches to law. Springer
Vujadinovic D (2023b) Theoretical-methodological premises of the feminist perspective. In: Actualidad Jurídica Iberoamericana, pp 13–49
Walby S (1989) Theorising patriarchy. Sociology 23:213–234
Walzer W (1983) Spheres of justice: a defense of pluralism and equality. Basic Books
Wing AW (2023) Critical race feminism: a different approach to feminist theory. In: Vujadinović D, Alvarez del Cuvillo A, Strand S (eds) Feminist approaches to law. Springer, pp 53–71
Wood May I (2022). https://www.magellantv.com/articles/justice-personified-who-is-lady-justice-and-how-did-she-come-to-be#:~:text=One%20answer%20to%20the%20question,form%20of%20the%20goddess%20Justitia
Young MI (1980) Throwing like a girl: a phenomenology of feminine body comportment motility and spatiality. Hum Stud 3(2):137–156
Young MI (1990) Justice and the politics of difference. Princeton University Press
Young MI (2001) Equality of whom? Social groups and judgements of injustice. J Pol Philo 9(1): 1–18
Zaharijević A (2014, 2019) Who is individual? Genealogic consideration of the idea of the citizen (Ko je pojedinac? Genealoško propitivanje ideje građanina). Karpos, Loznica

Dragica Vujadinović is a Full Professor at the Faculty of Law, University of Belgrade, teaching Political and Legal Theories and Gender Studies in undergraduate studies, and Introduction into the EU Political System in the Masters in European Integration (MEI) program. She is the Head of MEI. She was the coordinator of University of Belgrade for the Erasmus Mundus project for the development of Master's Study Program Law and Gender—LAWGEM, lawgem.ius.bg.ac.rs (2019–2029). She was also the coordinator for University of Belgrade for the UniSAFE project (2019–2022), as well as the member of the Faculty of Law team for the Horizon project Building Gender Equality through Gender Budgeting for Institutional Transformation—BUDGET IT (2022–2025). She is the University of Belgrade coordinator for the Erasmus Mundus Design Measures project (EMDM) (2023–2024, 15 months), which Orebro U gained together with UB and LUMSA U, for preparing the future joint master program Law, Gender, Intersectionality and Diversity (LAWGID). She is a co-editor with V. Stanimirović, *Gender Studies*, Beograd 2017, 2019. with Z. Antonijević eds. *Gender Equality in Higher education: Concepts, Practices, Challenges*, Novi Sad 2019; co-author with Lj. Kovačević, T. Marinković, I. Krstić, M. Davinić, *Achieving Gender Equality at the University of Belgrade Faculty of Law: Research and Policy Study*, Belgrade 2020; co-editor with M. Froechlich, Th. Giegerich, *Gender Competent Legal Knowledge*, Springer 2023; with Lj. Kovačević and M. Evola, *Intersectional Discrimination of Women and Girls with Disabilities and Means of Their Empowerement*, Belgrade 2022; with A. Alvarez de Cuvillo, S. Strand, *Feminist Approaches to Law - Theoretical and Historical Insights*, Springer 2023.

She is the co-editor with Ivana Krstić of the Springer book series *GENDER PERSPECTIVES IN LAW*, and she published numerous chapters related to gender issues and feminist analysis.

Adriana Zaharijević is a Principal Research Fellow at the University of Belgrade, Institute for Philosophy and Social Theory. Her work combines political philosophy, gender studies and social history. She authored four books, the latest being Judith Butler and Politics (Edinburgh University Press, 2023), and has published in Signs, European Women's Studies Journal, East European Politics and Societies: and Cultures, Redescriptions and Women's Studies International Forum. Her texts were translated into Albanian, German, Hungarian, Italian, Macedonian, Portuguese, Slovenian, Turkish and Ukrainian, and she herself has translated philosophy and feminist theory into Serbian. Zaharijević is also the proud holder of the Emma Goldman Snowball Award.

Human Dignity in Feminist Vocabulary

Duška Franeta

Contents

Abstract This chapter traces the most typical uses of the concept of human dignity in feminist discourses. The main idea through which dignity entered these discourses is objectification. This concept is based upon the Kantian principle that people should never be treated only as a means, here being applied to specific social practices or behaviors that downgrade women to the level of things, particularly those related to sex (including rape, prostitution and pornography). In the case of certain authors, human dignity is used as an argument for the legal abolition of sexual harassment and exploitation, which are regarded as typical phenomena of objectification. In the second type of feminist discourses, human dignity is critically approached as an element of (in Peter Sloterdijk's terms) the *thymotic* conceptual arsenal that closely ties it with independence, autonomy, impartiality, justice, etc. When connected to this set of ideals, human dignity is considered as disruptive for the recognition and appreciation of some important moral phenomena and values, such as care, empathy, interdependence, and trust, and even as being supportive to men's dominance over women. The third type of dignity use focuses on shame societies and the relation between shame and dignity, and juxtaposes ancient *dignitas*, shaming practices, patriarchal rank, and honor with those societies respectful of the human dignity of women. Patriarchal shame practices, honor societies, and public shaming practices in general, not only disadvantage women, but also directly or indirectly contribute to destroying their dignity and lives. Three identified uses of

---

D. Franeta (✉)
Union University, Belgrade, Serbia
e-mail: duska.franeta@flv.edu.rs

N. Lacey et al. (eds.), *Reassessing Feminist Legal Theories*, Gender Perspectives in Law 5, https://doi.org/10.1007/978-3-031-75423-4_5

human dignity in feminist discourses differently address contemporary morality, law, or practical philosophy. This chapter explains in what way they call for a more consistent protection of human dignity, a more nuanced approach to the idea of dignity, or challenge certain fundaments of contemporary law and morality.

1 Introduction

Human dignity occupies a particularly important place in contemporary law and ethics. Despite there being no singular discourse on human dignity and its varied meanings being situated in different philosophical and jurisprudential frameworks, there are some influential strands of its interpretation that can be identified. In terms of law, these include human dignity as a fundamental legal value,[1] as the universal legal status of human beings,[2] as right to rights,[3] as a request for the balanced protection of different groups of rights,[4] as a specific right with a restricted core and a more flexible margin,[5] as a legal principle balanced with other principles so as to yield an absolute right,[6] etc. In terms of ethics, but at the same time or subsequently often in terms of law too, dignity has been opposed to *dignitas*,[7] it has been associated with the capability of virtue and duty,[8] with the ideas of personality, subjectivity, autonomy, and reason,[9] with autonomy and authenticity,[10] identity,[11] self-esteem, self-respect and recognition,[12] etc.

Despite its importance and widespread place in contemporary moral and legal thought and practice, the idea of human dignity is prone to criticisms in different aspects.[13] Still, it is beyond any doubt that dignity, at least as present in contemporary constitutions and international law, addresses both men and women. In spite of this, the concept of human dignity has been differently viewed and evaluated in discourses directly addressing the problem of women's oppression (feminist discourses). These assessments of the idea of human dignity include its repeated uses as

---

[1] Dürig (1956).

[2] Waldron (2012).

[3] Enders (1997).

[4] Habermas (2011).

[5] Herdegen (2010).

[6] Alexy (1994).

[7] Pöschl and Kondylis (2004).

[8] Cicero (1913).

[9] Kant (1977).

[10] Dworkin (2013).

[11] Tiedemann (2006).

[12] Ricoeur (2007).

[13] On the main problems of the idea in: Franeta (2015).

a conceptual central pillar to confront women's oppression as well as its outright challenges.

In this chapter I will identify the main contexts in which human dignity appears in feminist discourses. I will only focus on philosophy, despite feminist thought and discourses having been developed and spread throughout literature and arts, the live and written words of social movements, etc. Along with identifying the main contexts of dignity use, I will explain and comment on its ties to associated concepts, the reasons for particular uses, and the way specific uses address contemporary law.

The chapter is divided into the following parts: Introduction; Objectification; Dignity Challenges; Shame and Dignity; and Conclusion. In the Conclusion I sum up the contextual niches, differences in use, applications and criticisms of human dignity in feminist discourses, and underline the valuable import made to this idea.

2 Objectification

Objectification is the main idea through which human dignity found its place in feminist discourses and became its important vehicle. According to Catherine MacKinnon, sexual objectification represents its cornerstone,[14] and the primary process of the subjection of women.[15] It is the result of linking sexuality and domination, and its paradigmatic institution is prostitution. MacKinnon holds that sexuality itself is objectified and controlled so as to oppress women, and that the ultimate aim of objectification is possession.[16] She considers the link between sexuality and dominance itself to be a threat to human dignity since it creates hierarchy and inequality, the major problem being that it is constituted at the level of desire ("erotizing of power"). In MacKinnon's view, sexual harassment and discrimination, pornography, and prostitution are just extreme manifestations of this fundamental cultural problem.

Andrea Dworkin, who significantly influenced and inspired MacKinnon's views, took the topic of objectification as the central one, and in some of her works heavily relied on the idea of human dignity.[17] She considered rape, prostitution, and pornography to be outputs of the underlining objectification and dehumanization of women. The result is that "you experience within yourself a lack of self-respect so bottomless that there is no self to respect",[18] explains Dworkin, indicating a psychological background to any legal and moral idea of dignity. Furthermore, she claimed that there was a different standard of dignity for men and women,[19] meaning

[14] MacKinnon (1987), p. 645.
[15] MacKinnon (1987), p. 645.
[16] MacKinnon (1989), p. 327.
[17] E. g. Dworkin (1997).
[18] Dworkin (1997), p. 156.
[19] Dworkin (1997), p. 164.

that different behavior was held appropriate for women–such as being dominated, and subjected–and for men, despite dignity being the issue of the rights of *human* beings.

Similarly to MacKinnon, Kathleen Barry focused upon sexual harassment and sexual exploitation, defining the latter as "the reduction of human beings to objects of others' sexual power (that – comment D. F.) destroys their human dignity"[20] and prevents them from enjoying their rights. Prostitution, either voluntary or involuntary, as the paradigm example of sexual exploitation, explained Barry, leads to psychological harms and distortion of self. This mostly happens through steps of distancing, disengagement, dissociation, disembodiment, and dissembling[21] on the personal level, while at the social level it comes about through the steps enforced by sexual industries. Since it is a violation of internationally protected human dignity and human rights, sexual exploitation should be legally abolished, concluded Barry.

From the point of view of all three mentioned authors, the objectification of women is a denial of personhood on a gender basis, and all three took the abolitionist stance regarding the practices of sexual harassment, prostitution, and pornography.[22]

On the other hand, contemplating the issue of women's oppression, other authors introduced additional nuances to the issue of objectification, or analyzed the problem somewhat differently.

Sandra Lee Bartky explained objectification as taking part for a whole.[23] She argued that objectification resulted in a specific situation of women in the world: in their bodies becoming spectacles, in their estrangement from the essential attributes of person, and, finally, in a disempowering shame.[24] Such a prevailing climate further leads to self-objectification, or a tendency to "to adopt an objectifying self-perspective," internalization of "objectifying gaze" and its reinforcement.[25]

Julia Kristeva considers the strong focus on sexual inequalities of the formerly mentioned feminist authors to be enabled by an earlier feminist theoretical focus and practical struggle for political, economic, and professional equality.[26] In that sense,

---

[20] Barry (1997), p. 29.

[21] Barry (1997), p. 31.

[22] Barry took the so-called objective approach, arguing that sexual exploitation was a violation of human rights even when the abused person consented to its specific acts since it was gendered and caused objective harm to the well-being, dignity and rights of the person as the member of her class, and conclusively to the whole subordinated class. The notion of harm here includes the fact of dehumanization ["that which is destructive to being human" (Barry 1997, p. 30)] and the fact of the exercise of power over the abused. (pp. 29–30).

MacKinnon successfully confronted and framed sexual harassment as a type of sexual discrimination in terms of law in the U. S. and also with Andrea Dworkin tried to confront pornography through civil rights law in the U. S. They also proposed criminal sanctions for selling and buying of sexual "services," which had already been officially accepted and introduced in Sweden in the late 1990ies and later in several other countries too.

[23] Bartky (1990), p. 27.

[24] Bartky (1990), p. 27ff.

[25] Winn and Cornelius (2020)

[26] Kristeva (1981), p. 21.

alongside sexual objectification and sexual inequality, there are also other types of objectification and inequality, as for example treating women as domestic machines, birth machines, or decoration, which are not necessarily derived from sexual objectification.

In her essay "Objectification" Martha Nussbaum explains this phenomenon as treating one thing as another,[27] treating person as an object, or, more specifically, as instrumentalizing someone, denying one autonomy, treating one as inert or lacking agency, fungible or interchangeable, violable or lacking boundary integrity, as being owned, or denying her or him subjectivity. Nussbaum here builds upon Kantian explanations of objectification in order to expose its multiple manifestations and to underscore that the core of various objectifications of human beings was not necessarily sexual. She maintains that under specific circumstances objectification is always objectionable,[28] but in the case of their lack, in her opinion, objectification is acceptable. Diverging from the mentioned abolitionists, Nussbaum does not propose legal restrictions on pornography and prostitution. As for the latter, Nussbaum even argues against the criminalization of prostitution, primarily on the basis that, in her opinion, legally supported stigma against prostitutes makes their situation worse, and instead advances the idea of taking a series of different measures promoting their well-being.[29] In short, Nussbaum maintains that objectification is often but not necessarily always a violation of human dignity and even when it is, it should not necessarily be directly legally prohibited.

Nussbaum's division of objectification into specific types brings some clarity to the concept and exposes certain existing background problems of the use of the terms subject-object in rethinking human nature and relations, but it also at the same time blurs and weakens the earlier presented issue and argument against women's oppression. By fragmenting objectification into specific types, by claiming that it is sometimes inevitable and that it is not necessarily offensive, she arrives at a somewhat different and more fluid concept of objectification than the one MacKinnon focuses on, at one which is no longer unambiguously and in all cases at odds with human dignity.

On the other hand, MacKinnon presses home the topic of objectification further and links it with the ideal of objectivity, claiming that the latter founded specific models of knowledge and verification, that she labels "male"[30] and that are biased, non-situated, distanced,[31] and only allegedly neutral. One of her usual examples is the legal treatment of the topic of the right to privacy which is typically treated as gender-neutral and abstract[32] instead of being exposed as favorable for men and

[27] Nussbaum (1999), p. 218.
[28] Nussbaum (1999), p. 214.
[29] Nussbaum (1999), pp. 288; 295.
[30] MacKinnon (1989), p. 327.
[31] MacKinnon (1987).
[32] MacKinnon (1987), p. 95ff.

oppressive for women (battery, home labor, sexual domination, etc. happening in privacy).

Despite the above described differences, it is clear that the narratives on women's objectification are deeply tied to the concept of human dignity and human rights. This concept here serves as one of the major conceptual vehicles in confronting women's oppression, either in just moral or both in moral and legal terms.

3 Dignity Challenges

Despite human dignity having been repeatedly invoked to address the problem of women's oppression, strong criticism of this concept in feminist discourses has not been lacking. Such challenges to the idea of dignity are usually deeply tied with opposing care and justice, and with dismissals of the ideals of independence and individuality.

Carol Gilligan did not address the concept of human dignity directly, but her research explicitly communicated the idea that there were essential moral phenomena beyond the concept of justice. What Gilligan related with the concept of justice in the 1970s—autonomy, selfhood, freedom, respect, rights, impartiality, competitiveness, and even aggression,[33] could easily have included the idea of dignity itself since the latter has been regularly and directly related with the first four. In the last decade, in his analysis of the cultural responses to the phenomenon of rage through European history, Peter Sloterdijk named the same sequence (justice-autonomy-selfhood, etc.) *thymotics*, reminding us of the foundational place of the Greek idea of *thymos* in this sequence, and introducing some slight additions if compared with Gilligan's line: he included human dignity, retribution and revenge into this list, and put an evident emphasis on its agonistic aspects.[34] In any case, one can read in Gilligan's lines that care is an essential moral phenomenon that does not belong to this (*thymotic*) sequence; moreover, it comes before justice or even as opposed to justice—it can be read in and in-between the lines of "In a different voice."

From that time on, differentiating or opposing justice and care has been repeatedly present in some feminist narratives. Care has been understood and pursued as a prerequisite for any other moral value, as an integral part and basis of any genuine human relationship, as empathy, intimacy, trust- and support-related, as partial,[35] as non-violent and dependency-related, as natality- and bodiliness-related, as contextual, and as the meaning of life.[36] Justice and its sequence have been challenged by means of every single one of these features, as well as by the dominance approach described in the previous section (MacKinnon and Dworkin). Finally, dissatisfaction

[33] Gilligan (2003), p. 173.

[34] Sloterdijk (2008).

[35] Gilligan (2003); Noddings (2013), p. 90.

[36] Tronto (2015), pp. 23–24.

with the status of women in society resulted in harsh criticisms of such a sequence, and, directly or indirectly, of the associated idea of human dignity. The following are some examples:

> In most dominant theories of justice, dignity is coupled with the capacity for autonomy... I believe there is much that is problematic in an approach that extols independence as the route to a dignified life and sees dependence as a denigration of the person. I worry that the emphasis on independence extols an idealization that is a mere fiction, not only for people with disability, but for all of us.[37]

> Liberals became gutless wonders who, instead of having a material standard for equality based on human dignity, accepted the dehumanization, humiliation, and injury of women in the sex industry as entertainment; liberals let women's bodies become the speech of pimps, a new chattel status— women's bodies became pimps' words and sentences and paragraphs, under law.[38]

> The most fundamental liberal value is a belief in the intrinsic dignity and worth of every human individual, a worth grounded in each individual's capacity for reason. Liberals express this value in their political theory through the demand for equality... In this chapter I shall show how liberal feminists have pushed the concept of equality so far that its instantiation threatens the basic structure of liberal political theory and even the liberal conception of human nature.[39]

> The feminist critique of liberalism that a view such as Nussbaum's misses is the more fundamental one that turning everyone into a liberal individual leaves no one adequately attentive to relationships between persons, whether they be caring relations within the family or social relations holding communities together. [...] Liberal equality doesn't itself provide or concern itself with the more substantial components of relationship. It is in evaluating and making recommendations for the latter that the ethics of care is most appropriate.[40]

With suspicion have particularly been regarded the ideas of the prevailing reciprocal exchanges between equals in a society, contractual social philosophy,[41] natural rights theory, specifically in the U. S.,[42] ahistoricity,[43] ideals of independence[44] and impartiality,[45] ethics of rules,[46] ideas of autonomy[47] and freedom understood as arbitrariness, and privacy-publicity division.[48] The way in which these ideas have been constructed and socially pursued has been charged with devaluing care, genuine relations, and morality, and particularly with harming women.

---

[37] Kittay (2011), pp. 50–51.

[38] Dworkin (1997), p. 194.

[39] Jaggar (1983), p. 173.

[40] E. g. Held (2006), p. 95.

[41] E. g. Held (2006); Hunter (2016)

[42] E. g. Gilligan (2003), p. XXVII.

[43] E. g. Becker (1999), p. 40.

[44] E. g. Noddings (2013), p. 151; Held (2006), p. 10.

[45] E. g. Noddings (2013).

[46] E. g. Gilligan (2003), pp. 20–21.

[47] E. g. Noddings (2013), p. 151; Held (2006), p. 10.

[48] E. g. MacKinnon (1987).

A combination of the above cited and described views developed into what would be labeled as a feminist critique of liberalism, which apparently included repetitive critical addresses to the concept of dignity. In 1997 Nussbaum wrote an article titled "The Feminist critique of liberalism" and addressed some of the raised charges. According to her, all three central arguments were dignity-related: the first related to individualism, the second to the abstractness of liberalism, and the third to the emotion-reason cleft in liberalism and dignity idea. The first one is connected with the devaluing of the importance of community for an individual and in the final run with making an individual self-sufficient and egoistic; the second with a historicity of liberalism or liberal essentialism; and the third with the undervaluing of emotional experience and worthy relationships.

Human dignity, according to Nussbaum, is related to the rational and moral core of personhood that all human beings share.[49] She considers dignity, alongside personhood, autonomy, rights, and self-respect as belonging to the conceptual framework of liberal enlightenment. Its essence is reason, the fact of choice, or, more specifically "the ability to plan a life in accordance with one's own evaluations of ends."[50] This idea, in Nussbaum's interpretation, opposes all types of exclusion and marginalization, and stresses that everybody, just by being human, is of equal dignity and worth, no matter where they are situated in a society. Therefore, prioritizing *individual* dignity is a necessary barrier to any kind of collective oppression and to downgrading an individual as an end in herself or himself.

In short, Nussbaum deems the charges to be in some type of their interpretation a relevant critique for certain strands of liberalism, but at the same time that the strongest version of liberalism, alongside with the idea of dignity, can resist them (although they remain, she adds, significantly enlightening in certain respects). Two important notes should be added to the above sketched union of freedom and dignity, if liberal ideas are to be taken in their strongest version, explains Nussbaum. First, the idea of reason is specifically practical reason (in Aristotelian sense), and not some abstracted logical capacity juxtaposed to emotions. Second, any hierarchy is inimical to the value of human dignity, argues Nussbaum, drawing upon Mill's treatise on women, and explaining that martial or domestic hierarchy is just an example of unjustly not pursing the ideals of equality, human dignity and freedom, not their inherent flaw.

Despite these important explanations and her relying upon a qualified type of liberalism, Nussbaum still faced the trouble of answering the difficult question of which choices could be deemed as genuinely free and which were the result of deprivation, oppression, manipulation, etc. In dignity scholarship this issue emerges as a specific paradox of freedom: is there a freedom to give your freedom away, which has, at least since Kant, often been solved by tying freedom and dignity to *Vernunft* (reason, mind). Trying to address this issue, Nussbaum resorts to the well-known capabilities theory of human rights, and the distinction between real choices

[49] Nussbaum (1997b), p. 4.

[50] Nussbaum (1997b), p. 4.

and adaptive preferences.[51] The result is the idea that there are certain social pre-requisites to be necessarily met for any selfhood and freedom; this idea indeed introduces important social conditions but at the same time still remains somewhat loose (e. g. the framework enabled Nussbaum to regard prostitution as a possibly genuine and dignified life choice).

The opponents assessed Nussbaum's moves as defensive, inadequate, and inconsistent with the basic liberal positions.[52] Moreover, according to critics, the capabilities list which should have corresponded to the freedom imagined as dignity is accessed in a monologist, armchair, and para-political manner.

On the other hand, some of the authors following the above described "care route" ended up in the ideas of women's ethics, hypostazing (*hypostasis*) women's social position along with the facticity of care. The criticisms followed that such a standpoint easily falls prey to traditional forms of life, reinforces stereotypes,[53] transforms women's unfavorable position into an ideology, promotes training in self-sacrifice, and indulges totalitarian views hostile to human dignity as associated with the individual as an end in itself.[54]

4 Shame and Dignity

It has already been noted in the first section that objectification has been associated with disempowering shame.[55] The feeling of shame, shaming practices, bodiliness, and imperfection make another discursive unit in which human dignity is addressed as related to the status of women. The feeling of shame is here opposed to the phenomenon of human dignity, despite it not necessarily being in general bluntly negatively assessed.

There is a familiar expression that could help in describing this intricate network connecting shame, dignity, self-respect, and humiliation practices. Gilligan used it when citing the diary of Sophie Tolstoy: "I developed a battered sense of dignity."[56] This expression sums up the way in which women often feel in the violent patriarchal environment, and what happens to their own sense of dignity. It connotes the connections between dignity and self-esteem, and at the same time points at the idea of dignity as a healthy mean between humbleness and arrogance, as Aristotle had already held it to be.

The subtle meaning of this expression is sometimes overheard in legal interpretations of human dignity which label it as inborn and inviolable. Paul Ricoeur got

---

[51] Nussbaum (1999), p. 40; Nussbaum (1997a).

[52] Jaggar (2006).

[53] MacKinnon (1987).

[54] Nussbaum (1999), p. 130.

[55] Bartky (1990), p. 27ff.

[56] Gilligan (2003), p. 124.

close to it when he described the connections between self-esteem and dignity, and particularly when he explained that self-esteem can be "neglected, contested, disputed, as well as scorned, belittled, choked back, and humiliated,"[57] which in the end results in feeling subhuman, degraded, worthless, and helpless.

In Martha Nussbaum's long and dense argument on shaming penalties,[58] the idea of dignity takes a wordily limited but essential place. To use the above expression here, she describes how a society based on shaming penalties develops into a group of people with a battered or choked sense of dignity. In a nutshell, she regards the underlying pattern as a familiar one and still deeply present in the contemporary world: people are publicly ashamed for who they are and this infantile device of shame wells up into an uncontrollable (often vindictive) rage and aggression. For Nussbaum, the background of the infantile emotions of shame and disgust is the lack in self-consciousness. These emotions are built and nurtured on the image of an omnipotent, perfect and narcissistic self, and any imperfection or failure of humanity is denied and repressed. The perfect image of human being is identified with those most powerful in a society, while those less powerful or minorities are despised, scorned, stigmatized, and regarded as inferior. Women in general, not necessarily particular women, belong to this second group. In conclusion, the fictions and phantasies of infantile shame create suffering, degraded identities, and broken spirits and induce a hardly reparable sense of dignity, destroying selves and society. Perpetuating shame through shaming penalties erodes human dignity by harming the individual self-esteem of society members, particularly of those most vulnerable, and by creating an atmosphere of humiliation, dehumanization, and disrespect.

Shaming practices are typical for the so-called honor societies. The concept of human dignity was developed as opposed to the concept of *dignitas* characteristic to the society of rank (or honor) which matches the status (dignity) with *officium* and honor.[59] Cicero contrasted human dignity with *dignitas*: the former belonging to everybody, the latter only to some Romans.[60]

An honor system is one of the "patriarchy's principal pillars."[61] Orit Kamir reminds that honor systems are typically based on honor codes that differently distribute honor and define the basic statuses of men and women in a society, which usually offends the human dignity of women. She explains that honor and dishonor manifesting as shame are measurable, and that lack of honor suggests some "inherent lack or circumstantial loss."[62] There is a pyramidal social structure[63] upheld by social norms representing what is honorable and what is not, often strictly dividing the ideas of the so-called male and female honor. "Female honor" has often

[57] Ricoeur (1986), pp. 124–125.

[58] Nussbaum (2004), p. 223ff.

[59] Pöschl and Kondylis (2004).

[60] Cicero (1913).

[61] Kamir (2019), p. 304.

[62] Kamir (2019), p. 310.

[63] Kamir (2019), p. 310.

been equated with chastity, subordinated under male discipline, and perceived as "potential dishonor to men."[64] Therefore, obedience is understood as another crucial "female" virtue, and women as objects or "vehicles of honor,"[65] goods in good condition or damaged ones. "Male honor" has usually been connected to *thymos*, competition with other men, bravery, authority and dominance, being superior, and making them subjects of honor.[66]

To sum up, human dignity is here used as a central argument against shaming practices, shame societies and cultures, particularly when the status and rights of women are concerned. Shaming practices result in degraded identities, outlawed groups, infantile identities and relations, disempowerment, and cultivation of rage. Combined with patriarchy, honor codes, and so-called male and female honor, shame becomes a powerful vehicle of the subordination of women. It strongly supports the foundational ritualization of life expressed in rigidly defined roles and following social expectations, leaving little or no space beyond the alternative of being submissive and being socially punished.

5 Conclusion

There are three main contexts in feminist discourses in which the idea of human dignity occupies an important role. The first one identifies the violation of human dignity of women in treating them as objects, familiar under the term objectification. Particularly, sexual objectification in its extreme manifestations such as rape, prostitution, sexual harassment, and pornography has been addressed by a group of authors as an outright violation of human dignity, not only in moral but also in the legal sense, therefore calling for their legal abolition. Multiple ways to objectify someone have been recognized, such as instrumentalization, denial of autonomy, treating persons as inert, lacking agency, fungible, interchangeable, violable or lacking boundary integrity, as being owned, etc. While some authors warned that objectification and associated violations of human dignity of women are rooted primarily in linking sexuality and dominance, others underlined economic and political marginalization of women (e.g., treating women as domestic machines) as equally relevant regarding the denial of their subjectivity and subsequent treatment as less than human.

The second context in which human dignity is repeatedly invoked are criticisms of theories of justice. Human dignity is here identified as an idea belonging to the line of *thymotic* or agonistic values which cannot embrace the phenomenon of care. Care is understood as a fundamental moral phenomenon and value that transcends the ideals of neutrality, impartiality, independence, and autonomy. Human dignity is

---

[64] Kamir (2019), p. 311.

[65] Kamir (2019), p. 313.

[66] Kamir (2019), p. 312.

therefore criticized as associated with the ideas supporting male domination that do not correspond to the reality of human interdependence, dependence, diminished or imperfect rationality and choice, inequality, and vulnerability.

The third context is related to the phenomenon of shame. Shaming practices that lead to humiliation are recognized as opposed to human dignity, as disabling a decent society, and as particularly oppressive to women, who are often its targets. Shame society or rank society, the patriarchy being its paradigm example, is built on the ideas of rank, honor, and shame that oppress women and violate their human dignity. By defining different standards of honor for men and women expressed in the foundational ritualization of life, rigid definitions of basic social roles, and following social expectations and sanctions, women are disempowered, ashamed, and their self-respect and selves shattered.

Some of the described dignity uses call for instant social and legal action and change, some are directed at reframing of the dignity idea and of the existing practical philosophy. The former includes those consistently applying or reforming existing legal standards related to the sexual oppression of women as well as those directed at a broader social opposition of dominance over women through reframing social roles and resisting gender stereotypes. The latter introduce the epistemological critique of the alleged legal objectivity as well as the introduction of the issues of care, empathy, and support as dignity-relevant. Grounding human dignity in rigid dualisms, such as indeterminism-determinism and subject-object, in individuality aspiring to self-sufficiency, connecting it to neutral and emotions-opposed rationality, or taking it as an absolute, foundational, and sole legal and moral value, proved to be not only inadequate but also hindering for the promotion of self-esteem and self-respect, the prerequisites of any human dignity. The processes of facilitating, supporting, developing, and restoring dignity, in the childhood as well as in other periods and aspects of life (close relations, illness, disability, poverty, old-age, trauma, etc.) are identified through the topic of care. They match certain continuous paths from passivity to activity, from involuntary to voluntary, from spontaneity to freedom, which need to be taken once and again, and that no one can take without any support to his or her own dignity; they match intricate connections among self-esteem, respect, recognition, shame, intimacy, support, empathy, gentleness, and care. Trying to sum up these delicate networks of empathy, dignity and justice, MacKinnon rightly put it that it was not about confronting morality of justice and morality of care, not about some different or female morality (as some authors indeed held), but about a morality in a higher register.[67] In that sense, the path of recognition, once described as a necessary struggle to life and death between master and slave by Hegel, started being envisioned as a less brutal but not less demanding path of communication, integrity, responsibility, solidarity, empathy, support, understanding, friendship, trust, and tolerance.

[67] MacKinnon (1987), p. 39.

References

Alexy R (1994) Theorie der Grundrechte. Suhrkamp, Frankfurt am Main
Barry K (1997) Prostitution of sexuality: a cause for new international human rights. J Personal Interpersonal Loss Int Persp Stress Coping 2(1):27–48. https://doi.org/10.1080/10811449708414404
Bartky SL (1990) Femininity and domination. Routledge, New York
Becker M (1999) Patriarchy and inequality: towards a substantive feminism. Univ Chicago Legal Forum 1:Article 3
Cicero MT (1913) De officiis. Harvard University Press, Cambridge
Dürig G (1956) Der Grundrechtssatz von der Menschenwürde. Archiv des öffentlichen Rechts 8: 117–157
Dworkin A (1997) Life and death. The Free Press, New York
Dworkin R (2013) Justice for Hedgehogs. Harvard University Press, Cambridge
Enders C (1997) Die Menschenwürde in der Verfassungsordnung. Mohr Siebeck, Tübingen
Franeta D (2015) Ljudsko dostojanstvo kao pravna vrednost (Human dignity as legal value). Centar za izdavaštvo i informisanje Pravnog fakulteta Univerziteta u Beogradu, Beograd
Gilligan C (2003) In a different voice. Harvard University Press, Cambridge
Habermas J (2011) Das Konzept der Menschenwürde und die realistische Utopie der Menschenrechte. In: Habermas J. Zur Verfassung Europas. Ein Essay. Suhrkamp, Berlin, pp 13–38
Held V (2006) Ethics of Care. Oxford University Press, Oxford
Herdegen M (2010) Kommentierung zu Art. 1 GG. In: Maunz T et al (eds) Grundgesetz Kommentar. C. H. Beck, München, Loseblattsammlung
Hunter R (2016) Contesting the dominant paradigm: feminist critiques of liberal legalism. In: Davies M, Munro VE (eds) The Ashgate research companion to feminist legal theory. Taylor and Francis, London
Jaggar A (1983) Feminist politics and human nature. Rowman&Allanheld, Sussex
Jaggar A (2006) Reasoning about well-being: Nussbaum's methods of justifying the capabilities. J Pol Philo 14(3):301–322
Kamir O (2019) A dignitarian feminist jurisprudence with applications to rape, sexual harassment and honor codes. In: West R, Bowman CG (eds) Research handbook on feminist jurisprudence. Edward Elgar, pp 303–320
Kant I (1977) Metaphysik der Sitten. Suhrkamp, Frankfurt a. M
Kittay EF (2011) The ethics of care, dependence, and disability. Ratio Juris 24:49–58
Kristeva J (1981) Women's time. Signs J Women Cult Soc 7(1):13–35
MacKinnon C (1987) Feminism unmodified. Harvard University Press, Cambridge
MacKinnon C (1989) Sexuality, pornography, and method: "Pleasure under Patriarchy". Ethics 92(2):314–346
Noddings N (2013) Caring: a relational approach to ethics and moral education. University of California Press, Berkley
Nussbaum MC (1997a) The feminist critique of liberalism. Lindley Lecture, University of Kansas
Nussbaum MC (1997b) Capabilities and human rights. Fordham Law Rev 46(2):273–300
Nussbaum MC (1999) Sex and social justice. Oxford University Press, New York
Nussbaum MC (2001) Fragility of goodness. Cambridge University Press, Cambridge
Nussbaum MC (2004) Hiding from Humanity. Princeton University Press, Princeton
Pöschl V, Kondylis P (2004) Würde. In: Brunner O et al (eds) Geschichtliche Grundbegriffe. Historische Lexikon zur politisch-sozialen Sprache in Deutschland 7. Klett-Cotta, Stuttgart, pp 637–645
Ricoeur P (1986) Fallible man (revised trans. Kelbley C). Fordham University Press, New York
Ricoeur P (2007) Reflections on the Just. The University of Chicago Press, Chicago

Sloterdijk P (2008) Zorn und Zeit. Suhrkamp, Frankfurt a. M
Tiedemann P (2006) Was ist Menschenwürde? WBG, Darmstadt
Tronto J (2015) Who cares. Cornell University Press, New York
Waldron J (2012) Dignity, rank and rights. Oxford University Press
Winn L, Cornelius R (2020) Self-objectification and cognitive performance. Front Psychol 11:20

Duška Franeta is a Professor of Philosophy of Law and Ethics at the Faculty of Law and Business Studies Dr Lazar Vrkatić, Union University, Serbia. Her primary research interests include legal axiology, with a particular focus on human dignity, moral ideals, philosophical and legal hermeneutics and professional ethics. She authored a book and a series of articles on human dignity, edited a book on Applied Ethics (with E. Protopapadakis), authored an introduction to Philosophy of Law, as well as many other publications including those on trust, the problem of impartiality, psychology ethics education, interpretation, etc.

What Has Gender Ever Done for Women? Considering the Potential of Gender as a Legal Concept

Lídia Balogh

Contents

Abstract What we understand by "gender" has become increasingly complex since the beginning of the 2010s. Currently, it is used with various meanings in academic and political discourse, as well as in public discourse and legal and public policy documents. In the past, within the latter areas, the constructivist interpretation of gender meant that it was primarily used as an analytical concept: it encompassed the social roles of women and men, as well as the social expectations, stereotypes, and power dynamics associated with female and male roles. However, recently, it has been increasingly used as an activist concept to articulate movement-related goals and with a different meaning than previously: to refer to gender identity experienced and defined by the individual. This shift has created new challenges for those who seek to conceptualize women's equality. This study concludes that gender as an analytical concept can still be useful in social science research and theory for understanding the relative positions of women and men and, in the realm of public policy, alleviating the specific social problems faced by women and men. However, as a legal concept, in contrast to the expectations of many, gender has proven to be rather irrelevant to women's rights, and as a political and movement slogan, it has instead done a disservice to women's issues. The study discusses the tumultuous history of the Istanbul Convention and, in connection with this, the heated debates about gender and women's rights. To put gender as a legal concept into perspective,

L. Balogh (✉)
Institute for Legal Studies, HUN-REN Centre for Social Sciences, Budapest, Hungary

N. Lacey et al. (eds.), *Reassessing Feminist Legal Theories*, Gender Perspectives in Law 5, https://doi.org/10.1007/978-3-031-75423-4_6

the study presents an analogous phenomenon: the development history of intersectionality, with the aim of questioning whether a thing should be used as a legal concept simply because it has proven to be a useful tool for social science analysis and achieved remarkable success in the realm of activism.

1 Introduction

There is an intentional reference in the chapter's title to a memorable scene from Monty Python's 1979 movie *Life of Brian*,[1] where the key question is asked during a political gathering: "What have the Romans ever done for us?" This scene is often invoked when someone, typically for the purpose of political mobilization, condemns clearly positive developments connected to (external) factors or players; for example, the opponents of Brexit frequently quoted it sarcastically, replacing "Romans" with "Europe." In the context of the debate surrounding *gender*,[2] we can relate to this scene because opponents of the latter in countries outside of Anglophone territories consider it a foreign concept imposed by (quasi) colonial powers, while its advocates continuously emphasize its beneficial social impact.

The writing of this chapter was motivated by the suspicion that *gender* as a legal concept is of questionable usefulness and may lead to dubious outcomes in terms of the realization of women's perspectives within the field of law. The latter element of this suspicion may seem counterintuitive, as *gender* was previously associated (by those who were aware of it, at least) primarily with feminism, that is, with the struggle for women's social empowerment. Accordingly, each section of the present chapter revolves around a question: What do people mean by *gender* nowadays? Is *gender* necessary for combatting violence against women? Can a sociological concept be applicable in law? What may one expect when criticizing the growing presence of *gender*?

Within the framework of a book chapter, these complex issues can only be discussed in limited depth. I do not intend to argue in favor of any particular approach to *gender* or to propose my own definition. My goal is to foster reflection, raise questions, and substantiate the relevance of the issues that are raised.

[1] *Monty Python's Life of Brian*, directed by Terry Jones (1979).

[2] Throughout the study, I use italics to indicate a distancing from the concept/term *gender* due to the lack of clarity associated with it and to indicate that I consider *gender* merely as a carrier or "vehiculum"; regarding the latter (semiotic) concept, see e.g.: Dobi (2019).

2 What Do People Mean by *Gender* Today?

Before discussing what (or how many things) we currently mean by *gender*, it is important to note that there are multiple narratives regarding the origin and history of *gender*, at least in terms of emphasis, and providing an overview of all these would exceed the framework of this study. I also have to reflect on my own position and my East-Central European (ECE) perspective.[3]

Hungary and the broader ECE region developed their relationship with *gender* in connection with their accession to the EU, as candidate countries had to demonstrate compliance with EU norms on equality between women and men, among many other requirements. Monitoring this process involved representatives from civil society and the academic sphere[4] who also contributed to promoting relevant policy concepts, particularly *gender* and *gender mainstreaming*. Importantly, the mere translation of these concepts posed a challenge in non-Anglophone societies.

In my direct context, in Hungary, there was no social debate surrounding *gender* or *gender mainstreaming* during the period surrounding EU accession. For most people (those who had even heard of these terms), the former seemed like an abstract concept from the social sciences, while the latter appeared to be a boring administrative complication. Later, however, the recognition that *gender* does not mean the same thing to everyone became inevitable for local proponents of the concept, although this was not entirely unexpected considering international trends. Still, the Hungarian Women's Lobby, an umbrella organization of women's NGOs, launched a thematic website in 2015 with the explicit mission of "clarify[ing] misconceptions and misinterpretations surrounding the concept of 'gender.'"[5]

But the confrontation with the ambiguity of *gender* could not be delayed for long,[6] and even the narrative surrounding its origins required revision. Apparently, *gender*, which gained significant importance in Western societies as a public policy concept, is not solely a product of (constructivist) social theory from the late twentieth century. The dominant narrative now acknowledges[7] that *gender* was initially used by a New Zealand sexologist-psychologist, John Money, in the 1950s, although his work remains controversial.[8] He first employed the term with

[3] On a personal note, I have been engaged with *gender* issues since the early 2000s, first while working for Hungarian NGOs, then as an academic researcher and an expert in European Union projects.

[4] See, e.g., a comprehensive report: Open Society Institute (2005).

[5] The webpage (http://sex.gender.hu/) is no longer available.

[6] It should be noted that even among those who view gender as the interplay of social and biological factors, there are various shades of opinion. The exact extent and significance of biology in different areas is a complex matter whose discussion goes beyond the scope of this chapter.

[7] Repo (2015).

[8] Bullough (2003).

the meaning of "gender role," then later as "gender identity."[9] The narrative now also recognizes that linguists have long used the term *gender*, derived from the Latin word "genus," to refer to a grammatical feature of certain languages.

The diverse meanings attributed to *gender* are effectively illustrated by philosopher Kathleen Stock in an essay from 2019,[10] where she identifies no fewer than five different interpretations: gender roles in society, stereotypes related to men and women, gender identity, biological sex (in English-speaking regions, *gender* is often used as a "polite" synonym for sex to avoid associations with sexuality), and the notion of *gender* according to Judith Butler's theory[11] (wherein even biological sex is basically considered a social construct). An essay by a Hungarian scholar, published a year earlier, also drew attention to the fact that *gender* is used with various senses; sometimes, it simply refers to women or to women's perspectives (the "gender analysis" of a policy may actually involve only examining a measure's impact on women).[12]

A notable development from the ECE region is that in Bulgaria, within the framework of a discourse criticizing Western liberal ideas, *gender* acquired a peculiar meaning and function in the late 2010s: the term (transliterated as *джендър*) became widely used as a noun,[13] roughly corresponding semantically to what is referred to as "LGBTQIA individuals" in liberal discourse; for example, a tabloid article in 2019 had the following headline: "Charlize Theron Raises Her Child to be a Gender."[14] While the Bulgarian example may seem comical, it is undeniable that by the early 2020s, addressing the topics of gender identity (transgender issues and self-identification) and sexual orientation (particularly the rights of same-sex couples) became mandatory in the context of EU policies under the heading of *gender*, while previously, these topics were referred to by the acronym SOGI (sexual orientation and gender identity),[15] while the very meaning of *gender* became diverse and ambiguous in EU documents.[16] For example, let us consider the definition provided by the European Institute for Gender Equality (EIGE), an institution operated by the EU: "Social attributes and opportunities associated with being female and male and to the relationships between women and men and girls

[9] Money and colleagues from Johns Hopkins University started from the assumption that we are psychosexually neutral at birth and that healthy psychosexual development depends on the appearance of genitalia. Based on this premise, they advised the parents of a male infant who was left without a penis due to a surgical error to raise the child as a girl, aiming to develop a female identity (which ultimately ended in failure). For more information on this case, see Diamond and Sigmundson (1997).

[10] Stock (2019).

[11] Her classic work on the issue: Butler (1990).

[12] Kováts (2018).

[13] Darakchi (2019).

[14] Stojanovski (2019).

[15] Nógrádi (2023).

[16] Kováts and Zacharenko (2022).

and boys, as well as to the relations between women and those between men."[17] This redundant yet inconsistent definition likely emerged due to the need for an explicit mention of sexual orientation, albeit raised further questions rather than providing answers. The change in meaning also affected "gender equality": previously, this simply served as a synonym for "equality between women and men," but for example, the EU's 2019–2027 Youth Strategy defines one of its goals as the "equality of all genders,"[18] which is a clear abandonment of the binary conceptualization.

Considering its blurred meaning, unsurprisingly, *gender* has become an effective tool for political mobilization by the radical right. For example, a comprehensive study (Kováts 2022). For a summary of the monograph in English, see an interview with the author: (Laczó 2022) about the politics of the governing coalition in Hungary since 2010 and a German opposition party, Alternative für Deutschland, presents why the metaphor of "gender as a Trojan horse" (which conveys the accusation that *gender* seemingly addresses the improvement of women's social position but actually seeks to abolish the concepts of man and woman) resonated so strongly.

3 Is There a Need for *Gender* to Combat Violence Against Women?

So far, *gender* has been discussed as a linguistic, sexological-psychological, sociological, public policy, activist, and political concept, acknowledging its uncertainties and contradictions. At this point, let me illustrate that even in the legal realm, the concept of *gender* is unstable, although stability is strongly expected of legal concepts. Not long ago, even in the mid-2010s, the topic of "law and gender" was closely related to feminist legal theory, and *gender*, in this context, served as an analytical tool for examining how social relations between women and men are reflected in case law and legal arguments.[19] However, a monograph from 2020, *Gender and Human Rights: Expanding Concepts*, positioned itself as follows: "This book is not about women and not about gender as a social corollary of sex. The book aims to disrupt the traditional association of gender with women and sex with biological binary."[20] Even more surprisingly, this book does not discuss the international legal documents that first applied the concept of *gender*: the Rome Statute of the International Criminal Court (1998),[21] which was negotiated as a treaty within

[17] EIGE (2023a).

[18] Council of the European Union (2018).

[19] Conaghan and Russell (2015).

[20] Krivenko (2020), p. 1.

[21] UN (1998).

the United Nations (UN) and the Istanbul Convention (2011)[22] of the Council of Europe (CoE).

As for the direct context, the term *gender* began to appear in international organizations' documents from the 1990s onwards, notably in the Beijing Declaration and Platform for Action adopted at the UN's Fourth World Conference on Women held in 1995. Even then, *gender* sparked debates and concerns, as evidenced by the conference report: a contact group was formed "to seek agreement on the commonly understood meaning of 'gender' in the context of the Platform for Action," which subsequently reported that: "there was no indication that any new meaning or connotation of the term [gender], different from accepted prior usage, was intended" by the drafters.[23] The report also includes interpretive statements on *gender* by the Holy See, committing to "the common meaning of that word, in languages where it exists [...] understood [...] as grounded in biological sexual identity, male or female"; excluding "dubious interpretations based on world views which assert that sexual identity can be adapted indefinitely to suit new and different purposes," but rejecting "the biological determinist notion that all the roles and relations of the two sexes are fixed in a single, static pattern."[24]

The Rome Statute from 1998 similarly seeks to clarify that "[f]or the purpose of this Statute, it is understood that the term 'gender' refers to the two sexes, male and female, within the context of society. The term 'gender' does not indicate any meaning different from the above."[25]

However, then came the Istanbul Convention (IC), which sparked debates in numerous countries and at the European level with its more sophisticated *gender* definition: "the socially constructed roles, behaviours, activities and attributes that a given society considers appropriate for women and men."[26] The IC also provides that "violence against women" "shall mean all acts of gender-based violence that result in [...] harm or suffering to women."[27] Furthermore, it provides a separate definition for "gender-based violence against women," understood as "violence that is directed against a woman because she is a woman or that affects women disproportionately."[28] However, within the text of the IC, the terms "violence against women," "gender-based violence," and "gender-based violence against women" are used in a virtually interchangeable way.

It is not possible here to provide a comprehensive evaluation of the IC's provisions, but one important feature, critically highlighted by several analysts,[29] deserves mention: while the IC considers inequality between women and men both the cause and consequence of violence against women, it approaches domestic

[22] CoE (2011a).

[23] UN (1995), Annex IV.

[24] UN (1995), Chapter V, para. 12.

[25] UN (1998), Article 7 (3).

[26] IC, Article 3 (c).

[27] IC, Article 3 (a).

[28] IC, Article 3 (d).

[29] Westendorp (2018), Jones (2018), Niemi and Sanmartin (2020).

violence as a basically gender-neutral phenomenon as it is claimed to cover "all acts of physical, sexual, psychological or economic violence that occur within the family or domestic unit or between former or current spouses or partners"[30]—acknowledging, however, that the phenomenon disproportionately affects women.[31] The European Women's Lobby (a civil society umbrella organization) stated no less (in a press release during the drafting of the IC) than this approach jeopardizes the main objectives of the CoE's initiative.[32] The UN Special Rapporteur on violence against women also expressed concern prior to the entry into force of the IC that a shift towards gender-neutrality suggests that assisting potential male victims of intimate partner violence would require resources of a similar magnitude to those dedicated to female victims; moreover, a shift like this depoliticizes the discourse surrounding the phenomenon and implies the abandonment of the goal of achieving "transformative change."[33]

Around the time when the IC entered into force, a legal analysis was published that is unique in terms of its approach, conclusions, and even its prognosis. Agnello's extensive critique,[34] supported by a massive reference apparatus, deserves to be presented, as it has become a point of reference, even beyond the academic world.

The author's main claim and primary concern is that the theoretically problematic *gender* concept of the IC is not only useless in terms of its goal, namely the protection of women, but also risky. He considers the IC's definition of "violence against women" as redundant and claims that there is no need for a concept of *gender* to emphasize that combating prejudice against women is important. As for the definition of *gender* itself, the author states that: "Opting for a socially-based 'gender' definition—it is well known—means, first of all, and at least, [...] affirm [ing] not just a distinction between 'gender' and 'sex,' but rather a substantial dichotomy between these concepts, thus denying the fact that these are even respectively linked."[35] Agnello believes that the best way to protect women would be to adopt a perspective that admits "the relevance of society and culture in assigning roles and duties to men and women" and affirms "the absolute equality between men and women in law and dignity," but does not affirm "the absolute irrelevance of the sex" but "recognizes the relevance of the biologically given differences and the necessity to affirm their juridical significance."[36] Agnello refers to the paragraph[37] of the IC's Explanatory Report concerning the IC definition of *gender*, which reflects the intention of some of the drafters of the IC to retain the biological basis (similar to the *gender* definition of the Rome Statute). He claims that

[30] IC, Article 3 (b).

[31] IC, Article 2 (1).

[32] European Women's Lobby (2010).

[33] Manjoo (2014), para. 61.

[34] Agnello (2014).

[35] Agnello (2014), p. 92.

[36] Agnello (2014), p. 95.

[37] CoE (2011b), para. 43.

the adoption of the IC was rushed: driven by its ambition of joining the EU and winning merit in the field of human rights, Turkey, then holding the presidency of the Committee of Ministers of the CoE, achieved the convention's adoption before the end of its presidential term, ensuring it would be associated with a historically important Turkish city, Istanbul. (It should also be noted that the IC was ultimately adopted without voting.[38])

Agnello's other major concern is the anti-discrimination clause in the IC: "The implementation of the provisions of this Convention by the Parties, in particular measures to protect the rights of victims, shall be secured without discrimination on any ground such as sex, gender [. . .or] gender identity [. . .]."[39] According to Agnello, this provision "at first sight could appear bizarre and senseless" but "becomes full of significance if read bearing in mind all the theories from which the social definition of gender stems and the goals pursued by them."[40] Additionally, he refers to the Explanatory Report's related paragraph, which elaborates that the prohibition of discrimination on the basis of gender identity "includes categories of individuals such as transgender or transsexual persons, cross-dressers, transvestites and other groups of persons that do not correspond to what society has established as belonging to 'male' or 'female' categories."[41] Agnello believes that this explanation "almost explicitly" extends the protection of women to people who "(having regard to their sex) are not women"[42] and introduces "striking consequences stealthily, by a back-door."[43] He concludes that "[w]hatever opinion one may have about the goodness" of initiatives in certain countries to introduce a third gender category or to recognize a self-identified gender, "all of these issues go beyond a convention on preventing and combating violence against women and domestic violence and should have been set aside."[44] Notably, during the preparation of the IC in 2009, the European chapter of the International Lesbian, Gay, Bisexual, Trans, and Intersex Association petitioned the *ad hoc* committee tasked with drafting the document, calling for explicit mention of "all transgender women, and not just those intending to undergo, or who have undergone, gender reassignment" in the provisions.[45] Although this request was not fulfilled, the "undefined definition" of *gender* in the IC enables lobbying for issues related to gender identity by influencing the monitoring committee of the IC (GREVIO).[46]

---

[38] CoE Committee of Ministers (2011).

[39] IC, Article 4 (3).

[40] Agnello (2014), p. 104.

[41] CoE (2011b), para. 53.

[42] Agnello (2014), p. 104.

[43] Agnello (2014), p. 105.

[44] Agnello (2014), p. 109.

[45] ILGA Europe (2009).

[46] Agnello (2014), pp. 105–106.

Agnello's study is occasionally cited by feminist scholars as a noteworthy contribution to the academic debate surrounding the IC[47] with regard to the issue of *gender* as a legal concept.[48] In Hungary, even audiences outside academic circles became aware of the paper in 2017 after the Hungarian government launched a public consultation on the proposed ratification of the IC. (Notably, Hungary signed the IC in 2014, when the same party coalition governed the country.) In response to this, the Hungarian branch of CitizenGO, an internationally operating conservative civil initiative, launched an online petition entitled "The ratification of the Istanbul Convention may serve as the Trojan horse of gender ideology for Hungary,"[49] directly referring to Agnello's study—although not endorsing the author's feminist perspective.[50] The governing Fidesz party's vice president repeatedly spoke out in the media against ratification—which was subsequently removed from the agenda—stating that the IC "is not about what they claim it to be" and through its provisions, which were "smuggled in from that politically correct world" it aims "to transpose gender philosophy."[51] In 2020, the Hungarian Parliament—following a formal initiative by MPs of the junior coalition party, the Christian Democratic People's Party—adopted a political declaration rejecting the ratification of the IC.[52] During the plenary debate,[53] one of the primary points of reference for those opposing ratification due to *gender* concerns was the Fundamental Law, and the case of Bulgaria was also mentioned, where in 2018, a constitutional court ruling found the IC's *gender* concept to be incompatible with the Bulgarian constitution.[54]

The ratification of the IC indeed faced obstacles in other countries as well, not only in Hungary,[55] and sparked numerous political debates, primarily in Eastern Europe.[56] But in Hungary, a notable element emerged in the discourse against ratification alongside the *gender* concept: the claim that the IC would encourage an undesirable influx of migrants through asylum-related provisions.[57] In this regard, the IC stipulates that "gender-based violence against women may be recognised as a form of persecution within the meaning of [. . .] the 1951 Convention relating to the Status of Refugees."[58] Although this is merely an interpretation of existing

[47] Jones (2018); Scotto Di Carlo (2023).

[48] Rudevska et al. (2018).

[49] See: https://citizengo.org/hu/fm/41487-az-isztambuli-egyezmeny-alairasa-gender-ideologia-trojai-falovat-jelentheti-magyarorszag.

[50] Human Dignity Centre (2017).

[51] ATV Hungary (2017).

[52] Parliament of Hungary (2020).

[53] See the records from 4 May 2022, at 19:30, https://bit.ly/3brwFe9.

[54] Vassileva (2018).

[55] Balogh (2020).

[56] Krizsán and Roggeband (2021).

[57] Drinóczi and Balogh (2022).

[58] Istanbul Convention, Article 60 (1).

legislation rather than an expectation of the expansion of legal provisions,[59] the assessment of this issue is complicated by the fact that the UN Refugee Convention's relevant provision does not explicitly include *gender* as a basis for persecution, and UNHCR guidance provides only a circular definition: "'Gender-related persecution' is a term that has no legal meaning *per se*. Rather, it is used to encompass the range of different claims in which gender is a relevant consideration in determining refugee status."[60]

Within the scope of a book chapter, it is impossible to provide an overview of the legal solutions that have proven effective or promising in combating violence against women. I have merely attempted to raise awareness of the fact that the consequences of applying *gender* in this context are unpredictable, partly because—despite the seemingly consolidated definition in the IC—the coherence of international implementation is jeopardized by the uncertainty surrounding the "denotation"[61] of *gender*. And even in the case of a rather fixed meaning, the normative applicability of an analytical concept remains questionable, as I will discuss below.

4 Is an Analytical Social Science Concept Useful in Law?

The aim of the detour that I take in this section is to put the story of *gender* as a legal concept into perspective by examining the evolution of another concept, namely intersectionality. I suggest that the story of the latter raises similar questions.

The theory of intersectionality was developed by Kimberlé Crenshaw in the late 1980s to increase understanding of the social difficulties experienced by African American women,[62] particularly due to the limitations of anti-discrimination law,[63] considering that the situation of this group is determined by the "intersection" of race and gender. (The fact that the perspectives and grievances of Black women in the US were not receiving sufficient attention from either the anti-racist movement or movements led by white women had already been problematized in several initiatives, such as the Combahee River Collective in the 1970s.[64]) While some opine that the concept of intersectionality cannot be separated from its original context,[65] the theory has gained international recognition since the early 1990s and contributed to the recognition in social sciences that social categories cannot be considered distinct

[59] Taramundi (2020).

[60] UN High Commissioner for Refugees (2002), point1.

[61] In semantics, the term "denotation" refers to "the relationship between the signifier and signified within the sign, and of the sign with its referent in external reality [...] the common-sense, obvious meaning of the sign" (Fiske 1990), pp. 85–86.

[62] See her comprehensive study: Crenshaw (1991).

[63] Crenshaw (2015).

[64] See, e.g., Leslie Bow et al. (2017).

[65] Davis (2020).

entities that identify homogeneous groups.[66] Feminist scholars in Europe began proposing the application of intersectionality as an analytical concept to understand the social situation of Roma women better,[67] and activists also started to use the term to draw attention to the multifaceted disadvantages faced by female members of Roma communities.[68]

Intersectionality, although initially proposed as a means of examining the legal tools for combating discrimination,[69] has basically become known as a sociological concept at the international level. Let us remember that *gender* also assumed a similar role in the eyes of the broader public. Intersectionality as an analytical concept or tool has had a significant impact, much like *gender*, and not only on academic thinking but also on public policy. It is used to critique legislation and jurisdiction, but its operationalization is far from straightforward within a legal context, similar to *gender*. Furthermore, the histories of both *gender* and intersectionality are closely linked to feminism, although it seems that women's perspectives have somewhat receded into the background in recent times in both cases.

Indeed, some have perceived changes in the conceptualization and use of intersectionality over time: that its role as a means of social criticism has diminished, and its interpretation has become ambiguous among stakeholders. The concept was eventually co-opted in the service of neoliberalism, where it is now employed in offering individual-level market-conforming solutions instead of advocating for systemic change.[70] In an interview from 2020, Crenshaw defended intersectionality by rejecting the accusation that it is nothing more than "identity politics on steroids";[71] however, the role of identity and individual experiences in relation to intersectionality had been a topic of discussion for some time in the academic discourse. For example, a theory of "intersectional invisibility" was developed "to understand the doubly marginalized experience of people with intersectional subordinate-group identities,"[72] then this approach was considered as "a kind of fragmented identity politics," involving abandoning the original role of intersectionality "as a counter to identity politics that emphasize [...] unidimensional versions of identity."[73]

In the meantime, the intertwining of intersectionality with identity has become dominant not only in scholarly discourse but also in public policy documents. EIGE defines intersectionality as an "[a]nalytical tool for studying, understanding and responding to the ways in which sex and gender intersect with other personal

---

66 Yuval-Davis (2006).

67 Kóczé (2009).

68 Curran (2016).

69 The critics of intersectionality theory problematize this approach; see, e.g., Zander (2017).

70 Hill Collins (2017).

71 Steinmetz, Katy (2020).

72 Purdie-Vaughns and Eibach (2008), p. 389.

73 Yuval-Davis (2015), p. 93.

characteristics/identities, and how these intersections contribute to unique experiences of discrimination,"[74] and the EU's Gender Equality Strategy for 2020–2025[75] employs a very similar definition.[76] This approach may lead to the neglect of knowledge acquired through social science research and to the stifling of political debate, as we "cannot have a discussion about subjective experience: the experience of suffering and identity is unquestionable."[77] Still, I am convinced that the original understanding of intersectionality and its application as a tool in social science has the potential to initiate "a process of discovery, alerting us to the fact that the world around us is always more complicated and contradictory than we ever could have anticipated";[78] and I do not doubt that intersectionality can be effectively utilized as an analytical concept in public policy.[79] However, I am skeptical about its viability as a legal concept for the reasons outlined below, while not disregarding the fact that the ambition of its legal application was present from the inception of the concept: Crenshaw herself approached the field of critical social theory with a legal background.

In the legal field, obviously, the term "intersectionality" is often simply used as a more fashionable synonym for "multiple discrimination"; this can be observed[80] in the aforementioned Gender Equality Strategy of the EU, where the phenomenon of "intersectional discrimination based on several personal characteristics" is illustrated with the following example: "a migrant woman with a disability may face discrimination on three or more grounds."[81]

In all other areas, including academia, public policy, and political activism, the same is happening: individual identity takes center stage, paradoxically, when addressing the issue of social disadvantages. An illustrative example of this phenomenon can be found in a report by the Center for Intersectional Justice (supported by the European Commission and the Open Society Foundations): "Systemic inequalities arise both from negative stereotypes attached to certain identities, or through positive stereotypes leading to implicit preference."[82] A psychological explanation like this not only appears shallow from a social theory perspective[83] as it diverts attention from economic and power interests, but it also has limited relevance when considering the legal toolkit developed to combat discrimination: it

[74] EIGE (2023b).

[75] For an analysis of the Strategy, with special attention to the concept of intersectionality, see Zacharenko and Kováts (2020).

[76] EC (2020), Preamble.

[77] Csányi and Kováts (2020).

[78] Davis (2008), p. 79.

[79] Balogh (2022).

[80] See: Zacharenko and Kováts (2020); Csányi and Kováts (2020).

[81] EC (2020), p. 18.

[82] Center for Intersectional Justice (2019).

[83] Fraser criticized the phenomenon of "psychologization" in the context of identity politics as early as the 1990s: Fraser (1996).

overlooks a significant factor, namely the phenomenon (and the legal concept) of indirect discrimination, where stereotypes do not necessarily play a role.

Returning to the origins of the concept of intersectionality, Crenshaw was interested in employment discrimination cases;[84] for example, she examined a case involving Black women whose employment had been terminated by General Motors[85] and argued that their lack of access to justice resulted from the failure of the law and its application to recognize the significance of intersecting disadvantages.

Decades later, the author of a study on the case law of the European Court of Justice critically claimed that intersectionality was either not considered or inadequately addressed in the relevant decisions, although EU anti-discrimination law would provide space for it, even in the absence of an explicit definition, and its use would have more advantages than disadvantages from a legal perspective.[86] As for the latter claim, those who represent the practice side of the law are not necessarily convinced: this was evident during a seminar by Equinet (a network of equality bodies in EU Member States) where participants acknowledged the significance of intersectionality in social sciences and public policy but considered the concept's relevance limited in the context of anti-discrimination law.[87] This is supported by a recent Hungarian legal case that concerned the discriminatory treatment of disadvantaged Roma women during maternity care, the court finding a violation of the principle of equal treatment (direct discrimination based on financial status, social background, and motherhood/pregnancy, and indirect discrimination based on Roma ethnicity) and imposed a deterrent sanction on the respondent without mentioning the term "intersectionality."[88] Apparently, a legal environment exists where effective action can be taken against discrimination that falls within the realm of intersectionality but without explicit provisions, thus avoiding the challenge of operationalizing the latter as a legal concept.[89]

The fact that Black women did not receive protection against labor market discrimination in the cases analyzed by Crenshaw[90] can be attributed to the peculiarities of the relevant US law[91] (analysis of the latter would exceed the scope of this chapter). Meanwhile, I do not doubt that the protection of the rights of those affected can be promoted if courts are "intersectionality sensible."[92]

In transitioning to the following section of the chapter, it is worth mentioning that despite the lack of clarity surrounding the concept, it has become a prominent slogan

---

[84] Crenshaw (2015).

[85] *DeGraffenreid v. General Motors,* 13 F Supp 142 (E D Mo 1976).

[86] Schiek (2018).

[87] Equinet (2016), p. 14.

[88] Balogh and Gellér (2020), pp. 32–33.

[89] See e.g.: O'Cinneide (2022).

[90] Crenshaw (2015).

[91] See about this issue: Farkas (2016), pp. 101–113.

[92] Xenidis uses the term "intersectional sensibility" in relation to the Court of the European Union: Xenidis (2018), p. 60.

of progressive social movements: "If your feminism isn't intersectional, it's bullshit!" It appears that there is strong pressure within the women's rights movement, particularly in the Western context, to enforce an intersectional perspective,[93] whatever this may mean (such as the inclusion of migrant women with Muslim backgrounds or transwomen in the movement).

5 What Should One Expect When Criticizing the Growing Presence of *Gender*?

As seen above, *gender*, through its various meanings, has acquired a particularly divisive force. In response to the question in this section's title, the straightforward answer is both praise and condemnation, depending on the context. Without aiming for a comprehensive global or European overview, I will highlight some trends and incidents.

During the 2010s, *gender* made spectacular strides worldwide in the political arena, particularly in non-Anglophone countries where the term may sound foreign. Some initially expressed bewilderment regarding this phenomenon, not progressing beyond raising the issue. This is seen, for example, in a 2016 report by the Commissioner for Human Rights of the CoE: "In recent years, both religious and secular critics of so-called 'gender ideology' and 'gender theory' have mounted a growing challenge against generally accepted human rights terminology and principles. During my country visits, I have even encountered objections to the very use of the word 'gender', particularly in the context of promoting the ratification of the [Istanbul Convention]. What should we in the human rights world make of this criticism?"[94]

As the societal mobilization and political discourse opposing *gender*—known as the "anti-gender" movement—have gained significant support in many countries, there has been an increase in interest from liberal-progressive social sciences in understanding this phenomenon. Authors dealing with this topic often refer to it as a "backlash," implying that critics of *gender*, particularly from conservative backgrounds, generally question the principle that women should have equal rights.[95] This interpretation was politically formalized within the EU framework by the European Parliament's resolution "on experiencing a backlash in women's rights and gender equality in the EU" (2019).[96]

A study from 2017, aiming for a deeper understanding, employed the metaphor of "gender as symbolic glue" to illustrate how *gender*, as a buzzword, can be associated

[93] Lawford-Smith and Phelan (2022).

[94] CoE Commissioner for Human Rights (2016), p. 20.

[95] See e.g.: Ebeturk (2018).

[96] EP (2019).

with numerous controversial issues (ranging from abortion to same-sex marriage and euthanasia) and connect various actors.[97]

The volume of social science literature that addresses the topic of "anti-gender" is dynamically increasing. However, I often notice a similar pattern in the structure and argumentation of these publications. (Listing all the publications I am familiar with would exceed the scope of a chapter's bibliography, and I would rather refrain from providing random examples to avoid singling out specific authors.) In the introduction to such studies, the author acknowledges that certain societal and political actors in a particular country or countries disseminate harmful and irrational views about *gender*, labelling it ideology. This claim is followed by a somewhat empathetic statement that the mentioned views seem to resonate with the frustration of people belonging to certain segments of society who have become disillusioned with politics and/or are facing economic hardship. At this point, the reader may get the impression that the author is genuinely interested in understanding the perspective of the population receptive to the "anti-gender" discourse. Subsequently, the study proceeds to present an overview of the developments—the unfolding of the "anti-gender" mobilization—in the given country in more or less detail and chronological order, accompanied by the enumeration of key actors accused of constructing an enemy image. These "anti-gender" actors are presented in a demonized way, and excerpts from their objectionable statements are cited as illustrative examples. Finally, towards the end of the study, the author reiterates the initial statements: that the campaign against "anti-gender" is worrisome, but with regard to the difficult economic and political climate of the present era, people are (regrettably, but to some extent understandably) receptive to it. The susceptibility to the criticism of progressive-liberal views is pathologized as a mental health problem—compulsive thinking—which could be addressed through some form of cognitive therapy. The pathologization of criticism towards *gender* appears most explicitly in the term "genderphobia."[98]

In certain Western European countries, those who are receptive to a feminist critique of some progressive-liberal demands under the umbrella of *gender*, specifically those related to gender identity,[99] can expect even less empathy. One example that comes to mind is the case of J. K. Rowling, who faced a wave of hostility that escalated into a hate campaign at some points because she publicly defended Maya Forstater, a British woman who lost her expert position at an international development NGO for expressing the opinion that a person's biological sex cannot be changed. Notably, this expression of opinion took place within the context of an ongoing political debate regarding the proposed reform of the legal recognition of (self-identified) *gender*. In 2019, the employment tribunal found that Forstater's "absolutist view" was "not worthy of respect in a democratic society"; then, upon appeal, it was eventually determined that her "gender critical" belief that sex is

[97] Grzebalska et al. (2017)

[98] Takács et al. (2022).

[99] Lawford-Smith (2022).

immutable and binary could be considered a "philosophical belief" protected by the law on equal treatment.[100]

Philosopher Kathleen Stock (whose essay on the meaning of *gender*[101] is cited above) resigned from her position at the University of Sussex in 2021 after becoming the target of a student group for being a "trans-exclusive radical feminist" (TERF) due to her expressed opposition to the legal recognition of self-identified gender without psychological or medical assessment. Additionally, it became known that Stock had signed a declaration on women's "sex-based rights,"[102] and the mere fact that such a declaration that establishes biological sex rather than *gender* as the basis for women's rights was deemed necessary by a group of feminists in 2019, brings us back to the question posed in the title of this study.

6 Conclusion and Final Thoughts

I deliberately chose a provocative title for this chapter. In that memorable scene from the movie *Life of Brian*, the expected answers to the question, "What have the Romans ever done for us?" included "Nothing!" or "Only bad things!" However, the audience provided a long list of positive contributions. Yet the conclusion of this piece does not conform to the expected response: in answer to the question "What has *gender* given to women?" my assessment does not yield a clearly positive outcome. However, we may also ask whether *gender* is beneficial to someone for something. I am currently inclined to think that if there are actors for whom *gender* is beneficial, it is they who are interested in advancing social-cultural, policy and legal demands related to gender identity—particularly those concerning self-identification and the legal recognition of non-binary gender identities. But it is evident that *gender* is serving women as a social group less and less effectively in various areas. Still, it is important to distinguish between different areas—namely, the field of social sciences, social movements, policymaking, and the legal domain—when assessing the usefulness of *gender*.

I have addressed the development of the concept of *gender* and touched upon the tension between its sociological and philosophical (Butlerian, queer feminist) uses. The latter approach, which focuses on the gender categories themselves, is the one that opens the door to social, cultural, political, and legal demands related to gender identity. The former uses *gender* as an analytical tool to examine the social relations between women and men.[103]

[100] *Maya Forstater v Center for Global Development & Others*, Appeal No. UKEAT/0105/20/JOJ.

[101] Stock (2019); see also: Stock (2021).

[102] Women's Declaration International (2019).

[103] Knapp (2018).

The realm of social movements and non-governmental organizations was also briefly mentioned, although delving into the related dynamics[104] would exceed the scope of this study. Regarding the meaning of *gender*, within progressive-liberal social movements, a shift towards using the word with the sense of "gender identity" can be observed.[105] Obviously, the usefulness of any abstract analytical concept is limited in the field of activism or mobilization. If the cause is advancing women's rights and coalition-building among movements, why not simply campaign by talking about women's rights?

As for the use of *gender* in policymaking, its meaning is actually shifting (within EU frameworks, for instance) into "gender identity," becoming a tool for advancing related demands. *Gender* still may be seen as an expedient analytical concept when considering the impact of proposed measures on women and men. However, for example, the EIGE thesaurus provides a circular definition concerning the concept of the "gender-needs of women": "Types of needs usually identified in a given society, namely practical gender needs and strategic gender needs."[106] This definition may be a (vague) paraphrase of the ideas of Molyneux,[107] who differentiates between the "practical gender interests" of women associated with a current situation and "strategic gender interests" with long-term significance.[108] However, it still raises the question of whether the definition would lose any meaning by replacing the term *gender* with "women's interests" (or "men's interests").

The remaining question here is whether *gender* can be used as a legal concept and, if so, whether its use benefits women. Although I do not call for *gender* to be expelled from the realm of law, I simply question its normative applicability. The law requires precisely defined and clarified concepts, so considering its nebulous meanings, *gender* is disqualified from use. Even if we regard it as an analytical concept, this still does not make it eligible for use as a legal concept, as the law requires concepts with fixed meanings. It is plausible to presume that even in the best-case scenario, the application of *gender* as a legal category does not lead to significant, tangible benefits for women and girls. For example, UNICEF uses the term "gender rights"[109] usually to refer to the (violation of the) rights of girls, or sometimes those of boys, while it is not clear (if we discard the assumption that the underlying aim is to raise gender identity-related issues on the agenda of child rights) why it would not be simpler to talk about "girls' rights" or "boys' rights."

---

[104] See e.g. Watkins (2018).

[105] Zacharenko and Kováts (2020).

[106] EIGE (2023c).

[107] Molyneux (1985).

[108] A vivid example of when the need for such differentiation may arise in relation to a policy question would be early retirement schemes for women. In certain situations, these can provide relief for women by allowing them to retire earlier. However, from the perspective of promoting women's economic independence as a strategic objective, such measures may still be perceived as negative due to the resulting lower pension benefits and increase in the amount of unpaid work within the family.

[109] UNICEF Europe and Central Asia (2023).

Regarding the elimination of violence against women, which is a straightforward goal, the study has aimed to demonstrate, through the example of the IC, that there may be a political cost associated with the use of *gender*. Some countries have refrained from ratifying the IC, with Turkey choosing to withdraw unilaterally. Ultimately, it is the women living in these— Eastern European—countries who have paid the price. The question remains whether women living in the countries that ratified the IC pay a price for the inclusion of the concept of *gender*: an important research endeavor would be examining how the latter is interpreted during the activities of the GREVIO (the monitoring committee of the IC) as time passes.

In 2023, the IC was eventually ratified by the EU despite the lack of consensus among the Member States on the issue. But at the time of writing this manuscript, the issue of a proposed EU directive on "combatting violence against women and domestic violence" is still pending.[110] The measures included in this proposal are built on the concept of *gender*, similar to the solutions of the IC. Thus, I foresee heated political debates that potentially overshadow the aim of protecting women.

Cases

Achbita, Samira and Centrum voor gelijkheid van kansen en voor racismebestrijding v. G4S Secure Solutions NV, C-157/15 EU: C:2017:203.

Bougnaoui, Asma and ADDH v. Micropole SA, C-188/15 EU: C:2017:204.

DeGraffenreid v. General Motors, 13 F Supp 142 (E D Mo 1976).

Forstater, Maya v. Center for Global Development & Others, Appeal No. UKEAT/0105/20/JOJ.

Parris, David L. v. Trinity College Dublin and Others, C-443/15 EU: C:2016:897.

References

Agnello F (2014) A new "Gender" approach definition in international law: the convention on preventing and combating violence against women and domestic violence. SYbIL 18:87–114. https://doi.org/10.17103/sybil.18.05

ATV Hungary (2017) Németh Szilárd: Soha nem fogjuk támogatni az isztambuli egyezményt [Szilárd Németh: We will never support the Istanbul Convention]

Balogh L (2020) The ratification status of the Council of Europe's Istanbul Convention Among EU Member States. MTA Law Working Papers

Balogh L (2022) Uncharted territories and cross-cutting publics: intersectional analysis within the framework of joint efforts of civil society reporting on mainstream and Romani Women's issues. In: Hojsik M, Munteanu G, Zentai V (eds) From the shadow to the limelight: the value of civil society policy monitoring knowledge in Roma equality struggles. CEU Press, Budapest, pp 135–154

[110] EC (2022).

Balogh L, Gellér J (2020) Reproductive rights of Romani Women in Hungary. Cause of action. European Roma Rights Centre, Brussels

Bow L, Brah A, Goeman M, Harriford D, Keating A, Tricia Lin Y, Pérez L et al (2017) Combahee river collective statement: a fortieth anniversary retrospective. Front J Women Stud 38:164. https://doi.org/10.5250/fronjwomestud.38.3.0164

Bullough V (2003) The contributions of John Money: a personal view. J Sex Res 40:230–236. https://doi.org/10.1080/00224490309552186

Butler J (1990) Gender trouble: feminism and the subversion of identity. Thinking gender. Routledge, New York.

Center for Intersectional Justice (2019) Intersectional discrimination in Europe: relevance, challenges and ways forward. European Network Against Racism (ENAR), Brussels

CoE (2011a) Convention on preventing and combating violence against women and domestic violence (Istanbul Convention), CETS No. 210

CoE(2011b) Explanatory Report to the Council of Europe Convention on preventing and combating violence against women and domestic violence (Istanbul, 11.V.2011)

CoE Commissioner for Human Rights (2016) 3rd Quarterly Activity Report 2016 by Nils Muižnieks Commissioner for Human Rights (presented to the Committee of Ministers and the Parliamentary Assembly), 1 July to 30 September 2016, CommDH(2016)37. Council of Europe, Strasbourg

CoE Committee of Ministers (2011) Draft Council of Europe Convention on preventing and combating violence against women and domestic violence (CM(2011)49-final, CM(2011)49-addfinal, Parliamentary Assembly Opinion No. 280 (2011) and DD(2011)232), 1111th meeting – 6-7 April 2011, Item 10.4

Collins PH (2017) The difference that power makes: intersectionality and participatory democracy. Investigaciones Feministas 8:19–39. https://doi.org/10.5209/INFE.54888

Conaghan J, Russell Y (2015) Talking law and gender. Fem Leg Stud 23:199–214. https://doi.org/10.1007/s10691-015-9288-2

Council of the EU (2018) Resolution of the Council of the European Union and the Representatives of the Governments of the Member States meeting within the Council on a framework for European cooperation in the youth field: The European Union Youth Strategy 2019–2027

Crenshaw K (1991) Mapping the margins: intersectionality, identity politics, and violence against women of color. Stanf Law Rev 43:1241. https://doi.org/10.2307/1229039

Crenshaw K (2015) Demarginalizing the intersection of race and sex: a black feminist critique of antidiscrimination Doctrine, feminist theory and antiracist politics. Univ Chicago Legal Forum 1989(1):139–167

Csányi G, Kováts E (2020) Intersectionality: time for a rethink. Social Europe

Curran S (2016) Intersectionality and human rights law: an examination of the coercive sterilisations of Romani Women. Equal Rights Rev 16:132–159

Darakchi S (2019) "The Western feminists want to Make Us Gay": nationalism, heteronormativity, and violence against women in Bulgaria in times of "Anti-gender Campaigns". Sex Cult 23: 1208–1229. https://doi.org/10.1007/s12119-019-09611-9

Davis K (2008) Intersectionality as buzzword: a sociology of science perspective on what makes a feminist theory successful. Fem Theory 9:67–85. https://doi.org/10.1177/1464700108086364

Davis K (2020) Who owns intersectionality? Some reflections on feminist debates on how theories travel. Eur J Women's Stud 27:113–127. https://doi.org/10.1177/1350506819892659

Diamond M, Sigmundson HK (1997) Sex reassignment at birth: long-term review and clinical implications. Arch Pediatr Adolesc Med 151:298. https://doi.org/10.1001/archpedi.1997.02170400084015

Dobi E (2019) Constringency as the basic category of representing the semiotic-textological meaning of texts. Argum 15:8–19

Drinóczi T, Balogh L (2022) The (non)-ratification of the Istanbul Convention by Hungary: lessons to be learned. Ost Eur Recht 68:42–60. https://doi.org/10.5771/0030-6444-2022-1-42

Ebeturk I (2018) Norms of gender equality and the backlash against Istanbul Convention. Orders Beyond Borders

EC (2020) Communication from the Commission to the European Parliament, the Council, the European Economic and Social Committee and the Committee of the Regions: A Union of Equality: Gender Equality Strategy 2020–2025

EC (2022) Proposal for a directive of the European Parliament and of the Council on combating violence against women and domestic violence, Strasbourg, 8.3.2022. COM(2022) 105 final, 2022/0066(COD)

EIGE (2023a) "Gender" entry in the Glossary and Thesaurus. European Institute for Gender Equality. https://eige.europa.eu/publications-resources/thesaurus/terms/1046?language_content_entity=en

EIGE (2023b) "Intersectionality" entry in the Glossary and Thesaurus. European Institute for Gender Equality. https://eige.europa.eu/publications-resources/thesaurus/terms/1050?language_content_entity=en

EIGE (2023c) "Gender needs of women" entry in the Glossary and Thesaurus. European Institute for Gender Equality. https://eige.europa.eu/publications-resources/thesaurus/terms/1351?language_content_entity=en

EP (2019) Resolution of 13 February 2019 on experiencing a backlash in women's rights and gender equality in the EU (2018/2684(RSP))

Equinet (2016) Fighting discrimination on grounds of race & ethnic origin (Summary Report), 9-10 November 2016, Office of the Commissioner for Fundamental Rights. Hungary, Budapest

European Women's Lobby (2010) The CAHVIO Process: Towards a Strong Convention on all forms of Male Violence against Women

Farkas L (2016) The meaning of racial or ethnic origin in EU law: between stereotypes and identities. European Network of Legal Experts in Gender Equality and Non-discrimination. LU: Publications Office of the European Union

Fiske J (1990) Introduction to communication studies. Studies in culture and communication. Taylor & Francis Group

Fraser N (1996) Social justice in the age of identity politics: redistribution, recognition, and participation (The Tanner Lectures on Human Values, Delivered at Stanford University April 30–May 2, 1996)

Grzebalska W, Kováts E, Pető A (2017) Gender as symbolic glue: how 'gender' became an umbrella term for the rejection of the (neo)liberal order. Polit Crit. https://politicalcritique.org/long-read/2017/gender-as-symbolic-glue-how-gender-became-an-umbrella-term-for-the-rejection-of-the-neoliberal-order/

Human Dignity Centre (2017) Az Emberi Méltóság Központ állásfoglalása az Európa Tanács nőkkel szembeni erőszak és a kapcsolati erőszak elleni küzdelemről és azok megelőzéséről szóló egyezményének ratifikálásával kapcsolatban: "Az Isztambuli Egyezmény ratifikálása a gender ideológia trójai falovát jelentheti Magyarország számára" [Position of the Human Dignity Centre regarding the ratification of the Council of Europe's Convention on preventing and combating violence against women and domestic violence: "The ratification of the Istanbul Convention may serve as the Trojan horse of gender ideology for Hungary"]

ILGA Europe (2009) Submission to the Council of Europe Ad Hoc Committee on Preventing and Combating Violence Against Women and Domestic Violence: The need to ensure that the Convention on violence against women addresses effectively the obligation of member states to prevent and combat violence against lesbian, bisexual and transgender women

Jones J (2018) The European Convention on Human Rights (ECHR) and the Council of Europe Convention on violence against women and domestic violence (Istanbul Convention). In: Manjoo R, Jones J (eds) The legal protection of women from violence. Routledge, pp 139–165

Knapp G (2018) Mut zur Kontroverse! Feministische Kritik zwischen Antigenderismus und akademischer Spezialisierung. In: Beier F, Haller LY, Haneberg L (eds) Materializing Feminism. Positionierungen zu Ökonomie, Staat und Identität. Unrast Verlag, pp 19–38

Kóczé A (2009) Missing intersectionality: race/ethnicity, gender, and class in current research and policies on Romani Women in Europe (with contribution from Raluca Maria Popa). CEU Press, Budapest
Kováts E (2018) The consequences of the differing meanings of gender in policy and activism for politics. LSE Blogs
Kováts E (2022) Genderőrületek Németországban és Magyarországon [Gender Madnesses in Germany and Hungary]. Napvilág Kiadó, Budapest
Kováts E, Zacharenko E (2022) The right-wing opposition to "Gender" in the light of the ambiguity of the meaning of the term in EU documents. Politické vedy 24:56–82. https://doi.org/10.24040/politickevedy.2021.24.4.56-82
Krivenko EY (2020) Gender and human rights: expanding concepts. Edward Elgar Publishing
Krizsán A, Roggeband C (2021) Politicizing gender and democracy in the context of the Istanbul Convention. Gender and politics. Springer International Publishing, Cham. https://doi.org/10.1007/978-3-030-79069-1
Laczó F (2022) What does right-wing anti-gender mobilization have to do with progressive gender trends? Eszter Kováts investigates the politics of Fidesz and AfD. RevDem
Lawford-Smith H (2022) Gender-critical feminism, 1st edn. Oxford University Press, Oxford
Lawford-Smith H, Phelan K (2022) The metaphysics of intersectionality revisited. J Polit Philos 30:166–187. https://doi.org/10.1111/jopp.12251
Manjoo R (2014) Report of the special rapporteur on violence against women, its causes and consequences. UN Human Rights Council
Molyneux M (1985) Mobilization without emancipation? Women's interests, the state, and revolution in Nicaragua. Fem Stud 11:227. https://doi.org/10.2307/3177922
Niemi J, Sanmartin AV (2020) The concepts of gender and violence in the Istanbul Convention. In: Niemi J, Peroni L, Stoyanova V (eds) International law and violence against women: Europe and the Istanbul Convention. Routledge, pp 77–94
Nógrádi N (2023) Navigating hostilities from one direction and pressures from others: exploring the realities of feminist Women's organizations in Central-Eastern Europe through the example of Hungary. In: Kováts E (ed) Culture wars in Europe. George Washington University, Washington DC, pp 291–309
O'Cinneide C (2022) Can intersectionality contribute to effective equality? – Address ECRI Annual Seminar. European Commission against Racism and Intolerance
Open Society Institute (2005) Equal opportunities for women and men: monitoring law and practice in new member states and accession countries of the European Union: overview. Central European University Press, Budapest
Parliament of Hungary (2020) OGY politikai nyilatkozata a gyermekek és nők védelmének fontosságáról, valamint az Isztambuli Egyezményhez való csatlakozás elutasításáról [Political declaration about the importance of protecting children and women, as well as rejecting the accession to the Istanbul Convention]
Purdie-Vaughns V, Eibach RP (2008) Intersectional invisibility: the distinctive advantages and disadvantages of multiple subordinate-group identities. Sex Roles 59:377–391. https://doi.org/10.1007/s11199-008-9424-4
Repo J (2015) The biopolitics of gender. Oxford University Press. https://doi.org/10.1093/acprof:oso/9780190256913.001.0001
Rudevska B, Roziņa G, Karapetjana I (2018) Interpretation of the concept gender in legal discourse. BJELLC 8:101–119. https://doi.org/10.22364/BJELLC.08.2018.07
Schiek D (2018) On uses, mis-uses and non-uses of intersectionality before the Court of Justice (EU). Int J Discrim Law 18:82–103. https://doi.org/10.1177/1358229118799232
Scotto Di Carlo G (2023) Defining 'Gender' Across Europe: a linguistic analysis of the definition, translation, and interpretation of the word 'Gender' from the Beijing Declaration to the Istanbul Convention. Int J Semiot Law 36:1217–1238. https://doi.org/10.1007/s11196-022-09944-z
Steinmetz K (2020) She coined the term 'Intersectionality' over 30 years ago. Here's what it means to her today. Time. https://time.com/5786710/kimberle-crenshaw-intersectionality/

Stock K (2019) Can you change your gender? The Philosopher 107
Stock K (2021) Material girls: why reality matters for feminism. Fleet, London
Stojanovski F (2019) How the word 'gender' became a slur in Bulgaria. Global Voices
Takács J, Fobear K, Schmitsek S (2022) Resisting Genderphobia in Hungary. Polit Gov 10. https://doi.org/10.17645/pag.v10i4.5528
Taramundi DM (2020) Gender-based violence against women and international protection needs: the contribution of the Istanbul Convention. In: Niemi J, Peroni L, Stoyanova V (eds) International law and violence against women: Europe and the Istanbul Convention. Routledge, pp 241–256
UN (1995) Report of the Fourth World Conference on Women, Beijing, 4-15 September 1995, UN Doc. A/CONF.177/20/Rev.1
UN (1998) Rome Statute of the International Criminal Court (United Nations, Treaty Series, Vol. 2187, No. 38544)
UN High Commissioner for Refugees (2002) Guidelines on International Protection No. 1: Gender-Related Persecution Within the Context of Article 1A(2) of the 1951 Convention and/or its 1967 Protocol Relating to the Status of Refugees. May 7
UNICEF Europe and Central Asia (2023) Gender rights. https://www.unicef.org/eca/topics/gender-rights
Vassileva R (2018) Bulgaria's Constitutional Troubles with the Istanbul Convention. *Verfassungsblog: On Matters Constitutional.* Fachinformationsdienst für internationale und interdisziplinäre Rechtsforschung (TEST). https://doi.org/10.17176/20180803-101332-0
Watkins S (2018) Which feminisms? New Left Rev 109:5–76
Westendorp I (2018) The Istanbul Convention; new perspectives for victims of domestic violence? Maastricht University Blog
Women's Declaration International (2019) Declaration on Women's Sex-Based Rights
Xenidis R (2018) Multiple discrimination in EU anti-discrimination law: towards redressing complex inequality? In: Belavusau U, Henrard K (eds) EU anti-discrimination law beyond gender. Hart, Oxford, pp 41–74
Yuval-Davis N (2006) Intersectionality and feminist politics. Eur J Women's Stud 13:193–209. https://doi.org/10.1177/1350506806065752
Yuval-Davis N (2015) Situated intersectionality and social inequality. Raisons Politiq 58:91–100. https://doi.org/10.3917/rai.058.0091
Zacharenko E, Kováts E (2020) How the new EU gender strategy fails east-central European women. Social Europe. https://www.socialeurope.eu/how-the-new-eu-gender-strategy-fails-east-central-european-women
Zander M (2017) Was ist problematisch an Intersektionalität? [What is problematic about intersectionality?]. Psychologie & Gesellschaftskritik:47–65

Lídia Balogh lives in Budapest, where she works for the HUN-REN Centre for Social Sciences Centre for Social Sciences, Institute for Legal Studies as a Research Fellow and as a visiting lecturer at the ELTE University Faculty of Social Sciences. As a freelance researcher, she participated in projects of the EU Agency for Fundamental Rights. She currently acts as a Gender Equality Expert within the framework of the European Network of Legal Experts in Gender Equality and Non-discrimination (EELN). She has been active in Hungarian civil society since the mid-2000s by contributing to projects and advocacy initiatives of various women's NGOs and Roma rights organizations.

Gender-Based Violence: A Conceptual Analysis

Francesca Poggi

Contents

Abstract The concept of gender-based violence is probably among the most significant contributions that feminist thought has made to legal theory. The concept is adopted in several international and supranational agreements and declarations, and it is also employed in some national legislations. The spread of this concept undoubtedly speaks to its political and social success. But it also raises problems, both theoretical and political. From a theoretical point of view, the concept is not at all clear. Different definitions of it circulate in the literature and the law, and they are often indeterminate. From a political point of view, the feminist struggle to assert the concept of gender violence has cast women in the role of victims, which has reinforced social stereotypes of female weakness, while at the same time placing an outsized emphasis on the recognition of new gender-oriented criminal offences. These political problems have been extensively debated, and I will briefly comment on that debate, but I suggest that it would be helpful to set the stage for that discussion with a conceptual analysis, to which the bulk of this essay is devoted, attempting to clarify the concepts of violence and gender and how they are related.

This research was funded by MUR (Ministero dell'Università e della Ricerca) grant "Dipartimenti di eccellenza 2023-2027".

F. Poggi (✉)
University of Milan, Milan, Italy
e-mail: francesca.poggi@unimi.it

N. Lacey et al. (eds.), *Reassessing Feminist Legal Theories*, Gender Perspectives in Law 5, https://doi.org/10.1007/978-3-031-75423-4_7

1 Introduction: Lights and Shadows of the Concept of Gender Violence

Of all the contributions that feminist thought has made to legal theory, few are as important as its work on the concept of violence. Feminist criticism has helped expand the concept of violence beyond the traditional boundaries of physical violence by identifying new forms of violent behaviour. To wit, we now speak of economic violence, psychological violence, emotional violence, symbolic violence, and verbal violence. Moreover, feminist thought has given us a new framework for analysing and classifying violence, by looking at its perpetrators, its victims, and its context. Thus, for example, we can now speak of institutional violence, structural violence, or obstetric violence. But the concept that probably best reflects and sums up feminist thinking on violence is that of gender violence, or gender-based violence (henceforth "GV"). GV covers different forms of behaviour (including economic violence, psychological violence, emotional violence, and verbal violence), is understood as a structural violence, and it encompasses obstetric as well as other types of violence (such as female genital mutilation and forced marriage).

The concept of GV has been adopted (and sometimes also defined) in several international and supranational agreements and declarations,[1] and it is also employed in some national legislations.[2] The spread of this concept doubtless testifies to its political and social success. The word "violence" carries a powerfully negative connotation, not only because of the strong symbolic force that can be exerted when something is so identified (as "violence"), but also because its use can set in motion processes of deep social transformation. This is especially true when the law itself embeds this concept, qualifying as "violence", and so as harmful and unjust, acts that might hitherto have been regarded as tolerable or normal.[3] Even so, the concept of GV also raises some problems, both theoretical and political. And it is to these problems that this essay is devoted, attacking them from both of those perspectives.

---

[1] These include General Recommendation No. 19 on Violence Against Women (GR 19), adopted in 1992 under Article 21 CEDAW (the 1979 UN Convention on the Elimination of All Forms of Discrimination against Women); DEVAW (the 1993 UN Declaration on the Elimination of Violence against Women); the Beijing Declaration (adopted at the 1994 United Nations Fourth World Conference on Women); the 1994 Belém do Pará Convention (Convención Interamericana para Prevenir, Sancionar y Erradicar la Violencia contra la Mujer); the 2003 Maputo Protocol (Protocol to the African Charter on Human and Peoples' Rights on the Rights of Women in Africa); and the 2011 Istanbul Convention (Council of Europe Convention on Preventing and Combating Violence against Women and Domestic Violence).

[2] Examples are legislation in Spain (Law No. 13/2007, Medidas de Prevención y Protección Integral contra la Violencia de Género); Salvador (Law No. 520/2011, Ley especial integral para una vida libre de violencia para las mujeres); Italy (Law No. 69/2019, Disposizioni in tema di violenza domestica e di genere); and Chile (Law No. 21.369/2021, Acoso Sexual, la Violencia y la Discriminación de Género en el Ámbito de la Educación Superior).

[3] See MacKinnon (1987); MacKinnon (1994); Klugman (2017).

From the theoretical perspective, the problem is that the concept of gender violence is not at all clear.[4] Different definitions circulate in the literature and the law, and they are often indeterminate. From a political point of view, we have the problem that the feminist struggle to assert the concept of gender violence has cast women in the role of victims, which has reinforced social stereotypes of female weakness or frailty, while at the same time placing an outsized emphasis on the recognition of new gender-oriented criminal offences, and I will argue that neither of these two outcomes advances the interests of women.

But I will also suggest that before we get to the political discussion, with its practical ramifications, we should first work through the problems we encounter on the theoretical plane. Which is precisely how I will proceed (Sect. 2), distinguishing two sets of questions—pertaining to the notion of violence (Sect. 2.1) and to that of gender (Sect. 2.2)—and clarifying how the two notions are related (Sect. 3). With that done, and in light of that analysis, I will turn to the political discussion (Sect. 4), briefly considering the aforementioned typecasting and the nearly exclusive focus on criminal offences.

The main thrust of this essay, then, is not that the concept of gender violence ought to be discarded but that it needs clarification. In fact, as I will indicate, while this concept has been put to effective symbolic, social, and political use, not all that has come out of that experience is unqualifiedly good, so it is essential that we clarify the concept's own (conceptual) boundaries before we put it to further use, especially in criminal law. The advantage we should be able to gain from such an analysis, in other words, is not just theoretical but can also be political, because in addition to deflecting the criticism of feminism as a partisan ideological position, the clarification I am calling for can help us forestall the distorting phenomena that work against women's interests.

2 What Does Gender Violence Mean?

As mentioned, the concept of GV is far from clear. Indeed, as we have seen, many forms and types of violence have been distinguished, but it is doubtful that they can be said to share any common set of properties. In what sense are they all the same phenomenon, namely, violence? The problem is not merely terminological. For if *anything* is violence, then *nothing* is. In other words, if we merely attach the label "violence" to certain behaviours without explaining why they are such, we risk diminishing the symbolic power of calling something "violence". This is a problem I will be addressing in the next section (Sect. 2.1).

At the same time, we have to ask, in what sense can an act of violence be said to be "gender-based"? A variety of definitions of GV circulate in the literature. According to the most widely used one, GV is violence directed against a woman

[4] See Pontara (1978); Coady (1986); Hamby (2017); Poggi (2019).

just because she is a woman. This definition makes an assumption about GV as specifically targeted (only against women),[5] neutral with regard to the perpetrators (who can include women), and requiring a specific psychological element, a specific *motive* that consists in intending to harm somebody "because she is a woman".[6] Thus, on this definition, GV would be a kind of hate crime, i.e. a crime motivated by hatred toward a specific group. However, the legal (national, international, and supranational) laws that adopt this definition do not just include crimes of this kind as examples or forms of GV. Thus, for example, the Istanbul Convention defines "gender-based violence against women" as "violence that is directed against a woman because she is a woman" (art. 3(d)), but then goes on to include within the scope of this definition a list of crimes—such as female genital mutilation, family abuse, forced marriage, and compulsory sterilization or abortion—that are not usually motivated by hate directed at "women" as such (as a class).[7]

But the definition we just saw is often supplemented by another one, according to which gender-based violence is violence that disproportionately affects women (see GR 19, pt. 6; Istanbul Convention, art. 3(d)). However, the latter (quantitative) definition is almost always taken as an alternative to the former, and it is difficult to say what exactly their relationship amounts to (see Sect. 3.1). In this regard, many authors stress that what the different definitions have in common is that gender violence always involves social expectations about gender roles: it is always "violence that occurs as a result of a normative role expectation associated with each gender, along with the unequal power relationships between the two genders, within the context of a specific society".[8] The main concern I have with this definition is that, as we will see (Sect. 3.1), in a patriarchal society, *any* violence could conceivably be considered gender-based so long as it is perpetrated by a man against a woman. It is not surprising, then, that some authors more or less explicitly confine GV to intimate partner violence (IPV), i.e. violence that takes place in affective relationships or between former partners. For in that sphere we can actually determine whether there are any unequal power relations at play and what the different

[5] In fact, all national, international, and supranational laws that adopt this definition deal almost exclusively with crimes against women. Other laws with similar content do not use the expressions "gender-based violence" or "gender violence" but use language that more specifically refers to violence against women: see, e.g., the Guatemalan Law No. 22/2008, "Ley contra el Femicidio y otras Formas de Violencia Contra la Mujer".

[6] See Vázquez (2019).

[7] The same goes for GR 19. By contrast, DEVAW, the Beijing Declaration, and the Belém do Pará Convention do use the expression "gender-based violence" or "action or conduct, based on their gender", but do not define these expressions. The same is true of the Maputo Protocol, which uses the expression "gender-based violence against women," but only in the preamble, while the main body of text refers to "violence against women". In any case, all of the declarations just mentioned provide for crimes usually not motivated by misogyny. Commenting on national legislation on femicide in Latin America, Vázquez (2019) points out that, while it does often define gender-based violence as "violence against a woman because she is a woman", this definition rarely figures among the crime's defining elements.

[8] Bloom (2008), p. 14.

role expectations are, since we are concerned not with society as a whole but with particular individuals.[9]

In the next sections, so as to proceed in an orderly fashion, I will first investigate the problems related to the notions of gender and violence, and will then examine the different forms in which gender and violence can be connected.

2.1 Concepts of Violence

There are many definitions of "violence", and I certainly cannot go through them all,[10] so I will confine myself to some general remarks on the most common notions. In a previous essay (Poggi 2019), I distinguished four main legal notions of violence, ranging from narrow to broad, suggesting that they map onto the common-sense understanding of violence, and that they can capture some salient features of most of the definitions circulating in the nonlegal literature.

On the narrow notion, violence consists in using physical force intentionally against one or more unconsenting individuals—as by shoving or hitting them or tackling them to the ground—and that counts as violence regardless of the outcome.[11] So, for example, if someone slaps someone else across the face without their consent, that, right there, is violence even if they suffer no physical injury as a result of the slap.[12]

We then have a moderately narrow notion, probably the most widespread in legal systems: it is just like the narrow notion except that it equates physical force with the threat, as a different way of executing the same crime. The notion of a threat is in turn almost invariably defined through that of "harm" or "evil": to threaten someone is to foreshadow some kind of harm or evil, to make it known to them that they will or may be made to suffer such a harm or evil, one that depends on the threatener's actions or is otherwise *presented* as such.

The intermediate notion includes physical violence, threats, and certain repeated forms of nonconsensual verbal insults and humiliation (e.g., those that constitute crimes such as domestic violence).

---

[9] See Giomi and Magaraggia (2017), as well as Hortal (2023), who writes: "The terms 'gender-based violence', 'dating violence', and 'domestic violence' refer to forms of violence or abuse occurring within relationships or families". Hortal (2023), p. 71, my translation. For criticism of such a reduction, see Martín Sánchez (2015).

[10] Parrott and Giancola (2007) estimated more than two hundred definitions, and certainly the number has since grown.

[11] It has often been observed that the narrow notion is the one that most closely tracks common sense: see, e.g., Coady (1986); Ó Murchadha (2006); Vázquez (2019).

[12] There are other approaches, especially widespread in social psychology, that by contrast distinguish between aggression and violence, defining the latter "as any aggressive act that has as its goal *extreme physical harm*, such as injury or death" (DeWall, et al. 2011, p. 246, italics added). For some criticisms see Hamby (2017).

Finally, the broad notion encompasses any intentional act or omission that results in physical, economic, or psychological harm (or all of the above).[13] It includes, for example, economic violence (i.e. controlling and limiting access to resources such as money and food) and emotional violence, implemented through repeated humiliation, isolation, disinformation, or the use of children to control the victim (or all of the above). This list is merely illustrative, since what matters, on the broad notion, is not the *form* the violence takes but its *effect*, namely, the harm suffered by those on the receiving end of violence.

To this list we must now add the notion of *structural* violence, a notion that, while foreign to law, has been exerting much influence on feminist studies. As Galtung puts it, "violence is present when human beings are being influenced so that their actual somatic and mental realizations are below their potential realization".[14] Violence is structural when there is no single actor who commits it. "The violence is built into the structure and shows up as unequal power and consequently as unequal life chances. [...] we shall sometimes refer to the condition of structural violence as social injustice".[15]

The point worth noting here that the five notions just listed may overlap but are not coextensive. So, for example, if we adopt the narrow notion, we will have excluded an entire range of acts which count as violence under the other notions—i.e. any act that does not involve a physical force. And if we adopt the broad notion, we will have excluded any act, including physical force and threats, that does not eventuate in harm,[16] and we will also have excluded structural violence, where the harm—broadly measured by the gap between what someone *in fact* achieves and what they could *potentially* achieve—cannot be attributed to an action or omission by any single individual.[17] Now, the problem we have can be stated thus: What do these different notions have in common? In what sense are they all violence?

---

[13]See, e.g., Harris (1980), p. 19: "An act of violence occurs when injury or suffering is inflicted upon a person or persons by an agent who knows (or ought reasonably to have known) that his action would result in the harm in question".

[14]Galtung (1969), p. 168. To give some examples from Galtung (1969), it is in the present day violence, on this definition, to die of tuberculosis or to have a life expectancy of 30 years (whether due to war or social injustice or both) or have a level of literacy lower than what is to be expected.

[15]Galtung (1969), p. 171. The main difference between structural violence and the broad notion of violence is that only the latter requires an element of intentional harm, or otherwise an intentional act or omission by one person to the detriment of another. Moreover, according to Galtung, structural violence, as well as personal violence, can also be latent. Latent violence "indicates a situation of unstable equilibrium, where the level of actual realization is not sufficiently protected against deterioration by upholding mechanisms" (Galtung 1969, p. 172).

[16]Consider a situation in which a stranger points a gun at me and demands that I hand over my handbag, whereupon a police siren goes off and the would-be mugger flees. Assuming that the attempted mugging does not cause me to suffer any psychological harm, there is no violence that, on the broad notion, can be said to have taken place here.

[17]Another key difference concerns omission. While on the broad notion and the structural one, omission—a typical example being child neglect—is a form of violence if it results in harm or social injustice, on the other notions there can be no such thing as violence by omission. On this problem

A common answer is that these notions all point to different forms of behaviour or action (including systemic or agentless action) under which other people's autonomy or self-determination is diminished. But apart from the fact that the concepts of autonomy and self-determination are much debated,[18] some forms of violence, that fall under the previously listed notions, do not diminish or otherwise affect autonomy or self-determination at all. If someone punches me in the face and gives me a black eye, this doesn't do anything to my autonomy or self-determination. And yet no one would say that punching someone is not a violent act. Moreover, there are forms through which other people's autonomy is affected that are not commonly perceived as violent. Think of illicit conduct such as fraud, or licit conduct such as manipulation, or all the lawful ways in which one can restrict the range of other people's options.[19]

According to Waldenfels, the semantic core of the different forms of violence lies in the concept of a violation. As suggestive as this proposal may be, it doesn't do much to advance the debate if one cannot identify what is to be meant by "violation".[20]

A more plausible solution focuses on the potential to cause harm: what all the previous notions of violence, including the narrow notion, have in common is that they all point to a likelihood of harm, to cases where someone may stand to suffer some kind of harm. However, this proposal raises three problems. First, the definition of "harm" is no less complex and contested than that of "violence".[21] Second, there also needs to be clarity around the concept of "likelihood of harm". As Hamby notes, there needs to be a high probabilistic link between the act or omission in question and the harm, since, on the one hand, "some obsessive or delusional

see, e.g., Galtung (1969); Harris (1980), chap. 2; Coady (1986); Krug et al. (2002); Bufacchi (2006); Hamby (2017).

[18] For an introduction see Buss and Westlund (2018).

[19] According to Galtung's definition of (structural) violence, these acts are indeed forms of violence, at least if the "somatic and mental realizations" they affect are valued in society (see Galtung 1969, p. 169). My point is that this definition does not reflect our ordinary intuitions about what violence is, nor it does reflect our legal definitions.

[20] Waldenfels (2006), p. 81, suggests that in order to identify a violation, we have to look at "bodily existence as a sphere of vulnerability", and stresses that violation does not amount to physical violence only. In fact, "we could distinguish between a peripheral and a central form of violence, referring to a scale which extends from the insistent gaze through lewd remarks and offensive conduct to torture, rape and murder. Making the further distinction between direct and indirect violence enables us to trace the evasive manoeuvres of violence, as in the case of reprisals [. . .]. Finally, there is a difference between on-going and structural violence [. . .]. Violence occurs momentarily when we suffer from disregard, attack or injury. But it can also be deposited in our body". Waldenfels (2006), p. 82. These are interesting observations, to be sure, and may all be true, but they still do not answer the question 'what is a violation?'. Why are all these examples cases of violation or violence? In fact, the whole argument may even be begging the question.

[21] See, e.g., Norris Turner (2014); Rabenberg (2014).

individuals may experience a romantic rejection as harmful",[22] but romantic rejection is not (necessarily) a violent act, and, on the other hand, someone can attempt to stab someone else and fail, yet even only assaulting someone with a knife (without battery or harm) has all the makings of a violent act. However, it is not easy to determine how the probabilistic link should be conceived. Does shoving someone amount to a likelihood of harm? That seems to depend on the circumstances, but so does the likelihood of harm from an assault with a knife. Third—and this is also a general criticism levied at the broad notion of violence—not every act or omission that is likely to result in harm is perceived as violence or is legally qualified as such. There are some unlawful acts (such as fraud and abuse of office) as well as many lawful ones that cause harm and yet are not ordinarily regarded as forms of violence.

Another solution to the problem of defining a single concept of violence consists in attempting a unified definition that encompasses both the effects of violence and the means by which it is perpetrated. So, for example, the World Health Organization (WHO) defines violence as the "intentional use of physical force or power, threatened or actual, against oneself, another person, or against a group or community, that either results in or has a high likelihood of resulting in injury, death, psychological harm, maldevelopment or deprivation" (Krug et al. 2002, p. 5). However, this kind of definition seems to raise more problems than it solves. Not only do the concepts of harm and likelihood of harm remain problematic (because undefined), but new problems arise relating to the definition of power and its connection with the occurrence of harm. Many cases in which the exercise of power results or is likely to result in harm are not generally considered forms of violence. For example, if a school panel recommends some students for retention, forcing them to repeat their current grade level, they are likely to suffer psychological harm.[23] It could be objected that the school panel has a *duty* to retain students if they perform poorly, taking the whole question of violence out of the picture. But then even soldiers in war may have to kill in order to fulfil their combat duties, and even police officers may have to use force in order to fulfil a duty to quell a riot, and yet these acts, although legitimate, still appear to be forms of violence.

In fact, even this last claim is disputed. On the one hand, some authors define violence as "the illegitimate or unauthorised use of force".[24] On the other hand, according to Hamby (2017), an essential element of violence lies in its nonessential

[22] Hamby (2017), p. 174. In other words, it seems particularly important to establish a high-probability link that can be assessed *a priori*, when the harm in question is psychological, for otherwise any determination as to whether this kind of harm has been sustained would be entirely contingent on each individual's psychological makeup and susceptibility.

[23] Of course, here too, the assessment depends on how we define psychological harm. Thus, if we were to take as our benchmark the rigid guidelines for psychological disorder set out in DSM-5 (American Psychiatric Association 2013), we would end up significantly restricting the range of cases that qualify as psychological harm, which by that standard would also exclude many forms of repeated nonconsensual verbal insult and humiliation.

[24] Wolff (1969) p. 606. See also Honderich (1980), p. 21. For some criticisms see Pontara (1978); Coady (1986).

or gratuitous nature. Violence "is not necessary for survival or fitness".[25] From both of these perspectives, neither soldiers nor police officers are acting violently, since they engage in legitimate, necessary, and nongratuitous behaviour. Thus, there is no agreement that legitimate violence, justified violence, violence in self-defence, and the like, still count as violence despite the legitimising qualifications.

As I think should be clear from the foreging overview, it is difficult to find a common core across the different notions of violence. We have different competing concepts, and some of them do not align with our most common linguistic intuitions. Certainly, theorists can advance normative arguments in favour of a certain redefinition (even one that departs from the common understanding), making a case for it in light of its political implications as well. In particular, feminist scholars usually support the broad or structural notions of violence on the supposition that they are better suited to the political agenda they are advancing. As I will argue (§4), however, such a supposition is questionable.

2.2 *Concepts of Gender*

It is obviously impossible to fully thrash out the complex concept of gender here. For my purposes, it will suffice to note that there are at least three distinct notions of gender, and that each one shapes GV in a different way.

On the first notion, gender equates with sex. This notion underpins all the definitions of GV that identify it with violence against women (or male violence against women).

On the second notion, gender is "a complex, multilevel cultural construct that determines the meanings of being female or male in a particular situational context".[26] Gender is a "social category imposed on a sexed body",[27] a constellation of beliefs, expectations, social roles, social norms, positions, tendencies, attitudes, tastes, etc., that are socially associated with one sex or the other (or rather, with appearing as belonging to one sex or the other); it varies across time and space, and it variously interacts with other markers of social difference, such as one's race, age, economic status, and profession. Those who subscribe to this notion argue that GV concerns the various ways in which gender mediates, moderates, interacts with, legitimises, or facilitates exposure (or the risk of exposure) to various forms of violence, with their severity, dynamics, and effects.

[25] For example, "bullying can be a successful means of attaining social status [...]. However, it is well within the behavioural repertoire of even school-age children to seek social status without resorting to bullying, and not all high-ranking children bully" (Hamby 2017, p. 170).

[26] Felipe Russo and Pirlott (2006), p. 180.

[27] Scott (1986), p. 1056.

On the third notion, finally, gender is an element of personal identity.[28] This third notion melds into the second insofar as the social constructions—the roles, expectations, attitudes, etc.—culturally associated with being (or appearing as) male or female can be internalised by individuals and be perceived as elements of their identity.[29] As much as the two notions may be inextricably connected, however, that connection does not amount to an equivalence. This for two reasons. First, if we perceive gender as an element of identity, this usually means that we cherish it as a value worth preserving, whereas if we conceive it as a heteronormative social construction, this often means, by contrast, that we have a problem with it and will try to deconstruct it. And, second, someone's gender identity may not coincide with the social expectations, roles, etc., assigned to them. For example, a trans woman may perceive herself as a woman (and not as a trans woman), and yet the stereotypes, expectations, social roles, etc., imposed on her relate to her being and appearing as a *trans* woman, and they are substantially different from those socially associated with biologically female individuals. Probably because the notion of gender as identity is closely bound up with the previous notion, it is not often thematised in studies on GV. True, we can find a definition of GV "as violence against an individual or population based on gender identity or expressions",[30] but then gender as identity is usually conflated with gender as a social construction.

3 Different Connections Between Gender and Violence

How are the different concepts of violence and gender connected? Or, stated otherwise, in what sense can violence be gender-based? The two concepts interact in some complicated ways that will be considered in the next section, but before that, in this section, we will look at two types of *clear* connection.

In the first place, violence is gendered. Violence exhibits different patterns between men and women and, making allowance for age and social and cultural variability, it is strongly associated with masculinity.[31] In most societies, men are expected to be more physically violent than women, to be able to react violently to physical violence, not to fear it. And, in fact, men do meet such social expectations and commit more violent crimes than women. So, for example, according to UNODC (2019a) about 90 percent of all homicides recorded worldwide in 2017 were committed by male perpetrators. This does not mean that women do not commit violent crimes, especially if we go with the narrow notion of violence, but

[28] This notion of gender is especially widespread in so-called difference feminism. See Gilligan (1982); Tronto (1989); McLaren (2001).

[29] See, e.g., Wood and Eagly (2015); Wood and Eagly (2012).

[30] Wies and Haldane (2011), p. 2.

[31] See, e.g., Hatty (2000); Ellis (2015); Poggi (2019).

statistically they commit fewer and less serious ones.[32] There is, however, an important exception: neonaticide.[33] Certainly, neonaticide is associated with gender—and so this kind of violence, too, is gendered—but not in the same way that male violence is. Male violence is gendered simply in the sense that masculinity is socially constructed as violent, while the association between neonaticide and the social construction of gender is more complex.[34]

Briefly, this first notion of gender violence mainly concerns cases under the narrow notion of violence, conceives of gender as a social construction, and focuses on the perpetrators. This notion is not about violence against women, but rather about the social roots of male physical violence. I think this notion is politically useful in working toward public policies for counteracting it, especially policies directed at school and kindergarten educators.[35]

In the second place, violence (in one of its meanings) can be a means by which to enforce the fulfilment of social expectations about gender or punish those who do not conform to these expectations. As examples where violence is used to impose a gender role, think of violence against homosexuals and transsexuals or the killing of girls who dishonour their families because they do not conform to gender expectations. Depending on the notion of violence one assumes, the use of violence to impose gender roles may also include nonphysical assault, like verbal assaults against little girls because they behave like "tomboys" or against little boys because behave like "sissies", at least if such assaults result in harm (in some sense of the term "harm"). This kind of GV links violence to gender as a social construction and as identity[36]; it can be carried out and suffered by both men and women; and it seems to require a specific intentional attitude, i.e. an intention to use violence against someone in order to force them to fulfil social expectations about gender or punish them if do not conform to these expectations. So understood, GV is also *legally* relevant: the law can provide that an intention to impose on someone an adherence to their socially assigned gender role, attitudes, etc., counts as a justification, excuse, or *extenuating* circumstance, or, on the contrary, the law can *exclude* any such

[32] So, for example, many studies report cases of mutual aggression in IPV, and so also cases where the aggression is by a female partner, but, as Reed et al. (2010) stress, male IPV is quantitatively greater and more serious if measured by its modalities and consequences. At the same time, however, other studies have shown that male IPV is *perceived* as more severe even if it is actually the same as female IPV. See, e.g., Hamby and Jackson (2010).

[33] For discussion (as well as some definitions) see Bourget and Bradford (1990); Putkonen et al. (2010); Almeida and Vieira (2017).

[34] The strongest predictors of maternal child homicide are maternal age (19 years or younger), education (12 years of schooling or less), single marital status, and late or absent prenatal care. See Overpeck et al. (1998); UNODC (2019b). However, more recent studies have indicated that a growing proportion of neonaticidal women are married and multiparous and suffer from mental disorders. See Tanaka et al. (2017).

[35] See Poggi (2019).

[36] It is violence to impose gender as (adherence to) a social construction against someone who does not identify with such construction, who does not perceive it as an element of their identity.

justification,[37] or it can provide that such an intention counts as an *aggravating* circumstance.[38]

However, if we frame this form of violence as structural violence, it becomes more nuanced and takes in all forms of injustice (including legal injustices) suffered by non-gender-conforming people. As much as it may be important to draw attention to these types of injustice, the question remains whether they are appropriately labelled as forms of violence.

3.1 Violence Inflicted on a Woman Just Because She Is a Woman

The two notions of violence previously distinguished seem pretty clear to me, and also legally and politically useful. However, although they come up in the literature and in statutory language, they do not figure prominently in either context. Indeed, for one thing, neither of the two notions, strictly speaking, refers to violence directed exclusively against women, and so neither one fits the standard definition of GV as violence against a woman just because she is a woman. And, for another thing, most legal regulations provide, as gender-based crimes, behaviours that may not be committed with physical violence and that are totally independent from the subjective intentions of their perpetrators to enforce the fulfilment of social expectations about gender or punish someone who do not conform to them (think of psychological or economic violence or female genital mutilation).

As mentioned (Sect. 2), GV is sometimes defined as violence that disproportionately affects women. Under this definition, violence (in the broad and structural senses) is connected with gender understood as sex, and there are good reasons for making that connection: if the victims' sex were irrelevant, we should expect a roughly equal percentage of male and female victims, but if the victims of a given violence are disproportionately of one sex, we should think that such violence does have to do with the victims' sex. However, this statistical definition is problematic, and I would point to three conceptual reasons why.

First, most victims of violent crimes are not women but men. According to the United Nations Office on Drugs and Crime (UNODC), around "81 per cent of homicide victims recorded in 2017 were men and boys, and the global homicide

[37] See the Istanbul Convention, Article 42 ("Unacceptable justifications for crimes, including crimes committed in the name of so-called 'honour'"): "Parties shall take the necessary legislative or other measures to ensure that, in criminal proceedings initiated following the commission of any of the acts of violence covered by the scope of this Convention, culture, custom, religion, tradition or so-called 'honour' shall not be regarded as justification for such acts. This covers, in particular, claims that the victim has transgressed cultural, religious, social or traditional norms or customs of appropriate behaviour".

[38] On both alternatives (the extenuating and the aggravating) see Poggi (2019).

rate for the male population is roughly four times the rate for women and girls".[39] Women are instead more often victims of some particular forms of violence, such as sexual violence and IPV.[40] If, on this statistical approach, we label the latter as violence against a woman just because she is a woman, then, by the same token, we should label all the other forms of violence as violence against a man just because he is a man.

Second, this notion doesn't shed any light on the relation between someone being a victim of violence and their being female, so it doesn't seem to be of much use politically. In other words, there may be a variety of reasons why women are statistically more likely to be victims of certain forms of violence. For example, women over the age of 44 are statistically more likely to be victims of purse-snatching. This has to do with a number of social rules about appearance and attire (handbags, heels, skirts) that make them less likely to react.[41] However, it is clear that the way in which sex is connected with victimisation in the case of purse-snatching is very different from the way it is, for example, in the case of IPV or sexual violence. The statistical notion of GV is completely silent on these issues. I will come back to this point later.

And third, there is a whole range of cases that this definition, by conflating sex with gender, fails to cover, where the violence bears some strong similarities to violence against women and yet is directed at persons who are not women. Think of violence against homosexual, transgender, and nonbinary people. Aren't these forms of violence gender-based as well? They certainly are, but only if we see gender as a social construction.

As mentioned, a widespread alternative definition of GV is the one that links it to the unequal distribution of power. A case in point is the Istanbul Convention, stating that GV is "a manifestation of historically unequal power relations between women and men, which have led to domination over, and discrimination against, women by men and to the prevention of the full advancement of women; [. . .]. [GV] is one of the crucial social mechanisms by which women are forced into a subordinate position compared with men" (Preamble). That is to say, according to this definition, GV is "against a woman just because she is a woman" in the sense that GV is a manifestation and a mean of the male domination. Of course, the perpetrators may not see it that way: as pointed out, many forms of gender-based violence listed in the Istanbul Convention itself are not easily qualified as hate crimes. In fact, this form of

[39] UNODC (2019a), p. 22.

[40] According to Eurostat (2023) statistics on victims of intentional homicide at the hands of family members or intimate partners in the EU in 2021, the ratio of female to male victims was 3.9 to 1.8 per million victims. In the US, according to Smith (2022), the percentage of females murdered by an intimate partner in 2021 was 5 times greater than for males. According to the WHO (2021), almost 1 in 3 women, or 30 percent, have been subjected to physical and/or sexual violence by an intimate partner or to nonpartner sexual violence, or both (data from 2000 to 2018 across 161 countries and areas). According to Kearl (2018), 81 percent of women and 43 percent of men in the US reported experiencing some form of sexual harassment or assault in their lifetime.

[41] See Poggi (2019).

violence is often regarded as structural, as embedded in society, while its perpetrators seem to be just cogs in the machine.

My main objection against such a definition is that it lacks clarity—so much so, in fact, as to be theoretically useless (and also politically harmful: see Sect. 4). In a patriarchal society, *any* violence perpetrated by a man against a woman could be regarded as gender-based. Likewise, if we subscribe to the structural notion of violence, *any* social injustice that affects a woman is *ipso facto* a form of GV. If John and Johanna fight over a parking space and John gets in first with a reckless manoeuvre, this is a form of GV. John has caused harm to Johanna (he has even put her bodily integrity at risk) in order to assert his male superiority through his reckless takeover of the parking space. However, if it is Johanna who acts this way, hers is no longer a form of gendered violence (against John). If John insults his wife, Johanna, because she cannot find a job, this is GV; if Johanna insults John because he cannot find a job, this is "just simply" violence. If Johanna drops out of high school or college, this can be considered structural GV[42]; if John does so, that wouldn't probably even be recognised as a form of structural violence. From a conceptual standpoint, this asymmetry is very odd.

Most importantly, this loose and inchoate definition obscures the fact that gender (as a social construction) can interact with and mediate violence in many different ways, as well as it can get commingled with other social markers (like age, ethnicity, and socioeconomic status). As we have seen, it is in very different ways that gender and violence connect in neonaticide, purse-snatching, and sexual violence: in neonaticide, the factors involved include social expectations of motherhood and lack of public assistance and medical care for postpartum depression; in purse-snatching, it is social norms of appearance and attire that make a woman an easy prey; with sexual violence, it is social stereotypes (including about appearance and attire) that can come into play, causing a rape victim to be perceived as blameworthy (victim blaming), while diminishing the perceived seriousness of the crime. True, all these expectations, social norms, and stereotypes are somehow related to the structural subordination of women, but in very different ways.

4 A Political Issue

We have seen that many feminist writers have worked from a broad and/or structural notion of violence coupled with the unclear definitions of GV analysed in the previous section (Sect. 3.1). And that, as I would argue, has had some negative political consequences.

As Coady stresses, a "wide definition seems to likely encourage the cosy but ultimately stultifying belief that there is one problem, the problem of (wide)

[42] The implication here is that Johanna's potential hasn't been realized, and the argument could be made that it hasn't because, as a woman, she is discriminated against in the educational system.

violence, and hence it must be solved as a whole with one set of techniques".[43] And if there is just one problem of violence—that of its victims, for if we have violence, then by definition we have victims—the one set of techniques can only be that of the criminal provisions needed to protect these victims. In other words, the emphasis the feminist struggle has placed on a wide and hazy concept of GV has engendered what Pitch calls the "victimization paradigm".[44] This paradigm fits into a political logic of good and evil, victim and enemy, on which we have blameless "good" victims on the one hand (those who have done their best not to be victimised) and evil enemies on the other, and the main objective therefore becomes to protect the former by neutralizing the latter. This all gets filtered through the lens of criminal law, where conflicts and claims "are placed on a horizontal level, thus ignoring or bypassing issues stemming from the unequal balance of political, economic, and social power".[45] So the paradox here is that feminist thinking on violence, in setting out to unveil the social and systemic roots of violence, has ended up contradicting its own assumptions. From a criminal perspective, violence is a matter of individual deviant perpetrators. Women are presented as victims, as vulnerable subjects who must be protected and must protect themselves—so much for women's empowerment and freedom. The growth of gender-oriented crimes recognised in the law has at best resulted in some stiffer penalties for IPV, and at worst in obscure legal provisions that jeopardise legal certainty.[46] And, most importantly, statistics show that this simplistic policy—one problem, one solution—is not bearing any fruit. Some of the most typical gender-based crimes—domestic violence, sexual assault, IPV—continue to be on the rise.[47]

To conclude, the gist of this chapter is not that the notion of GV ought to be dispensed with, but that it needs to be more fully thought through and refined. If we are to implement effective public policies, we need to delve into the ways in which gender, as a social construct, interacts with different types of oppression and discrimination, and above all we need to distinguish violence from other forms of social injustice: only with the former should the policy response lean on criminal law, among other measures, while the latter calls for a different suite of policies, based on a structural and intersectional understanding of the root causes of different forms of oppression and discrimination that should not be bundled into a single concept of violence. As Hamby comments, "[m]any bad things happen that are not violence".[48]

---

[43] Coady (1986), p. 12. This is a claim that Coady makes about the structural notion of violence, but I think that the claim holds as well for the definitions of GV analysed in Sect. 3.1.

[44] Pitch (2022).

[45] Pitch (2022), p. 33, my translation.

[46] For a detailed analysis on crimes of femicide see Vázquez (2019).

[47] See Kearl (2018); WHO (2021); Morgan and Thompson (2022); Smith (2022); Eurostat (2023).

[48] Hamby (2017), p. 170.

References

Almeida F, Vieira DN (2017) Profiling in violent crimes: the perpetrator and the victim in cases of filicide. In: Petherick W, Sinnamon G (eds) The psychology of criminal and antisocial behavior. Academic, Amsterdam, pp 167–209
American Psychiatric Association (2013) The diagnostic and statistical manual of mental disorder, (DSM-5). American Psychiatric Association Publishing, Washington
Bloom SS (2008) Violence against women and girls: a compendium of monitoring and evaluation indicators. Carolina Population Center, Chapel Hill
Bourget D, Bradford JMW (1990) Homicidal parents. Canadian J Psy 35(3):233–238
Bufacchi V (2006) Violence by omission. In: Ó Murchadha F (ed) Violence, victims, justification. Peter Lang, Bern, pp 95–114
Buss S, Westlund A (2018) Personal autonomy. In: Zalta EN (ed) The Stanford Encyclopedia of Philosophy. <https://plato.stanford.edu/archives/spr2018/entries/personal-autonomy/>
Coady CAJ (1986) The idea of violence. J Appl Philosophy 3(1):3–19
DeWall CN, Anderson CA, Bushman BJ (2011) The general aggression model: theoretical extension to violence. Psychol Violence 1(3):245–258. https://doi.org/10.1037/a0023842
Ellis A (2015) Men, masculinities and violence: an ethnographic study. Routledge, London
Eurostat (2023) Crime statistics. https://ec.europa.eu/eurostat/statistics-explained/index.php?title=Crime_statistics#intentional_homicides_in_the_EU_in_2021.2C_the_lowest_value_in_2008-2021
Felipe Russo N, Pirlott A (2006) Gender-based violence. Concepts, methods, and findings. Ann N Y Acad Sci 1087:178–205. https://doi.org/10.1196/annals.1385.024
Galtung J (1969) Violence, peace, and peace research. J Peace Res 6(3):167–191
Gilligan C (1982) In a different voice: psychological theory and women's development. Harvard University Press, Cambridge
Giomi E, Magaraggia S. (2017) Relazioni brutali. Il Mulino, Bologna
Hamby S (2017) On defining violence, and why it matters. Psychol Violence 7(2):167–180
Hamby S, Jackson A (2010) Size does matter: the effects of gender on perceptions of dating violence. Sex Roles 63:324–331. https://doi.org/10.1007/s11199-010-9816-0
Harris J (1980) Violence and responsibility. Routledge, London
Hatty SE (2000) Masculinities, violence, and culture. Sage, London
Honderich T (1980) Violence for equality. Pelican, London
Hortal A (2023) Combatiendo la violencia de género a través de políticas públicas conductuales: Alcances y limitaciones. Retos 13(25):9–83. https://doi.org/10.17163/ret.n25.2023.05
Kearl H (2018) The facts behind the #metoo movement: a national study on sexual harassment and assault. Stop Street Harassment, Reston
Klugman J (2017) Gender based violence and the law. World Development Report Background Paper. © World Bank, Washington DC. http://hdl.handle.net/10986/26198
Krug EG, Dahlberg LL, Mercy JA, Zwi A, Lozano R (2002) World report on violence and health. WHO, Geneva
MacKinnon CA (1987) Feminism unmodified: discourses on life and law. Harvard University Press, Cambridge—London
MacKinnon CA (1994) Rape, genocide and Women's human rights. Harv Wom Law J 17:5–16
Martín Sánchez M (2015) El género en la "violencia afectiva": clave para un examen de constitucionalidad. Estudios Constitucionales 13(1):203–236
McLaren M (2001) Feminist ethics: care as a virtue. In: DesAutels P, Waugh J (eds) Feminists doing ethics. Rowman & Littlefield, Lanham (MD), pp 101–118
Morgan RE, Thompson A (2022) Criminal victimization. NCJ 301775. https://bjs.ojp.gov/library/publications/criminal-victimization-2020
Norris Turner P (2014) "Harm" and Mill's harm principle. Ethics 124(2):299–326
Ó Murchadha F (2006) Introduction: violence, discourse and human interdipendence. In: Ó Murchadha F (ed) Violence, victims, justification. Peter Lang, Bern, pp 9–22

Overpeck MD, Brenner RA, Trumble AC, Trifiletti LB, Berendes HW (1998) Risk factors for infant homicide in the United States. New England J Med 339:1211–1216
Parrott DJ, Giancola PR (2007) Addressing "the criterion problem" in the assessment of aggressive behaviour. Aggress Violent Behav 12:280–299
Pitch T (2022) Il malinteso della vittima. Gruppo Abele, Trapani
Poggi F (2019) Sobre el concepto de violencia de género y su relevancia para el derecho. Doxa 42: 285–307
Pontara G (1978) The concept of violence. J Peace Res 15(1):19–32
Putkonen H et al (2010) Child murder and gender differences: a nationwide register-based study of filicide offenders in two European countries. J Forensic Psychiatry Psychol 21(5):637–648
Rabenberg M (2014) Harm. J Ethics Soc Philosophy 8(3):1–32
Reed E, Raj A, Miller E, Silverman JG (2010) Losing the "gender" in gendered-based violence: the missteps of research on dating and intimate partner violence. Violence Against Women 16(3): 348–354
Scott JW (1986) Gender: a useful category of historical analysis. Am Hist Rev 91(5):1053–1075
Smith EL (2022) Female Murder Victims and Victim-Offender Relationship, 2021. NCJ 305613: https://bjs.ojp.gov/female-murder-victims-and-victim-offender-relationship-2021
Tanaka CT, Berger W, Valença AM, Coutinho ES, Jean-Louis G, Fontenelle LF, Mendlowicz MV (2017) The worldwide incidence of Neonaticide: a systematic review. Arch Womens Ment Health 20(2):249–256. https://doi.org/10.1007/s00737-016-0703-8
Tronto J (1989) Women and caring: what can feminists learn about morality from caring? In: Jaggar AM, Bordo S (eds) Gender/body/knowledge: feminist reconstructions of being and knowing. Rutgers University Press, London, pp 172–187
UNODC (United Nation Office against Drugs and Crime) (2019a) Global Study on Homicide. https://www.unodc.org/unodc/en/data-and-analysis/global-study-on-homicide.html
UNODC (United Nation Office against Drugs and Crime) (2019b) Global Study on Homicide: Killing Children and Young Adults. https://www.unodc.org/documents/data-and-analysis/gsh/Booklet_6new.pdf
Vázquez C (2019) Técnicas legislative del feminicidio y sus problemas probatorios. Doxa 42:193–219
Waldenfels B (2006) Violence as violation. In: Ó Murchadha F (ed) Violence, victims, justification. Peter Lang, Bern, pp 72–94
WHO (World Health Organization) (2021) Violence against women prevalence estimates, 2018. WHO, Geneva. https://www.who.int/publications/i/item/9789240022256
Wies JR, Haldane HJ (2011) Ethnographic notes from the front line of gender-based violence. In: Wies JR, Haldane HJ (eds) Anthropology at the front lines of gender-based violence. Vanderbilt University Press, Nashville, pp 1–18. https://doi.org/10.2307/j.ctv16b78b5.4
Wolff RP (1969) On violence. J Philosophy 66:601–616
Wood W, Eagly AH (2012) Biosocial construction of sex differences and similarities in behavior. Adv Exp Soc Psychol 46:55–123. https://doi.org/10.1016/B978-0-12-394281-4.00002-7
Wood W, Eagly AH (2015) Two traditions of research on gender identity. Sex Roles 73:461–473. https://doi.org/10.1007/s11199-015-0480-2

Francesca Poggi (PhD) is full professor at the Department "Cesare Beccaria" of the University of Milan, where she teaches Legal Philosophy, Law and Bioethics and Legal Gender Studies. She is also professor in Masters and post-lauream courses. She is the scientific coordinator of the PhD in legal studies "Cesare Beccaria" at the University of Milan. She is member of different research groups within national and international research projects. She is member of the Scientific Boards of the journals "Revus", "Notizie di Politeia", and "Storia, metodo, cultura". She is member of the Edotorial Boards of the journals "Analisi e diritto" and "GenIUS". Her main scientific interests concern legal interpretation, bioethics and legal gender studies.

Trans* Citizenship: A Feminist Socio-Legal Analysis of Theories and Practices

Zara Saeidzadeh

Contents

Abstract Feminist approaches to citizenship have for a long time problematized the traditional view of male, white, heterosexual, and able-bodied citizenship. Nonetheless, many feminist theories on citizenship are based on the gender binary system and the idea of universal rights for all, which tend to erase differences and structural inequalities (Monro and Warren, Sexualities 7(3):345–362, 2004; Monro, The limits of gendered citizenship: contexts and complexities, Routledge, 2010; Monro and Van der Ros, Crit Soc Policy 38(1):57–78, 2018; Kuhar et al., Crit Soc Policy 38(1): 99–120, 2018). In this chapter, I discuss how feminist politics address trans* people's citizenship using the concept of trans* citizenship developed by Surya Monro (Crit Soc Policy 23(4):433–452, 2003), Monro (The limits of gendered citizenship: contexts and complexities, Routledge, 2010), while engaging with Nancy Fraser's understanding of recognition (Fraser, New Left Rev 1(3):107–120, 2000; Fraser, Crit Inq 34(3):393–422, 2008). Thus, I focus on the politics of recognition that emphasises the status and needs of citizens in achieving social justice. Through examining the use of

Z. Saeidzadeh (✉)
Örebro University, Örebro, Sweden
e-mail: zara.saeidzadeh@oru.se

N. Lacey et al. (eds.), *Reassessing Feminist Legal Theories*, Gender Perspectives in Law 5, https://doi.org/10.1007/978-3-031-75423-4_8

some theoretical concepts in feminist politics, I discuss how the limits of identity-based politics of recognition in feminist theories and practices have amounted to social injustices and denial of trans* people's needs, affecting their citizenship. Thus, I maintain that trans* citizenship needs feminist socio-legal researchers, practitioners, and policy makers' attention to social status and needs of trans* people with respect to people's diversity of knowledge and experiences.

1 Introduction

Citizenship is about rights, duties, participation, belonging while it addresses the lack of right, duties, participation, and non-belonging that is to include and exclude certain groups of people from participating in society.[1] Citizenship is conceptualized not only as a legal status but also as a practice which reflects people's lived experiences.[2] Furthermore, struggles for social justice, equality and recognition of legal and social status are characterized as struggles for citizenship.[3]

What constitutes a citizen varies in different parts of the world.[4] Thus, citizenship is context specific as its understanding is vastly contingent on the historical, cultural, legal, and political complexities. The common modern characteristic of citizenship is the relationship between the individual and the state. However, from a feminist point of view, citizenship is constructed and contested in civil society in relations to individuals as well as non-state organisations which means that the territorial state is not always a necessary component of citizenship.[5]

Citizenship has been discussed as a contested, problematic, and slippery concept in feminist theories and empirical studies since the nineteenth century.[6] Debates on citizenship in the Western world emerged through building on the liberal understanding of citizenship based on the trio of civil, political, and social rights developed by Marshall in the 1950s (2013).[7] Feminists began to problematize traditional Marshallian view of citizenship that focuses on male, white, heterosexual, middle class citizens,[8] for failing to account for ethnicity, race, and nationality.[9] Citizenship in a liberal definition is more about individualistic ways of pursuing own interests rather than collective participation in public which means less collective in political

[1] Lister et al. (2007a); Roseneil (2013); Roseneil et al. (2012).

[2] Lister (2017).

[3] Predelli et al. (2012).

[4] Lister et al. (2007b).

[5] Predelli et al. (2012).

[6] See Lombardo and Verloo (2010); Predelli et al. (2012); Roseneil (2013).

[7] Marshall (2013).

[8] Strasser (2012).

[9] Hines (2007).

activities. In liberal citizenship, citizens are bearers of universal rights. However, feminists criticize liberal citizenship for not addressing universal rights of women and diversity of human experiences in both private and public spheres.[10] Sylvia Walby[11] upholds that citizenship is not complete without theorization of gender and gender relations. According to Walby:[12] "access to citizenship is a highly gendered and ethnically structured process." If people are denied participation in society because of gender, then "gender matters to citizenship [...] Citizenship is about gender and the transformation of the form of patriarchy as much as it is about class, nation/ethnicity and capitalism".[13] Furthermore, Leti Volpp discusses how liberal understandings of citizenship assumes multiculturalism contradictory to citizenship and argues that "citizenship is both a cultural and anti-cultural institution".[14] Can citizenship support gender equality? is a recurring question in feminist discussions which concerns the extent to which citizenship can be developed to promote gender equality without the interests of subordinated groups becoming subsumed and dispersed by the institutions and by the processes of being associated with state machinery.[15]

Ruth Lister maintains that the basis of feminist theory for citizenship is the approach that synthesizes rights and participation as she calls it an 'internationalist approach' to citizenship by feminists.[16] Lister upholds[17] "citizenship is constructed both as a status and a practice" in relation to women by which she explains the importance of women's agency, not as passive victims, while acknowledges the structural problems. Lister proposes[18] the notion of "differentiated universalism" emphasizing on inclusion of women's different rights and needs as well as reconciliation of universalism in feminist theories of citizenship, which she thinks elaborates on diversity of women and other oppressed groups.

Although the notion and vocabularies of citizenship is originated in the West.[19] the work of feminist scholars from non-Western contexts have contributed to the limits of understanding citizenship and therefore have reworked the notion citizenship as Surya Monro and Dianne Richardson[20] show how multiple factors such as war, violence, poverty and the importance of women's agency impact the construction of citizenship in countries like Iran and Turkey. Monro and Richardson[21] further

[10] Lister (1997, 2017).
[11] Walby (1994).
[12] Walby (1994), p. 391.
[13] Walby (1994), p. 392.
[14] Volpp (2007), p. 574.
[15] See Roseneil et al. (2012); Roseneil et al. (2013); Volpp (2017).
[16] Lister (1997).
[17] Lister (1997), p. 42.
[18] Lister (1997), p. 42.
[19] Lister et al. (2007b).
[20] Monro and Richardson (2014).
[21] Monro and Richardson (2014).

explain that citizenship entails discussions on both gender and sexuality as they are not separable. Yet again, the dominant understandings of the concepts of gender and sexuality is based on the Western scholarship which is often rooted in binaries. Nonetheless, the Western conceptualization of gender and sexual categories are applied as universal terms in human rights documents and policy making. On the other hand, de-gendering citizenship has limits in theory and practice patriarchy,[22] while it eludes problematising patriarchy.[23]

Intersectionality approach to citizenship is advanced to pay attention to different underlying forces that shape social structures and people's experiences.[24] This is referred to as "lived citizenship"[25] by some scholars to accounts for national and sub-national differences of experiences across gender, class and ethnicity for better understanding of gendered citizenship. Lister et al. write[26]: "The notion of 'lived citizenship' is about 'the meaning that citizenship actually has in people's lives and the ways in which people's social and cultural backgrounds and material circumstances affect their lives as citizens." Although studies on gender and citizenship have developed adopting intersectionality approaches to elucidate gender, sexuality, migration, occupation, education, race, ethnicity, religion, age and ability of citizenship, studies on LGBT citizenship are still underdeveloped.[27]

Citizenship is inclusionary because it has been helpful for social, political and legal gains for women and it is exclusionary, because it is tied to individualistic neoliberal "Westphalian nation-state".[28] Hence, the state enacts violence and discrimination against the nation by defining citizenship. Roseneil also reminds us about the dominance of feminist theorization against trans* people in the West. Therefore, she suggests that: "feminists concerned with citizenship need to address this kind of blind spot in feminist thinking and take ownership of their own roles in perpetuating certain types of inequality".[29] The concept of citizenship has been reworked by feminist scholars and activists to better help achieving social justice, equality and participation for the racialized, disabled, poor, marginalized, gender and sexual nonconformist people.[30]

Trans* people around the world have been reclaiming citizenship through recognition of their existence as equal members of society that is social participation, ability to contribute to the development of society as well as access to structural and institutional resources.[31] Despite decades of robust activism and social movements,

---

[22] Hearn et al. (2010).

[23] Connell (2012).

[24] Hearn et al. (2010).

[25] Lister et al. (2007a).

[26] Lister et al. (2007b), p. 168.

[27] See Monro and Richardson (2014); Kuhar et al. (2018).

[28] Roseneil (2013), p. 2.

[29] Roseneil (2013), p. 15.

[30] Predelli (2012).

[31] See Currah et al. (2006); Hines (2010); Platero (2020).

trans* people are still denied citizenship in many countries which means they are not provided with basic needs, nor are they allowed participation in society. For example, in a social welfare country like Sweden, which claims to be running a feminist government, trans* people are still denied access to legal change of gender without medical diagnosis. Moreover, there is no legal recognition of gender for non-binary trans* people in Sweden as the legal gender functions on a binary male and female system. In Norway, too gender binarism is legally, culturally, and politically institutionalized.[32] The lack of legal recognition and medical pathologisation have led to misrecognition of trans* people's status in society, resulting in denial of trans* people's citizenship by pushing them to the margins and preventing them from participating in society with their desired gender as equal citizens. In a similar position, the Islamic republic of Iran legally recognizes trans* people as citizens if only they undergo gender affirmation surgery which involves forced sterilization. In the same vein, the state of Florida in the United States of America, has banned health care for trans* youth through Bill 1421 which came into force in March 2023, forbidding young trans* citizens from accessing medical transition.[33]

In this chapter, I discuss feminist politics towards trans* citizens status and needs by elaborating on specific theoretical concepts to show how theories and practices that are based on identity politics of recognition don't really helped trans* people to enjoy equality of status and needs in society.

2 Feminist and Trans* Citizenship

The early 1970s witnessed what is known as a watershed period in the shared history of trans* movement with gay, lesbians and feminist liberation groups in the US which caused alienation between some feminists who chose hostile approaches to trans* people.[34] The hostility of some feminist groups towards trans* people are rooted in the epistemological questions of who constitutes as a woman[35] and who has the right to be part of feminist agendas along with the global movements' shift to identity in the early 1970s.[36] Since the growth of feminists' antagonistic positions towards trans* people, and later the emergence of gender critical feminists, trans* people's citizenship has been denied even more so through exclusion,

---

[32] Monro and Van der Ros (2018).

[33] DeSantis government has pushed for limited access to hormone treatments and procedures for children and minors will be allowed to such treatments under the condition of more evaluations and bureaucratic processes in the state of Florida. Medicaid coverage is also eliminated by Florida's Agency for Health Care Administration. They argue that this bill is to bring justice for those who are tricked into a sexual mutilation. See: https://thehill.com/homenews/3883279-florida-bill-targets-gender-affirming-health-care-for-trans-youth-adults/.

[34] Morgan (1977); Daly (1978); Raymond (1979).

[35] Hines (2010).

[36] Saeidzadeh and Strid (2020).

discrimination, and violence. Gender critical feminists' politics today focuses on the interests of non-trans and cisgender women, another words, gender critical feminism involves those who were born with *female genitalia*.

Despite feminists' work and the development on sexual and intimate citizenship beyond traditional understandings, these forms of citizenships are still based on gender binarism, and the negligence of complexities and fluidities of gender and sexuality, excluding trans* citizens.[37] Monro and Warren[38] discuss intimate citizenship focuses on personal and intimate life involving the right to body, feelings, relationships, eroticism in the Western world. Thus, oversees the structural problems with which trans* people grapple. Moreover, sexual citizenship refers to the right to participate in sexual activity, sexual pleasure as well as right to sexual self-determination and self-expression[39] is anchored to the notion of universal citizen, a whole and free individual in contrast to the 'other' living under oppression.[40] According to Volpp sexual citizenship bears negative vibes as it is based on Euro-American definitions in which anti-immigrant, racist policies deny some people equal social participations.[41] Moreover, sexual citizenship refers to experiences of and expression of sexual minorities rather than gender and gender relations which are the concerns of trans people.[42] Evans talks about "trans-citizenship" in a limited and controlled way of entitlement to material rights and freedom under medical and legal systems.[43]

Gender binary account of citizenship discriminates trans* people in terms of employment and prevents them from creating their family of choice. Thus, nonbinary gender people lack citizenship in most countries around Europe.[44] Trans* citizenship calls for the establishment of civil identities such as birth certificate and passport, be able to marry or be parents and have the right to employment.[45]

I build on the notion of trans* citizenship developed by Surya Monro[46] to emphasise on trans* citizenship's structural phenomena such as law and society rather than individual phenomena such as rights and identities. Monro developed the notion of transgender citizenship [sic] emphasising "participatory democracy" on path to change social organisation of gender.[47] Transgender citizenship for Monro

---

[37] Monro (2003); Hines (2007); Monro and Van der Ros (2018).

[38] Monro and Warren (2004).

[39] Richardson (2000).

[40] Volpp (2017).

[41] Volpp (2017), p. 14.

[42] Monro and Warren (2004); Hines (2006).

[43] Evans (1993).

[44] Monro and Van der Ros (2018).

[45] Monro (2003).

[46] Monro (2000, 2003, 2010).

[47] Monro (2003).

"questions the conceptualisation of gender in politics and policy making".[48] Thus, trans* citizenship challenges the results of social policy implications such as right to parenthood, freedom of psychiatric diagnosis, access to medical care, and job opportunities.[49]

Trans* citizenship underlines diversity of trans* experiences and their needs at intersection with race, class, age, sexual orientation, nationality, religion, and ability. Trans* citizenship is gendered and involves variety of underlying forces of social structure. Thus, trans* citizenship concerns reproduction, sexual intimacy, independence and the need to earn.

Studies have shown that trans* people's citizenships have been denied largely due to structural inequalities, discrimination, violence, institutionalised exclusion and erasure which is framed by Volpp as 'disposability and social death' that constraints individuals' citizenship.[50] This is what Fraser encapsulates as 'social subordination' that denies a person status in society.[51]

Liberal discourses on citizenship for trans* people can be limited and universalistic, because the idea of "universal equality erases differences and structural inequalities".[52] Neoliberal focus on consumers rights has enabled trans* people to access services as consumers. It has enabled trans* people to access private health care for transition and fertility treatments, but it has also created problems for gender diverse people who are erased in society and cannot have access to services because they are not able to participate in society. Needless to say, trans* people's difficult life trajectories usually prevent them from active participation in society on the ground of race, class, ethnicity, age and (dis)ability which expose them to discrimination and exclusion. Trans* people's experiences and identities are diverse which makes trans* citizenship a complex and contested terrain. Furthermore, Monro writes: "the universality of rights in citizenship can be overcome by particularities of citizenship".[53] But the universal claims to equal rights tends to homogenise differences as well as particularities under the frame of fundamental human rights.[54] For instance, the fundamental human rights to family. Therefore, the focus on *needs* of trans* citizens is deemed necessary rather than *rights* or universal human rights. I subscribe to approaching citizenship through synthesis of participation and needs which solves the problem of universalism and exclusionary in providing equal participation for people of diverse gender and sexuality.

---

48 Monro (2003), p. 435.

49 Monro (2003, 2010).

50 Volpp (2017), p. 16.

51 Fraser (2000).

52 Monro (2003), p. 437.

53 Monro (2003), p. 448.

54 Hines (2009).

3 The Limits of Identity-Based Recognition in Feminist Politics Towards Trans* People

Here, I discuss how the two theoretical concepts of Autogynephilia and Rapid Onset Gender Dysphoria are used and advocated by some feminists to negatively impact trans* citizenship, denying trans* people status and social participation. For the past couple of decades, the growing emergence of anti-trans feminists including gender critical feminists in the UK and the US have reinforced the use of these concepts against trans* people. These concepts are based on biological determination of gender rooted in identity politics that purports condemnation of gender transition and misrecognition of trans* people.

3.1 Autogynephilia

The notion of autogynephylia is used by anti-trans feminists and more increasingly by gender critical feminists' via online platforms 4thWaveNow since 2014 to insinuate trans women are "sexually deviant men".[55] Autogynephilia as a concept was first used by an American Canadian sexologist Ray Blanchard in 1989 to refer to trans women as people who become aroused by the thought of themselves being women, a "misdirected heterosexual sex drive" and [...]primary cause of gender dysphoria.[56] Moreover, Blanchard used autogynephilia to explain "different erotic abnormalities; those who are interested in gay men and those who are attracted to heterosexual men".[57]

Despite series of publication by Blanchard on the concept of autogynephilia in the 1980s, it only received attention during 2000 when J.Michael Bailey's book, The Man Who Would be Queen: The Science of Gender Bending and Transsexualism was published.[58] The use of this term for trans women is criticized as Serano explains Blachard did not base his theory on empirical study.[59] Moreover, later research show that autogynephilia is a different form of embodied fantasy that could be taken by any cisgender person too.[60] That is to say autogneyphilia has no bearing in trans* people's gender identity but is used by anti-trans groups including feminists to deny existence of trans women.[61]

55 Serano (2020), p. 764.

56 Serano (2010), p. 176.

57 Serano (2020), p.765.

58 Serano (2010), p. 178.

59 Serano (2020).

60 Moser (2009).

61 Serano (2010, 2020).

According to Serano autogynephilia is rooted in gender essentialism in nature because it implies that if a person does not conform to innate gender roles, then that person is a man or a woman with "feminized or masculinized brains".[62] Moreover, Serano reminds us that in a patriarchal and misogynistic society the idea of becoming a woman is startling and it is usually assumed becoming a woman is an excuse for sexual reasons which is in itself degrading, reproduces sexualization of women and reinforces inferiority of women's positions in society.[63] Thus, authognephilia invalidates trans women's gender portraying them as men who are psychopaths. Therefore, Serano writes[64]: "it is hypocritical for any self-identified feminist to resort to these same tactics (via invoking Blanchard's autogynephilia theory) in their attempts to exclude trans* people."

3.2 *Rapid Onset Gender Dysphoria*

The term Rapid Onset Gender Dysphoria known as ROGD was also first used and popularized by anti-trans feminists on the 4thWaveNow website in 2016 aiming to oppose gender affirming care.[65] The term has been recorded to be coined by an American physician Lisa Littman who defines it as "a phenomenon where the development of gender dysphoria is observed to begin suddenly during or after puberty in an adolescent or young adult who would not have met criteria for gender dysphoria in childhood".[66] Moreover, ROGD basically insinuates the idea of a mistaken belief among youngsters who think they are trans*, but they are not really trans*, they are mentally ill persons who are exposed to internet communities and social contagion which also attributes transition due to devaluation of womanhood and sexualization of women's bodies.

The proponents of ROGD believe that medical transition does not benefit young trans* people, it rather harms them because they grow up not to be trans adults.[67] Littman[68] bases her argument on a quantitative survey study of 256 parents claiming ROGD is a result of scientific research. However, trans* scholars and activists question her claim for not being scientific and ethical. Florence Ashley explains that ROGD is a weak and poorly theorized concept or a "scientific sounding language" to mobolise parents of young children who identify as trans*, especially those who were assigned female at birth.[69] Furthermore, Ashley argues that ROGD

---

[62] Serano (2020), p. 774.

[63] Serano (2016, 2020).

[64] Serano (2020), p. 775.

[65] Ashley (2020).

[66] Littman (2018), p. 37.

[67] Ashley (2020).

[68] Littman (2018).

[69] Ashley (2020).

is turned into "a political discourse to prevent gender transition for young people".[70] These beliefs are based on an outdated type of research known as "desistance research" which was used in the 1980s.[71]

Ashley provides a lengthy discussion about the lack of plausibility of the theoretical and empirical grounds of ROGD forwarded by Littman among which she argues that the absence of trans* youth voices themselves rather than their parents in the study is not only unethical but also is biased and ideologically prejudiced.[72] Thus, she writes: "Denying trans people's epistemic agency and credibility is one of the ways in which transantagonistic attitudes are operetionalised".[73] Pathologisation of trans* people is not new. There are decades of history of trans activism and literature around the world against pathologisation, while there is little evidence to indicate gender affirming care is harmful to people. On the contrary, many studies have shown how gender affirming care helps trans* people's quality of life.[74]

3.3 Discussion

Anti-trans* theory of ROGD is used to refer to people who are assigned female at birth and it is supported by those who are against banning conversion therapy. The theory is backed up by homonationlist views which infers ROGD is the result of traumatization of women lesbians in sexist society. Similarly, Autogynephilia is used for people assigned male at birth supported by homonationalist ideas that insinuate men who suffer in heteronormative societies undergo transition.[75]

These theories aim to deny the existence of trans* citizens by subscribing to gender identity being constructed on the basis of biological determination, something that feminists themselves have been questioning for a long time.[76] Heavily invested in identity politics, such theories deny trans* people's existence. Moreover, feminist supporters of these theories contribute to epistemic misrecognition which results in social injustice reflected in policy making and social practices against trans* people. One example is the ban on hormone therapy for young trans* people in many countries including Sweden. As a result, In November 2022, a motion was sent to the Swedish parliament by two middle-aged men from the right-wing political party called Swedish Democrats demanding that GAS must be banned for people under the age of 2524F,[77] arguing that GAS is a form of legal FGM exercised

[70] Ashley (2020), p. 780.

[71] Ashley and Baril (2018).

[72] Ashley (2020).

[73] Ashley (2020), p. 789.

[74] Dhejne et al. (2014); Kahlenberg et al. (2018).

[75] Ashley (2020).

[76] McKenna and Kessler (2006).

[77] https://www.riksdagen.se/sv/dokument-lagar/dokument/motion/_HA02542.

on children and also they use the concept of Rapid Onset Gender Dysphoria in the motion as another reason for banning GAS for youngsters.

The stigmatization, sexualization and pathologisation effects of the concept of autogynephilia make trans women less of a human which results in social exclusion and violence.[78] Moreover, Ashely and Baril explain that theories of autogynephilia and ROGD are another form of strategy to discredit trans* people and oppose their need to gender affirming care.[79] Ashely and Baril further illuminate on the fact that ROGD being based on 'social contagion' follows the old tactic against those who identified as gay, lesbian and bisexuals who were regarded as being mistakenly under influence which wrongs their knowledge and amounts to epistemic injustice and violence against trans* people.[80]

ROGD is also discussed as the result of testimonial injustice which causes epistemological violence.[81] Furthermore, using the lable of Autogynephilia to refer to trans women reinforces epistemic violence, especially when it is advocated by feminists who systematically render trans* women as inferior members of society. Thus, deny them citizenship.

4 The Limits of Identity-Based Recognition in Trans* Citizenship Policy Making

Here, I discuss how the use of two identity-based theoretical concepts of cisgender and transphobia in policy making and practices which aim to combat social injustices have reinforced marginalisation of trans* citizens and inability for legal protection against inequalities and discrimination.

4.1 Cisgender

Feminist biologist and trans* scholar Julia Serano popularized the terms cissexual and cisgender in 2007 in the field of trans* studies. However, Dana Leland Defosse, biologist first used the term cisgender publicly in 1994,[82] and Emi Komoya had already written about cisgender and cissexual in her weblog in 2002.[83] It should be noted that the term cisgender emerged in the context of the US trans* activism via

[78] Serano (2010, 2020).
[79] Ashley and Baril (2018).
[80] Ashley and Baril (2018).
[81] Ashley (2020).
[82] Enke (2012), p. 61.
[83] http://www.eminism.org/interchange/2002/20020607-wmstl.html.

Camp Trans, and thus is usually used by people who transcend normative gender roles/expression.

Cisgender aims to de-centralizes the dominant group exposing it as one possible alternative rather than a norm. Moreover, cisgender has become an identity category and a political act that is not usually been subject to race, ability, nationality, or class analysis. According to Enke,[84] the use of cis "reinforces self-evident and autonomous category" to indicate non-trans identity will continue to negatively affect the marginalization of trans* existence that Enke puts as: "requiring trans to appear through an ever-narrower set of signifiers, cis meanwhile never needs to prove itself".[85] It is not fair that trans* people have to constantly prove themselves as citizens in society while non-trans people do not have to justify their narratives and limits, but using an identity lable like cisgender compromises trans* people's lives, especially those who never come out as trans* after transition. Enke upholds that the dichotomy of cis and trans* is a product of neoliberal politics in which identity categories are constructed to privilege even more the normative.[86] Afterall, cisgender is a product of CampTrans which is part of identity politics-based activism.

I uphold that cisgender reinforces otherness of trans* people as a minority group. It forces people to fit/identify in either of these groups. On the other hand, Serano advocates for the term cisgender arguing that identifying as cis will mark the person with the privilege they regularly experience and are blind to it.[87] I side with Enke who argues: " just when queer and trans theory remind us that gender and sex are made and have no a priori stability (one is not born a woman), cisgender arrives to affirm not only that it is possible for one to stay "a woman" but also that one is "born a woman" after all." Evidently, trans* people need theories and concepts to describe their experiences and perspectives to non-trans persons, but cisgender is not one of them".[88]

4.2 Transphobia

Transphobia is broadly defined as an emotional disgust towards individuals who do not conform to society's gender expectations.[89] It is also understood as a "hostile response to perceived violations of gender norms and/or challenges to the gender binary".[90] Furthermore, transphobia is an explanation for the cause of violence

[84] Enke (2012), p. 67.

[85] Enke (2012), p. 76.

[86] Enke (2012).

[87] Serano (2013a).

[88] Enke (2012), p. 62.

[89] Hill and Willoughby (2005), p. 532.

[90] Bettcher (2014), p. 249.

against trans* people.[91] Thus, transphobia is measured through examining intolerant attitudes towards trans* and gender variant people.[92] The measurements of transphobia are set through examining how people are ridiculed or embarrassed of their trans* identity, or because of gender expression and appearance or being made fun of or being a victim of jokes.[93] Therefore, based on transphobia, the social injustices and inequalities including violence against trans* people are explained as a result of hate motivated acts.

Bettcher upholds transphobia happens in a "cisgenderist broad social contexts where trans people are systematically disadvantaged through anti-trans practices".[94] However, she (ibid.) emphasizes that it does not seem prudent to have a fixed account of transphobia, first because it is manifested differently in different cultures, second because transphobia separates itself from other forms of power relations such as racism, classism, sexism, colonialism etc. that is to say not all trans* people experience violence because of their transness. For example, a trans* woman might be the subject of violence because of sexism, racism and misogyny.[95] Moreover, it is not quite possible to explain the violence or discrimination experienced by trans* people as a form of transphobia when the perpetrators of violence themselves identify as trans*. Serano equals cissexism to transphobia defining it as "how individuals, organizations and governments refuse to respect trans people's lived experience",[96] but I argue that classifying anti-trans positions including feminists as transphobic does not solve the structural and institutional problems trans* people face in society, nor does it validate the existence knowledge and experiences of trans* people. Thus, I maintain that anti-trans theories and practices have institutional and structural roots which should not be reduced to individual fear of trans* people.

I argue that transphobia tackles an individual reaction or psychological response to violence experienced by trans* people rather than problematising the structural constraints facing trans* citizens in everyday life. Therefore, transphobia's focus on identity reduces the existence of trans* citizens to representation, expression and appearance. I also maintain that transphobia is a product of identity politics. It is a negative concept which means fear towards trans* people. It might mean differently in different places, and it might not apply to every trans* person. For example, transphobia invalids a trans woman's identity if she sees herself as a woman, "then the use of transphobia in her case invalids her gender identity".[97] Moreover, it excludes other intersecting elements of analysis like race, class, ethnicity similar to

[91] See Hill (2002); Bettcher (2007); Browne et al. (2011); Turner et al. (2009); Nemoto et al. (2011); Jauk (2013); Markenson Sarah (2014).

[92] Nagoshi et al. (2008).

[93] Jauk (2013), p. 812.

[94] Bettcher (2014), p. 20.

[95] See Serano (2007, 2013b); Namaste (2005).

[96] Serano (2013a), p. 45.

[97] Bettcher (2014), p. 249.

what Enke explains in relation to the concept of cisgender, which lacks intersectional analysis.[98]

4.3 Discussion

The identity-based politics of recognition overlooks the status of trans* people in society as well as their social relations. It also fails to understand the institutionalized and structural subordination of trans* people, because identity politics sees misrecognition as a cultural devaluation, therefore, to overcome injustice it demands representation rooted in discourse instead of problematising socially grounded forces.[99] Thus, The identity-based recognition focuses solely on the rights discourses to express gender identity. It pressures individuals to conform to a group which denies diversity and complexity of people's lives.[100] Social status recognition is important, because access to resources and equal participation in society it is due to recognition of the status of trans* people in society. Furthermore, practices of violence and exclusion are rooted in the work of social institutions which define and regulate relations, interactions and thus make some people normative and some inferior who are consequently denied participation in society.[101]

The focus on identity recognition has created discussions of inclusion and exclusion of trans* people in feminist agendas. Such debates have dismissed active engagement of Western feminism with trans* people in the process of knowledge production and ignores the history of political coalitions between trans* people and feminist groups altogether.[102] It is therefore deemed necessary for more feminist theories to be developed about the status versus identity of trans* citizens in law and society. More research has to be done on the needs versus the rights discourse approach to highlight trans* citizenship which can elaborate on trans* people's participation and redistribution of resources in society.[103] Hines writes: "Narratives of moving beyond a transgender identity are characteristic of 'claims to citizenship'.".[104] In the same vein, I propose focusing on the recognition of trans* people's social status and needs in order to address the structural inequalities including violence experienced by trans* people. Here, I discuss how identity-based theories and practices of cisgender and transphobia are not fully equipped to tackle the problems of denying trans* people's citizenship.

[98] Enke (2012).
[99] Fraser (2000).
[100] Fraser (2000).
[101] Fraser (2000).
[102] Hines (2013, 2014); Bettcher (2007); Martinez (2017); Saeidzadeh and Strid (2020).
[103] Fraser (2000).
[104] Hines (2007), p. 190.

Laws and policies are one of the formal ways of recognizing or denying citizenship, for example, Sofia Aboim shows how legal recognition of gender identity in three countries: the UK, Portugal and Nepal has not only restricted people but also reproduced institutionalized gender binary and homogenization of gender identities.[105] The focus on the construction of identity and, the politics of difference, reinforces 'otherness' of the person, Focusing on the construction of identity and the politics of differences reinforces marginalization, inequality and discrimination.[106] Similarly Van der Rose explains how the Norwegian welfare system has reproduced misrecognition and institutionalisation of cisgendersim through restrictive legal gender recognition.[107] In other words, the state has washed its hands of the responsibilities towards trans* citizens by giving the power to the one and only medical centre in the country to diagnose gender dysphoric for legal gender recognition. Van der Rose draws on affirmative form of recognition as opposed to transformative recognition to explain how the Norwegian state has failed its trans* citizens by institutionalising heteronormative gender binary system. As a result, many trans* people have been denied access to resources including the healthcare, because they have refused to be diagnosed with gender dysphoria.[108]

Despite the legal recognition of gender identity in 38 European countries, trans* people still do not have full citizenship within the EU as EU citizens, especially, "trans people who transition from male to female face more challenges".[109] Although legislations on equality, hate crime and anti-discrimination recognize gender diverse people in many countries, trans* people have limited social and political participation due to high rate of unemployment and being absent in decision making positions.[110] For example, Hungarian Act on Equal Treatment and Promotion of Equal Opportunities recognises gender identity as well as anti-discrimination laws in countries like Croatia, Serbia and Bosnia but,[111] "none of the examined countries provide full legal protection for their trans* citizens". I maintain that the limitation of identity-based recognition has brought minimum changes in realities of trans* people's lives. Identity-based legal and social policies overlook the realities and people's experiences in obtaining diverse identities by going through different processes of individual, institutional, and structural transitioning. Acknowledging gender identity is helpful only when the provisions and needs for acquiring such identities are not denied or neglected. Recognizing identity does not necessarily mean that trans* people with different identities are given social status and are provided access to resources.

---

[105] Aboim (2020).

[106] Aboim (2020).

[107] Van der Ros (2017).

[108] Van der Ros (2017).

[109] Lashyn (2022), p. 213.

[110] Kuhar et al. (2018).

[111] Kuhar et al. (2018), p. 101.

In Serbia, for example, there is no official legal policy for changing legal documents but some people in some institutions have learned the legal loopholes to be able to change legal documents for trans* citizens. In the south part of Serbia, however, institutions reject such applications for receiving diagnosis saying that it is not addressed by law.[112]

In Sweden legislators added gender identity as a ground for prohibition of discrimination in 2008 but continued to force sterilization on trans* people who wished to change legal gender until 2013. In Norway irreversible forced sterlisation was a practice against trans* people who wished to change legal gender until July 2016. As of today, twenty countries in the EU force trans* people into sterilisation before legal change of gender including Finland and Switzerland.The Norwegian anti-discrimination law did not even address the ground of gender identity and gender expression until 2014.[113] Despite legal recognition of trans* identity, both Sweden and Norway as examples of welfare states have failed to recognise the needs and status of their trans* citizens through forcing sterilisation and imposing medical diagnosis as prerequisite to legal change of gender as well as banning of hormone blockers for youth, limiting access to health care.

The life condition of LGBT people is not as comfortable as the other members of society, but trans* people suffer in a more particular way as they are not perceived suited to be citizens because of the way trans* deconstructs the notion of gender and gendered relations, disrupts the traditional institution of marriage and because it engages with medical and legal systems. That's why the anti-gender groups are increasingly targeting trans* people to the extent that policy makers, politicians and a portion of the public do not see it fit to include trans* in the lesbian, gay and bisexual agendas because "they enjoy a certain form of citizenship they did not have before".[114]

I maintain that feminist theories and practices of citizenship on trans* people should foreground status recognition, because emphasising on the status recognition accounts for the existence of a person encompassing all the relations and practices at different levels of individual, institutional, and structural in society. In the identity model of recognition, matters related to realities, social standing and gender relations and practices as well as materiality of needs rather than identity and individual rights are not given room for analysis. Identity-based politics of recognition that tend to see the problem of misrecognition in individual psychology instead of social relations.

---

[112]Kuhar et al. (2018).

[113]Van der Ros (2017).

[114]Kuhar et al. (2018), p. 115.

5 Conclusion: Status-Based Politics of Recognition in Trans* Citizenship

In this chapter I have discussed how trans* citizenship is construed through the recognition of status and needs of trans* people within law and society, rather than recognition of merely individual rights to express identity. In my understanding of trans* citizenship, I have used the concept of status recognition defined by Nancy Fraser who explains misrecognition constitutes violation of justice and thus suggests that the person's status is misrecognised when they are marginalised in everyday life including through the process of policy making.[115] Fraser explains misrecognition is '[t]he process of being negatively recognised and subjected to social subordination', rather than being unappreciated as an identity group or cultural norm.[116]

If people are subordinated in society, it is because their status is misrecognized. Status misrecognition denies parity participation in society through "institutionalised relations of subordination and violation of justice" or "parity impeding norms".[117] In Fraser's view, status is specific to individuals and cannot be universalised. Therefore, trans* citizenship should not be about a set of universal rights. Moreover, misrecognition should not be treated as a "free-standing cultural harm" but as "institutionalized relations of social subordination" Social institutions create parity impeding norms that constitute some people as normative and some as deficient or inferior through formal (legal, administrative, and professional) and informal (customs, traditional, and socio-cultural) practices.[118] Hence, to recognize one's citizenship, the status subordination should be remedied. "Status subordination includes sexual harassment, objectifying, demeaning, violence and disparagement in everyday life".[119] Status subordination can be remedied by providing the person access to resources; redistribution of wealth and allow them to participate in politics at least in decision-making about their own affairs.[120]

Feminist politics is well equipped and best situated in contributing to revitalize theories and practices around trans* citizenship and I think that some groups of feminists' denial of trans* citizens cannot be deemed as idiosyncratic responses, but rather to be tackled as institutionalised and structurally embedded problems. Feminist theories on the existence of trans* citizens and citizenship are crucial as: "citizenship rights affect trans* people's lives; freedom from violence and discrimination, care and reproductive rights",[121] all of which have already been the goals of feminist projects for decades.

[115] Fraser (2000, 2008, 2013).

[116] Fraser (2000), p. 114.

[117] Fraser (2000), p. 113.

[118] Fraser (2000).

[119] Fraser (2013), p. 163.

[120] Fraser (2000, 2008, 2013).

[121] Kuhar et al. (2018), p. 116.

References

Aboim S (2020) Fragmented recognition: gender identity between moral and legal spheres. Soc Polit Int Stud Gend State Soc 29(1):71–93
Ashley F (2020) A critical commentary on 'rapid-onset gender dysphoria'. Soc Rev 68(4):779–799
Ashley F, Baril A (2018) Why 'rapid-onset gender dysphoria'is bad science. The Conversation
Bettcher TM (2007) Evil deceivers and make-believers: on transphobic violence and the politics of illusion. Hypatia 22(3):43–65
Bettcher TM (2014) Trapped in the wrong theory: rethinking trans oppression and resistance. Signs J Women Cult Soc 39(2):383–406
Browne K, Bakshi L, Lim J (2011). It's something you just have to ignore: understanding and addressing contemporary lesbian, gay, bisexual and trans safety beyond hate crime paradigms. J Soc Pol 40(4):739–756
Connell R (2012) Transsexual women and feminist thought: toward new understanding and new politics. Signs J Women Cult Soc 37(4):857–881
Currah P, Juang RM, Minter S (eds) (2006) Transgender rights. University of Minnesota Press
Daly M (1978) Gyn/ecology: The metaethics of radical feminism. Beacon Press
Dhejne C, Öberg K, Arver S, Landén M (2014) An analysis of all applications for sex reassignment surgery in Sweden, 1960–2010: prevalence, incidence, and regrets. Arch Sex Behav 43(8): 1535–1545
Enke F (ed) (2012) Transfeminist perspectives in and beyond transgender and gender studies. Temple University Press
Evans D (1993) Sexual citizenship: the material construction of sexualities. Routledge
Fraser N (2000) Rethinking recognition. New Left Rev 1(3):107–120
Fraser N (2008) Abnormal justice. Crit Inq 34(3):393–422
Fraser N (2013) Fortunes of feminism: from state-managed capitalism to neoliberal crisis. Verso Books
Hearn J, Oleksy EH, Golańska D (2010). Introduction: The lmits of gendered citizenship: Jeff Hearn, Elżbieta H. Oleksy, and Dorota Golańska. In The Limits of Gendered Citizenship (pp. 12–35). Routledge.
Hill DB (2002) Genderism, transphobia, and gender bashing: a framework for interpreting anti-transgender violence. Underst Dealing Violence Multicult Approach 4:113–137
Hill DB, Willoughby BL (2005) The development and validation of the genderism and transphobia scale. Sex Roles 53
Hines S (2006) Intimate transitions: transgender practices of partnering and parenting. Sociology 40(2):353–371
Hines S (2007) (Trans) forming gender: social change and transgender citizenship. Sociol Res Online 12(1):181–194
Hines S (2009) A pathway to diversity?: human rights, citizenship and the politics of transgender. Contemp Polit 15(1):87–102
Hines S (2010) Recognising diversity? The gender recognition act and transgender citizenship. In: Hines S, Sanger T (eds) Transgender identities. Routledge, pp 101–119
Hines S (2013) Gender diversity, recognition and citizenship: towards a politics of difference. Springer
Hines S (2014) "I am a Feminist But. . .": transgender men and women and feminism. In: Reger J (ed) Different wavelengths. Routledge, pp 57–80
Jauk D (2013) Gender violence revisited: lessons from violent victimization of transgender identified individuals. Sexualities 16(7):807–825
Kahlenberg CA, Nwachukwu BU, McLawhorn AS, Cross MB, Cornell CN, Padgett DE (2018) Patient satisfaction after total knee replacement: a systematic review. HSS J 14(2):192–201
Kuhar R, Monro S, Takács J (2018) Trans* citizenship in post-socialist societies. Crit Soc Policy 38(1):99–120

Lashyn S (2022) Transgender EU citizens and the limited form of union citizenship available to them. Feminist Legal Stud 30(2):201–218
Lister R (1997) Citizenship: towards a feminist synthesis. Feminist Rev 57(1):28–48
Lister R (2017) Citizenship: feminist perspectives. Bloomsbury Publishing
Lister R, Williams F, Anttonen A et al (2007a) Gendering citizenship in Western Europe: new challenges for citizenship research in a cross-national context. Policy Press
Lister R, Williams F, Anttonen A et al (2007b) Vocabularies of citizenship since the 1970s. In: Lister R, Williams F, Anttonen A et al (eds) . Policy Press, Gendering citizenship in Western Europe, pp 47–74
Littman L (2018) Rapid-onset gender Dysphoria in adolescents and young adults: a study of parental reports. PLoS One 13(8)
Lombardo E, Verloo M (2010) Towards feminist citizenship: contentious practices and European challenges. In: Oleksy EH, Hearn J (eds) The limits of gendered citizenship. Routledge, pp 42–61
Markenson Sarah B (2014) What is a hate crime? Fighting bias and violence against transgender individuals. Int Law News 43(4):16
Marshall TH (2013) Citizenship and social class, 1950. In: Lazar S (ed) The anthropology of citizenship: a reader. Wiley Blackwell, Malden, pp 52–61
Martínez J (2017) Beyond Diversity Ventriloquism: How Mujer T Is Transing Inclusion in Bogotá. Hypatia, 32(3):679–695
McKenna W, Kessler S (2006) Blurring the boundaries of gender. In: Davis K, Evans M, Lorber J (eds) Handbook of gender and Women's studies. Sage Publications, p 342
Monro S (2000) Theorizing transgender diversity: towards a social model of health. Sex Relatsh Ther 15(1):33–45
Monro S (2003) Transgender politics in the UK. Crit Soc Policy 23(4):433–452
Monro S (2010) Introducing transgender citizenship. In: Oleksy EH, Hearn J, Golańska D (eds) The limits of gendered citizenship: contexts and complexities. Routledge
Monro S, Richardson D (2014) Citizenship, gender and sexuality. In: van der Heijden H-A (ed) Handbook of political citizenship and social movements. Edward Elgar Publishing, pp 60–85
Monro S, Van Der Ros J (2018) Trans* and gender variant citizenship and the state in Norway. Crit Soc Policy 38(1):57–78
Monro S, Warren L (2004) Transgendering citizenship. Sexualities 7(3):345–362
Morgan R (1977) Going too far: the personal chronicle of a feminist. Random House, New York
Moser C (2009) Autogynephilia in women. J Homosex 56(5):539–547
Nagoshi JL, Adams KA, Terrell HK, Hill ED, Brzuzy S, Nagoshi CT (2008) Gender differences in correlates of homophobia and transphobia. Sex Roles 59(7–8):521
Namaste V (2005) Sex change. Soc Change Reflect Identity Inst Imperialism:11–32
Nemoto T, Bödeker B, Iwamoto M (2011) Social support, exposure to violence and transphobia, and correlates of depression among male-to-female transgender women with a history of sex work. Am J Public Health 101(10):1980–1988
Platero RL (2020) Redistribution and recognition in Spanish transgender laws. Polit Gov 8(3): 253–265
Predelli LN, Halsaa B, Thun C (2012) 'Citizenship is not a word I use': how women's movement activists understand citizenship. In: Roseneil S, Halsaa B, Sümer S (eds) Remaking citizenship in multicultural Europe: Women's movements, gender and diversity. Palgrave Macmillan, London, pp 188–212
Raymond JG (1979) The transsexual empire: making of the she-male. Teachers College Press, New York
Richardson D (2000) Constructing sexual citizenship: theorizing sexual rights. Crit Soc Policy 20(1):105–135
Roseneil S (2013) Beyond citizenship? Feminism and the transformation of belonging. Palgrave Macmillan UK, pp 1–20

Roseneil S, Halsaa B, Sümer S (2012) Remaking citizenship in multicultural Europe: Women's movements, gender and diversity. Palgrave Macmillan UK, pp 1–20
Roseneil S, Crowhurst I, Santos AC, Stoilova M (2013) Reproduction and citizenship/reproducing citizens: editorial introduction. Citizsh Stud 17(8):901–911
Saeidzadeh Z, Strid S (2020) Trans* politics and the feminist project: revisiting the politics of recognition to resolve impasses. Polit Gov 8(3):312–320
Serano J (2007) Whipping girl: A transsexual woman on sexism and the scapegoating of femininity. Seal Press: Berkeley
Serano J (2013a) Excluded: making feminist and queer movements more inclusive. Seal Press
Serano J (2013b) Outspoken: a decade of transgender activism and trans feminism. Switch Hitter Press, pp 151–155
Serano J (2016) Reconceptualizing 'autogynephilia'as female/feminine embodiment fantasies
Serano J (2020) Autogynephilia: a scientific review, feminist analysis, and alternative 'embodiment fantasies' model. Soc Rev 68(4):763–778
Serano JM (2010) The case against Autogynephilia. Int J Transgend 12(3):176–187
Strasser S (2012) Rethinking citizenship in multicultural Europe: critical encounters with feminist, multicultural and transnational citizenship. In: Roseneil S, Halsaa B, Sümer S (eds) Remaking citizenship in multicultural Europe: Women's movements, gender and diversity. Palgrave Macmillan UK, London, pp 21–40
Turner L, Whittle S, Combs R (2009) Transphobic hate crime in the European Union. Press for Change, London
Van der Ros J (2017) The Norwegian state and transgender citizens: a complicated relationship. World Polit Sci 13(1):123–150
Volpp L (2007) The culture of citizenship. Theor Inq Law 8(2):571–602
Volpp L (2017) Feminist, sexual, and queer citizenship. In: Shachar A, Bauboeck R, Bloemraad I, Vink M (eds) The Oxford handbook of citizenship. Oxford University Press, pp 153–177
Walby S (1994) Is citizenship gendered? Sociology 28(2):379–395

Zara Saeidzadeh is a researcher in Gender Studies at Örebro University in Sweden, where she also completed her PhD. Zara holds an MA in Sociology of Law from Lund University, Sweden and has earned her LLM in International Human Rights Law from the School of Oriental and African Studies (SOAS) in the UK. For the past decade, Zara has been conducting research on socio-legal recognition of trans* people. In her current research project, she carries out an empirical study to examine the social and legal recognition of trans* women in Sweden through the lenses of epistemic recognition and trans* citizenship.

Reassessing the Notion of Vulnerability: The Feminist Debate

Fabio Macioce

Contents

Abstract The issue of vulnerability has gained particular relevance within the feminist debate: first, it has been analyzed by scholars of legal and political feminism, to propose new anthropologies or political and legal approaches mindful of the link between privilege and gender oppression. Second, it has been developed specifically in relation to the status of women and the issue of gender-based violence. In this latter perspective, the concept of vulnerability has been harshly criticized, because it has been considered by many to be an expression of unjustified essentialism, and likely to favour or reinforce exclusion and victimhood. The aim of this essay is to show how a reassessment of the notion of vulnerability, and group vulnerability in particular, can be theoretically coherent and sound as well as politically positive, that is, productive of politically useful and relevant forms of collective agency. The collective dimension of vulnerability can be a prerequisite for challenging dominant structures of power, opening new arenas of discourse, proposing different narratives, and aggregating otherwise marginalized interests and needs.

F. Macioce (✉)
LUMSA University, School of Law, Rome, Italy
e-mail: f.macioce@lumsa.it

N. Lacey et al. (eds.), *Reassessing Feminist Legal Theories*, Gender Perspectives in Law 5, https://doi.org/10.1007/978-3-031-75423-4_9

1 Introduction

The notion of vulnerability has progressively gained relevance in philosophical debates, in the language of the social sciences, as well as in international legal instruments, guidelines and policies. However, vulnerability is, in itself, a polysemic concept, which is often used to designate categories of persons or individuals either based on their assumed physical fragility, their reduced autonomy, or their presumed inability to express free consent. At the same time, this concept is used to identify situations of different exposure to risk due to economic, environmental, social, and legal factors, in a process of accumulation of "social handicaps".[1]

The fact that the concept of vulnerability is polysemic, however, does not mean that it is useless, legally or philosophically.[2] On the contrary, vulnerability is a "heuristic device"[3]: the ambiguity and broad applicability of the concept allow it to be used to construct critical perspectives in the legal or political sphere, to raise new questions and elaborate new solutions to social and political challenges.

For example, if we look at its possible legal applications, this concept can be used to justify preventive interventions, additional burdens of proof, and enhanced forms of protection for specific assets (e.g., territories, artistic heritage...) or rights. To be more precise, group vulnerability has been used by Courts and International Bodies to both justify the recognition of specific rights and activate forms of protection based on other grounds. In this last perspective—for instance, in the case-law of the ECHR—the particular vulnerability of certain groups has been used to justify the application of a stronger interpretative mechanism concerning the need for specific forms of protection by public institutions. This has been done by determining a stricter standard for the definition of inhuman or degrading treatment, by widening or facilitating the admissibility of individual complaints, or by reducing the margin of appreciation of the States.[4]

Similarly, the concept of vulnerability has a strong critical value from a political point of view, as it can be used to challenge discriminatory policies and practices. Focusing on groups, rather than on single individuals, it allows conditions of vulnerability to come out that would otherwise not be perceived, as well as the emergence of counterpublics crucial to the claiming of rights and guarantees. Vulnerable groups can unmask power differences and systemic oppression operating in the society, and open alternative opportunities for discussion, which are usually silenced.[5] In this sense, vulnerable groups can influence the context of oppression and privilege, being able to orient the debate and propose different narratives, formulating different or alternative points of view. Additionally, the presence of

---

[1] Ferrarese (2016), p. 151.

[2] Casadei (2015), p. 75.

[3] Fineman (2008), p. 9.

[4] Peroni and Timmer (2013); Ippolito and Iglesias Sanchez (2015).

[5] Fraser (1990).

groups in the public arena allows the level of collective needs to emerge from the level of individual interests, thereby guaranteeing a fairer distribution of resources.

The issue of vulnerability has gained particular relevance within the feminist debate, both in the sense that it has been developed and analyzed precisely through the reflection of many feminist scholars, and because the question concerning women's vulnerability has been specifically discussed within this debate. More precisely, on the one hand, the question of vulnerability has been raised patently within the analyses of legal and political feminism, even to propose new anthropologies or political and legal approaches mindful of the link between privilege and gender oppression. On the other hand, the issue of vulnerability has been developed specifically in relation to the status of women and the issue of gender-based violence. In this latter perspective, the concept of vulnerability has been used from a perspective of empowerment, and collective agency, but it has also been criticized on the theoretical and political level: on the theoretical level, because it has been considered by many to be an expression of unjustified essentialism, and on the political level, since it is likely to favour or reinforce exclusion and victimhood.

The aim of this essay, therefore, is to show how a reassessment of the notion of vulnerability, and group vulnerability in particular, can be theoretically coherent and sound as well as politically positive, that is, productive of politically useful and relevant forms of collective agency.

2 The Notion of Vulnerability, within the Feminist Debate

The analyses concerning vulnerability, and principally those discussions which to a greater or lesser extent explicitly trace back to feminist thought, have touched on several aspects. First of all, the dialectic with the liberal paradigm of the autonomous, independent, rational, and productive subject must be mentioned.[6] In particular, the reflections elaborated by feminist scholars have highlighted how the liberal conception can neither adequately take into consideration the condition of constitutive dependence of the human being, nor the relational and progressive character of the construction of the self.[7] It is certainly true that the "liberal paradigm" is far from being homogeneous, and criticisms of this model are not common to any feminist perspectives.[8] And yet within liberalism, as a family of theories, the intuition of the fundamental equality (in terms of dignity) of every human being, regardless of their status and role in society, arises directly from their capacity to elaborate life plans and choices in accordance with one's subjective values and goals.[9]

[6] Kittay (1997); Fineman (2004); Fineman and Grear (2013).

[7] Dodds (2014), p. 181.

[8] Nussbaum (1997), p. 5.

[9] Nussbaum (1997), p. 4.

Criticism of the liberal model, therefore, focused on such a conception of the person as fully autonomous, self-determining, and independent. Not only has the excessive individualism of such a view been pointed out[10] but feminist scholars[11] highlighted that the premise of such independence is the (unpaid) care labour performed by women: therefore, such a perfectly independent (or rather: falsely independent) subject is essentially a male, whose independence is won at the expense of that of women.[12] Again, the liberal ideal of justice has been deemed as excessively formal, and therefore inadequate to manage and modify systemic injustices that depend on mechanisms of power and culture.[13] Finally, this model has been criticized as generally hyper-rationalistic: it tends to devalue the significance of emotions and caring tasks in public life, thus contributing to placing the question of vulnerability in the private sphere.[14] The idea—especially in the so-called feminism of difference and in critical theories—is that the liberal model has taken a disembodied subject as its reference: therefore, it is unable to appreciate relationships of care, as well as the constitutive dependence of the human being, and it is more generally blind to the relational character of human existence, arising from patriarchal premises that allow these aspects not to be considered,[15] insofar as it confines them to the private sphere and delegates them (in a logic of exploitation) to the unpaid labor of women.[16]

A second thematic horizon led to a positive interpretation of vulnerability, precisely in opposition to this dominant liberal anthropology and the social models consistent with it. From this perspective, many feminist scholars emphasized the positive value of notions such as those of dependence, care, relationality, and need, which the liberal model had instead qualified in a purely negative sense.[17] Therefore, they proposed a different, more complex image of the subject, where the recognition of vulnerability can deconstruct the distinction between autonomous and non-autonomous subjects.[18] Interpreting vulnerability beyond the distinction between autonomy and dependence, and in a way that is not exclusively negative, justifies a political shift: the passage from institutions conceived to maximise freedom and competition between autonomous and rational subjects—the *myth of autonomy*, according to Fineman,[19] to a responsive state, in which the intervention of the state is primarily oriented towards guaranteeing substantial equality between

[10] Sandel (1981); Kymlicka (1989).

[11] MacKinnon (1987); Abbey (2014).

[12] Okin (1989), p. 138–39.

[13] Young (1990), p. 114.

[14] Jaggar (1989); Lloyd (1993).

[15] Tronto (1993).

[16] Gilligan (1982); Pateman (1988).

[17] Kittay (1997), pp. 219ff; Fineman (2004); Fineman and Grear (2013).

[18] Fineman (2008), p. 11.

[19] Fineman (2004), pp. XIII–XXIV.

people, understood as being intrinsically and inevitably bound by relationships of dependence.[20]

A third question raised by many scholars concerned the universal or particular character of vulnerability. The dialectic with the liberal paradigm has led some scholars to highlight the constitutive dependence of human beings, understanding vulnerability as an ontological, and therefore universal, trait. Conversely, the idea of a constitutive and universal vulnerability has been paired with reflections on specific, contextual, and individual forms of vulnerability. Indeed, many feminist scholars have pointed out that while all human beings are vulnerable, not all are vulnerable in the same way: vulnerability varies in intensity, characteristics, and extent, due to the power structures and systemic inequalities that characterize our societies, regarding gender, race, class, physical conditions, etc.

From the first perspective, Martha A. Fineman argues that the abstract autonomous subject of Western metaphysics does not reflect the human condition, which is instead marked by a universal vulnerability. The self-sufficient, rational, independent, adult and archetypically masculine subject, which constitutes the protagonist of all modern political thought, understands individual freedom and personal responsibility as fundamental legal and political ideals.[21] At the same time, this model devalues vulnerability, dependence, and embodiment, and excludes them from the development of public policies, legal doctrines, and legal practices. Therefore, Fineman proposes a new conception of the political subject, organized around the recognition of vulnerability as a "primal human condition," and not linked to a condition of passivity, femininity, or need. Vulnerability, according to Fineman, is a condition that is universal, constant, complex, and particular. It is universal in the sense that it is a condition shared and inevitably experienced by the totality of human subjects. It is constant because human dependence is not a contingent condition, but accounts for the legal and political institutions, social relations, and material infrastructure present in human societies. It is then a complex characteristic because it manifests itself in a plurality of conditions and modes throughout a person's life, and it is particular because physical, mental, and intellectual characteristics are not socially neutral, and "historical reaction to some human variations, particularly race and gender, has led to the creation of hierarchies, discrimination and even violence".[22]

From the second perspective, others emphatically stressed the particularity of vulnerability, and highlighted the weight that gender, class, and race factors (among others) can play in determining a person's specific condition of vulnerability. Judith Butler, with a dichotomy intentionally aimed at avoiding the use of the concept of vulnerability for its victimizing repercussions, introduces the difference between precariousness and precarity, precisely to distinguish between ontological vulnerability, and that produced by (or consequent to) a differential distribution of resources

[20] Fineman (2010).

[21] Fineman (2020), p. 54.

[22] Fineman (2013), p. 637.

and capabilities.[23] Thus, while precariousness qualifies that vulnerability that all human beings share because of their bodily condition, namely finitude and limitation, exposure to need and suffering,[24] precarity depends on and is modulated by the social, political, economic and relational forms that qualify our lives. For Butler, precariousness and precarity are, in effect, two sides of the same coin. Existential vulnerability is in fact experienced, by each individual, within social, political, and economic structures that shape its intensity and draw its boundaries. From the biopolitical logic of contemporary power, the removal of the condition of vulnerability (as precariousness) for some subjects is the premise for a differential distribution of vulnerability (as precarity), such that some are rendered vulnerable, and qualified as fragile, exposed, dependent, etc. Vulnerability, in short, must be thought of within the horizon of power.[25]

In a similar vein, other scholars further specify the distinction between precariousness and precarity by distinguishing existential vulnerability, situational (or context-specific) vulnerability, and conditional (or pathogenic) vulnerability.[26] In the first group, one can place conditions of vulnerability that depend on the existential characteristics of the subject, and his or her living conditions: these conditions, while not necessarily expressive of vulnerability may become so under certain circumstances and range from dispositional or occurrent vulnerability.[27] The second group concerns those conditions of vulnerability that are caused or aggravated by environmental, political, social, economic, and other factors. These factors may be interrelated with those that are "existential", but they depend first and foremost on the context and the specific situation in which the subject finds himself/herself, although the effects of such vulnerability may vary greatly in intensity depending on the subjective resources, and the degree of resilience of people in that given context.[28]

Finally, some scholars introduced the notion of pathogenic vulnerability, when the vulnerability is the outcome of a situation marked by an imbalance of power, or by forms of oppression and discrimination, or by economic need, or even by the actual functioning of systems and institutions geared (at least in theory) toward reducing vulnerability.[29] This third category of vulnerability is certainly shared by different individuals and groups, but it is useful for understanding the embodied experience of domestic and sexual violence, including the significance of psychological, as well as physical, wounds and injuries. A large part of feminist thinking on vulnerability has focused on the violence/vulnerability conceptual pair, highlighting the social structures and gendered discourses through which violence can be made

---

[23] Butler (2006, 2016).

[24] Cavarero (2007).

[25] Butler (2006), p. 44.

[26] Rogers et al. (2012), pp. 11–38; MacKenzie et al. (2014), pp. 7–9.

[27] MacKenzie et al. (2014), p. 8.

[28] MacKenzie et al. (2014), p. 8.

[29] MacKenzie et al. (2014), p. 9.

meaningful and legitimate, thereby inspiring phenomenological work on violence and the vulnerable feminized subject. Feminist phenomenologies of violence have analyzed the experience of vulnerability highlighting how violence can be politically and legally justified, rendered invisible, neutralized, unrepresented, and denied.[30]

3 Essentialist and Anti-Essentialist Approaches to Vulnerability

Among the many issues raised by the concept of vulnerability, some are particularly relevant when discussed from a feminist perspective. The most general question relates to the theoretical possibility of using a group perspective without falling into an essentialist fallacy: can women, in other words, be considered a group? And more specifically: can they be considered a vulnerable group?[31] A second question relates to the political consequences of this notion: assuming that women can be considered—somehow—a vulnerable group, is this a politically useful outcome, or does it produce negative consequences?

For some scholars, vulnerability itself is a troubling concept when it is understood from a gendered perspective, since it conveys ideas of dependence, weakness and victimhood.[32] As Judith Butler, Zeynep Gambetti, and Leticia Sabsay argue, "there is always something both risky and true in claiming that women or other socially disadvantaged groups are especially vulnerable"[33] because this can reinforce paternalist outcomes and deprive people of agency. Additionally, any approach focused on groups risks being essentialist: it risks taking certain characteristics of a specific object as necessary (in the sense of non-contingent) properties of that object, such as to explain its functioning, behaviour, manifestations, as well as to represent an element of its identity.[34] To say, for example, that women are vulnerable because they are victims of violence, discrimination and/or marginalisation, would be like saying that such a condition is a necessary characteristic, which explains practices, claims, experiences, narratives, and which in a certain way identifies the subjects that belong to this group, distinguishing them from the *others*, i.e. from all those who do not belong to the group. As has been correctly noted, "the most pernicious effect of the segmenting of a general population so that only some are designated as vulnerable ... is that such segmentation suggests that the rest of us are not vulnerable".[35]

Constructing categories of individuals and groups identified in terms of a certain characteristic or condition of vulnerability often functions as a barrier, which can

[30] Frazer and Hutchings (2017), pp. 690 ff.

[31] Witt (1995), pp. 321–344.

[32] Chouliaraki (2013); Knudsen and Stage (2017).

[33] Butler et al. (2016), p. 2.

[34] Stone (2004).

[35] Fineman (2012), p. 1751.

consolidate processes of marginalization. The members of a vulnerable group, precisely because, as subjects, they are less able than necessary, less rational, less capable of defending themselves, less competent, are accorded less autonomy and reduced agency, regardless of an assessment of subjective competence.[36] In other words, group vulnerability is likely to function as a device of "disempowerment", producing induced vulnerability, especially when group identification disregards a context analysis but occurs in general and abstract terms.[37]

It is no accident, therefore, that many feminist, queer, and critical race studies scholars have turned to other concepts instead of vulnerability. Butler herself, for example, has used the concepts of precarity and precariousness, rather than vulnerability: in Butler's words, "vulnerability cannot be the basis of group identification without strengthening paternalistic power".[38] In the same vein, others have pointed out the risk that the concept of vulnerability may lead to a "labeling approach", being likely to obscure the specific needs of individuals in a given context,[39] becoming a source of stereotyping and discrimination.

From a different perspective, others argue that the concept of vulnerability—even when referred to women—should be preserved and used. Alyson Cole, for example, criticized the attempt to redefine vulnerability in contrast to victimization, because if victims are not seen as such, this may justify policies that do not prioritize changing injustices. Above all, denying relevance to vulnerability can "unwittingly dilute perceptions of inequality and muddle important distinctions among particular vulnerabilities, as well as differences between those who are injurable and those who are already injured."[40]

Even more explicitly, Young emphasizes that conceptualizing certain forms of vulnerability (or oppression) as referring to a group of people is necessary to both make evident, and unhinge, the operation of power systems that are at the origin of such oppression, and that would otherwise be difficult to perceive. To conceptualize women as a collective allows us to go beyond liberal individualism, which considers oppressive any categorization from elements such as race, gender, class, citizenship, and religion. As Young writes, "this individualist ideology, however, in fact obscures oppression. Without conceptualizing women as a group in some sense, it is not possible to conceptualize oppression as a systematic, structured, institutional process".[41] Oppressive mechanisms and structures do not simply affect multiple women at the same time but affect women *as such* within the existing system of power. It is only when a group perspective is taken that the power mechanisms and systemic prejudices that every woman experiences, as such, become perceptible.

---

[36] Brubaker (2006).

[37] Morondo Taramundi (2018), pp. 188–189.

[38] Butler (2016), p. 25.

[39] Hurst (2008), p. 191; Luna (2009), pp. 121 ff.

[40] Cole (2016), p. 262.

[41] Young (1994), p. 718.

This raises the challenging question of how to hold together the necessary group perspective, on the one hand, and the rejection of an essentialist and reductionist approach, on the other. More specifically: how can vulnerability be interpreted, in the light of the experience of groups, avoiding at the same time employing an essentialist reading? Two approaches are possible, and both can be not only theoretically convincing but also politically useful.

In a first sense, it is possible to consider women as a group from a "positional" perspective, that is, considering their vulnerability as dependent on a similar positioning within a specific risk context. Such positioning does not convey any identity trait but is the result of a common condition of vulnerability with respect to the presence of specific factors. It is a social collective without common attributes, a "seriality", a group where individuals are included in the "series" only as long as common risk factors persist.[42]

It is also possible to use the notion of group, with reference to women, in a stronger sense. It is possible to speak of vulnerable groups when vulnerability mainly depends on systemic forms of violence or oppression, directed toward specific persons *as* members of a group. The group dimension, in this sense, is at least to some extent identity-based: it is the systemic oppression perpetrated against a group that creates a form of group identity, even if the group exists as such only in the eyes of others, and it is perceived externally as something homogeneous and internally consistent. At the same time, this common experience of oppression is at the origin of common practices of contestation or resistance activated not as individuals, but as groups.[43] The historical experience of feminism, in this respect, is illuminating; women began to act and enter the public scene as a group in order to bring about a change in the basic ideology of human society.[44]

From this perspective, it is not necessary to qualify women as a group on an essential level, that is, assuming that there is, somewhere, a common essence, or characteristic that can ground and determine female identity. It is sufficient to admit, on the one hand, that women are exposed to the systemic phenomena of oppression, which may vary in intensity according to individual characteristics (of race, orientation, class, etc.) but are nonetheless present for all. On the other, this common dimension is necessary for understanding social phenomena and their occurrence in certain ways: for instance, we cannot understand femicide rates and the characteristics of such phenomena without taking gender oppression into account.[45]

With a small but interesting example, Cudd admits this necessity in order to explain otherwise incomprehensible social practices: the social practice that required men to open the door for women is not comprehensible in its asymmetrical and incapacitating bearing if placed at the merely individual level (at this level, it is indistinguishable from politeness or courtesy), but becomes revealing of an

[42] Young (1994), p. 728. Woodly (2015), p. 221.

[43] Calhoun (1991); Cerulo (1997), pp. 385 ff.; Wall (2000).

[44] Cavarero and Restaino (2002), p. 159.

[45] Taylor and Jasinski (2011), pp. 341 ff.

asymmetry of power and role if understood at the group level.[46] Similarly, the vulnerability of women in clinical trials depends not only on the condition in which each individual, at any given point in her life, finds herself, but also on the fact that the clinical and pharmacological research system structurally tends to under-represent women[47] for multiple reasons, including (1) the consideration of males, often of Caucasian race, as the "normal" study population; (2) the assumption of a "male point of view" in the conduct of the study, and thus, for example, in the formulation of informed consent models (3) the idea that physiological differences are a negligible factor in drug response; (4) the idea that women are more complex and more costly subjects because of changing hormone levels; and (5) the risks associated with the effects of drugs on fetal development, risks that led first to the exclusion of pregnant women from the trial, and then to the limited inclusion in general of women of childbearing age, especially in the early stages of research. Such a context produces an increased exposure to risks—ranging from a higher incidence of adverse drug reactions, to a risk of overmedication related to dosages not calibrated to the female body, to the use of informed consent models designed for the so-called universal-neutral-male individual,[48] and to worse—that has nothing to do with the characteristics of the single individual woman, but becomes perceptible when a group perspective is taken.

4 Reassessing Group Vulnerability as a Politically Positive Notion

It is difficult to translate the notion of vulnerability into a political concept, moving it from the realms of philosophy and anthropology to that of political agency.[49]

The consideration of socio-political factors that shape human vulnerability is not sufficient to make the question of vulnerability a political issue. According to Rancière,[50] in order to move to a political level, vulnerable people must prove capable of sustaining claims on the public scene, of demanding power and a different distribution of power itself, of articulating dissent, and of being alternative to the existing power structure. As many experiences within the horizon of feminism show, the analyses must be accompanied by an uprising, for there to be a real change in the existing structures of power.

On the one hand, vulnerable groups shed the light on power systems that are at the origin of their conditions of vulnerability, and that would otherwise be difficult to

---

[46] Cudd (2006), p. 47.

[47] Zucker and Prendergast (2020); Khan et al. (2020).

[48] H2020, *Improving the guidelines for Informed Consent, including vulnerable populations, under a gender perspective* (i-CONSENT), at https://i-consentproject.eu/it/.

[49] Cole (2016), p. 272; Ferrarese (2016), p. 156.

[50] Rancière (2006), p. 6.

perceive. In Young's words, the discourse of liberal individualism denies the reality of groups and obscures oppression.[51] In this vein, the exclusion of a single woman from a clinical trial, or a member of an ethnic minority, could be either justified due to individual factors or unfairly discriminating if motivated by prejudice or other non-legitimate reasons. However, when a group perspective is assumed (and it is made clear that this exclusion affects women as such, and not only some of them) power mechanisms and systemic prejudices that every woman experiences become perceptible: for instance, being induced to take drugs which are tested mainly, if not exclusively, on men.

On the other hand, focusing on groups makes it possible to recognise them as political actors, which cannot be done simply through the interpretation of their vulnerability as situational or pathogenic. Vulnerable groups can be understood as political actors,[52] as opportunities for resistance and dissent, as well as voices that cannot be silenced within the public debate. In other words, the group vulnerability allows for the occupation of public space, gives social exposure, and allows the level of collective needs to emerge from the level of individual interests, thereby fostering processes of inclusion for marginalised people.

In other words, focusing on groups highlights that the vulnerability experienced by each individual is not reducible to a merely private matter and that the object of claims, as well as the aim of the political action, is in itself a meta-individual element. What is not fully grasped by theories on situational vulnerability, is the fact that groups can forge new political subjectivities, as well as new forms of participation in public life, being the vulnerability a shared condition that influences relations between human beings. As Young correctly writes, the democratic discussion is "a process in which differentiated social groups should attend to the particular situation of others and be willing to work out just solutions to their conflicts and collective problems from across their situated positions".[53] Therefore, focusing on the condition of single individuals not only overshadows our opportunities to understand the systemic dimension of their vulnerability but makes it also difficult for people to perceive themselves as connected by structures that are beyond their will. Even if relational understandings of vulnerability (where the system of social, political and institutional relations is correctly taken into consideration) makes intelligible the significance of such relations for the experience and opportunities of any vulnerable person, the consideration of groups highlights the conditions that create the possibility for people to collectively make claims.[54] While relational theories and consideration of situational vulnerability correctly conceptualize the impersonal and systematic forces that affect individual lives, the recognition of groups fosters people's mobilization for change and redress of their conditions.

[51] Young (1994), p. 718.
[52] Cixous (1975).
[53] Young (2000), p. 7.
[54] Woodly (2015), p. 214.

Talking about women as a vulnerable group is not only possible on a theoretical level, but also politically important. The #MeToo campaign, or movements such as Ni Una Menos, are examples of how the public articulation of experiences of wounding, trauma, and violence can become a powerful global movement, a site of political agency. A sum of individual voices, sharing a vulnerability in the two senses just indicated, can give rise to a feminist movement for emancipation, justice and change.[55]

Thus, while it is true that feminist, queer, and anti-racist debates have blamed some of these movements (#MeToo, for example) for exposure to the risk of whitewashing and the exclusion of trans and queer identities, and the prevailing focus on the experience of cisgender (and affluent) women, it is also true, on the other hand, that it has favoured demands for visibility and struggles for recognition, occupying public space and making heard otherwise inaudible voices.

Even more strikingly, NUM's intersectional and cross-cutting approach has led to public affirmation of a different notion of vulnerability, no longer linked to unqualified femininity (and referred to as weak, passive), but highlighting more properly the differential distribution of precarity, a "politically induced condition that makes some lives more vulnerable than others".[56] The NUM movement does not have merely punitive aims but proposes a different narrative of violence and vulnerability, in which gender and sexual violence are linked to patriarchal structures and the state, issues of social inequality and justice, and transnational dynamics.

NUM's charter bears the following statement: "Nosotras no nos reconocemos como víctimas—hayamos o no sido victimizadas—ni nos dirigimos a otras mujeres, incluso las que sufren o sufrieron violencia, como víctimas, sino como sujetas de creación, potencia de hacer, voluntad de transformación (...) El punitivismo y el manodurismo, por otra parte, son usados contra nuestro legítimo derecho a la protesta social. Decimos: no en nuestro nombre".[57]

As a group, then, individuals who experience conditions of vulnerability can enter public space, deconstructing the illusion that it is a regulated and neutral arena in which anyone can discuss issues of public importance. On the contrary, these groups can enter this space as alternative publics, changing conceptualization of the process of public debate, its rules, and spaces. Above all, they can subvert it, proposing new themes and new modes of discourse, new perspectives and new points of view that would otherwise be excluded from it.[58]

In this context, vulnerable groups—that is, groups that from their condition of vulnerability challenge dominant structures of power and discourse—are afforded the opportunity to open new arenas of discourse, propose different narratives, and aggregate otherwise marginalized interests and needs.[59] In doing so, they perform a

---

[55] Koivunen et al. (2018), p. 1.

[56] Nijensohn (2018), p. 9; Nijensohn (2022).

[57] Ni Una Menos, Carta Orgànica, at: https://niunamenos.org.ar/quienes-somos/carta-organica/.

[58] Fraser (1990), p. 66.

[59] Young (2000), p. 167.

powerful emancipatory action: on the one hand, they enable people to share their experiences, and thus show that these experiences are not related to contingent and individual circumstances but to the functioning of social systems. On the other hand, they operate as sounding boards for demands for recognition, opening up spaces for political action and arenas for discussion, helping to orient the political agenda for the benefit of individuals, and beyond their individual possibilities.[60]

Once placed into the focus of ethical, juridical, and political reflection the notion of vulnerability becomes inevitably, and fully, political significant. Such a shift makes visible what is normally hidden, and bring to centre stage what is marginalized. Moreover, such a shift fosters the development of political and publicly relevant arguments by those (individuals and groups) whose voice is rarely heard: to the extent the classical liberal anthropology is the cultural reference for public debates, vulnerable people are in a subordinate position, and their argument are often dismissed within a logic of charity and social solidarity. Feminist thought, in many of its variants, has often emphasised this change of perspective, and reassessed the notion of vulnerability as a new form of strength, alternative to models oriented towards possession and domination, a place of redemption, and an opportunity to shape different social relations and models. Looking at reality from the perspective of vulnerability, in short, means looking at inequalities and marginalisation from a different point of view: it means arguing for redemption and resistance, moving from a logic of acceptance or assistance to that of dissent, opening new spaces for resistance, and new demands for visibility and struggles for recognition.[61]

This way of understanding vulnerability, which tends to highlight its positive and emancipatory value, is consistent with an approach that abandons the myth of perfect independence and individual autonomy, and reaffirms the value of bodies and human dependence. At the same time, it conveys an enabling conception of justice, where the need for public intervention towards vulnerability goes along with the need to keep vulnerability separate from mere disadvantage. Above all, it is a model that emphasises the active and not merely passive character of vulnerability, and highlights potentialities rather than defective characteristics. Vulnerability, in other words, is a potential, rather than simply an unpleasant or negative condition; it certainly includes passivity, awe, but also susceptibility to change and openness to sociality. In Gilson's words, "Taken in this way, as a fundamental state, vulnerability is a condition of potential that makes other conditions possible (. . .) Vulnerability is not just a condition that limits us but one that can enable us".[62]

This positive and enabling dimension of vulnerability is particularly evident if we place the discourse on a collective level, alongside the individual. In other words, the positive and enabling value of vulnerability is even more evident when we refer to vulnerability as a collective condition, a condition that is peculiar to groups of people as well as individuals. The vulnerability of groups can be interpreted as a

---

[60] Fraser (1990), p. 71.

[61] Bernardini et al. (2018).

[62] Gilson (2011), p. 310.

constitutively political dimension, an opportunity for resistance and a place for dissent, and as a point of departure to develop demands for visibility and struggles for recognition.[63] I am aware that these struggles can also take place as single individuals' claims; however, it is the collective dimension that, par excellence, allows for the occupation of public space and visibility, as well as for the participation to the public debate and have one's voice heard. On the one hand, because in order to enter the public space, it is necessary to be able to show that the vulnerability that each subject experiences is not reducible to a private matter, but is in fact a shared condition that influences relations between human beings. On the other hand, because by doing so, vulnerable subjects prove themselves capable of building new political subjectivities and new forms of participation in public life.

References

Abbey R (2014) The return of feminist liberalism. Routledge, London

Bernardini M, Casalini L, Giolo O, Re L (a cura di) (2018) Vulnerabilità, etica, politica e diritto. IF Press, Roma

Brubaker R (2006) Ethnicity without groups. Harvard University Press, Cambridge

Butler J (2006) Precarious life: the powers of mourning and violence. Verso Books, New York

Butler J (2016) Frames of war: when is life grievable? Verso Books, New York

Butler J, Gambetti Z, Sabsay L (eds) (2016) Vulnerability and resistance. Duke University Press, Durham

Calhoun C (1991) The problem of identity in collective action. In: Huber J (ed) Macro-micro linkages in sociology. Sage, Newbury Park

Casadei T (2015) La vulnerabilità in prospettiva critica (vulnerability and the approach of critical theory). In: Giolo O, Pastore B (eds) Vulnerabilità. Analisi multidisciplinare di un concetto. Carocci, Roma

Cavarero A (2007) Horrorism: naming contemporary violence. Columbia University Press, New York

Cavarero A, Restaino F (2002) Filosofie femministe, due secoli di battaglie teoriche e pratiche (*Feminist Philosophies. Two centuries of theoretical and practical battles*). Bruno Mondadori, Milano

Cerulo K (1997) Identity construction: new issues, new directions. Annual Rev Soc 2:385–409

Chouliaraki L (2013) The ironic spectator: solidarity in the age of posthumanitarianism. Cambridge Polity Press

Cixous H (1975) La jeune née. Unione générale d'éditions, Paris

Cole A (2016) All of us are vulnerable, but some are more vulnerable than others: the political ambiguity of vulnerability studies, an ambivalent critique. Crit Horiz 17(2):260–277

Cudd A (2006) Analyzing oppression. Oxford University Press, Oxford

Dodds S (2014) Dependence, Care, and Vulnerability. In: MacKenzie C, Rogers W, Dodds S (eds) Vulnerability. Oxford University Press, New Essays in Ethics and Feminist Philosophy

Ferrarese E (2016) Vulnerability: a concept with which to undo the world as it is? Crit Horiz 17(2): 149–159

Fineman MA (2004) The autonomy myth a theory of dependency. The New Press, New York

[63] Macioce (2022), p. 132.

Fineman MA (2008) The vulnerable subject: anchoring equality in the human condition. Yale J Law Fem 20:1
Fineman MA (2010) The vulnerable subject and the responsive state. Emory Law J 60:251
Fineman MA (2012) Beyond identities: the limits of an antidiscrimination approach to equality. Boston Univ Law Rev 92:1713–1770
Fineman MA (2013) Equality, autonomy, and the vulnerable subject in law and politics. In: Fineman MA, Grear A (eds) Vulnerability. Reflections on a new ethical foundation for law and politics. Ashgate Publishing
Fineman MA (2020) Beyond equality and discrimination. SMU Law Rev Forum 73:51–62
Fineman MA, Grear A (eds) (2013) Vulnerability: reflections on a new ethical Foundation for law and Politics. Routledge
Fraser N (1990) Rethinking the public sphere: a contribution to the critique of actually existing democracy. Soc Text 25(26):56–80
Frazer E, Hutchings K (2017) Feminist Approaches to Violence and Vulnerability. In: Garry A, Khader SJ, Stone A (eds) The Routledge Companion to Feminist Philosophy. Routledge, London-New York
Garry A, Khader SJ, Stone A (eds) (2017) The Routledge companion to feminist philosophy. Routledge, New York
Gilligan C (1982) In a different voice. Psychological theory and women's development. Harvard University Press, Cambridge
Gilson E (2011) Vulnerability, ignorance, and oppression. Hypatia, 26(2): 308–332
Hurst SA (2008) Vulnerability in research and health care; describing the elephant in the room? Bioethics 22(4):191–202
Ippolito F, Iglesias Sanchez S (eds) (2015) Protecting Vulnerable Groups: the European Human Rights Framework. Bloomsbury Publishing, London
Jaggar AM (1989) Love and knowledge: emotion in feminist epistemology. In: Jaggar AM, Bordo SR, Bordo S (eds) Gender/body/knowledge: feminist reconstructions of being and knowing. Rutgers University Press
Khan SU, Khan MZ, Raghu Subramanian C et al (2020) Participation of women and older participants in randomized clinical trials of lipid-lowering therapies: a systematic review. JAMA Netw Open 3(5)
Kittay EF (1997) Human dependency and Rawlsian equality. In: Meyers DT (ed) Feminists rethink the self. Westview Press, Boulder
Knudsen BT, Stage C (2017) Affective methodologies. Developing cultural research strategies for the study of affect, Palgrave, New York
Koivunen A, Kyrölä K, Ryberg I (2018) Vulnerability as a political language. In: Koivunen A, Kyrölä K, Ryberg I (eds) The power of vulnerability. Mobilising affect in feminist, queer and anti-racist media cultures. Manchester University Press, Manchester
Kymlicka W (1989) Liberal individualism and liberal neutrality. Ethics 99(4):883–905
Lloyd G (1993) The man of reason: 'Male' and 'Female' in Western philosophy. Routledge, New York
Luna F (2009) Elucidating the concept of vulnerability: layers not labels. IJFAB: Int J Fem Approach Bioeth 2(1):121–139
Macioce F (2022) The Politics of Vulnerable Groups: Implications for Philosophy, Law, and Political Theory. Springer Nature
Mackenzie C, Rogers W, Dodds S (eds) (2014) Vulnerability: new essays in ethics and feminist philosophy. Oxford University Press, Oxford
MacKinnon CA (1987) Feminism unmodified. Discourses on life and law. Harvard University Press, Cambridge
Morondo Taramundi D (2018) Un nuovo paradigma per l'eguaglianza? La vulnerabilità tra condizione umana e mancanza di protezione (A new paradigm for equality? Vulnerability between human condition and lack of protection). In: Casalini B, Giolo O, Re L (eds) Vulnerabilità: etica, politica, diritto (vulnerability, ethics, politics and law). IF Press, Roma

Nijensohn M (2018) Por un feminismo radical y plural: Repensando las coordenadas teóricas y políticas de un nuevo feminismo desde una lectura cruzada de Judith Butler, Ernesto Laclau y Chantal Mouffe. Cadernos pagu, e185411
Nijensohn M (2022) Precarity and counter-hegemonic articulation: from the massification of feminisms toward a radical and plural feminism. Inter Fem J Polit 24(1):133–152
Nussbaum MC (1997) The feminist critique of liberalism. The Lindley Lecture, University of Kansas Department of Philosophy
Okin SM (1989) Justice, gender, and the family. Basic Books, New York
Pateman C (1988) The sexual contract. Polity Press, Oxford
Peroni L, Timmer A (2013) Vulnerable groups: the promise of an emerging concept in European Human Rights Convention law. Int J Constit Law 11(4):1056–1085
Rancière J (2006) The ethical turn of aesthetics and politics. Crit Horiz 7(1):1–20
Rogers W, Mackenzie C, Dodds S (2012) Why bioethics needs a concept of vulnerability. IJFAB: Int J Fem Approach Bioeth 5(2):11–38
Sandel M (1981) Liberalism and the limits of justice. Cambridge University Press, New York
Stone A (2004) Essentialism and anti-essentialism in feminist philosophy. J Moral Philosophy 1(2): 135–153
Taylor R, Jasinski JL (2011) Femicide and the feminist perspective. Homicide Stud 15(4):341–362
Tronto J (1993) Moral boundaries: a political argument for an ethics of care. Routledge, New York
Wall E (2000) The problem of group agency. Philos Forum 31(2):187–197
Witt C (1995) Anti-essentialism in feminist theory. Philos Top 23(2):321–344
Woodly D (2015) Seeing collectivity: structural relation through the lens of youngian seriality. Contemp Polit Theory 14(3):213–233
Young IM (1990) Justice and the politics of difference. Princeton University Press, Princeton
Young IM (1994) Gender as seriality: thinking about women as a social collective, signs. J Women Cult Soc 19(3):713–738
Young IM (2000) Inclusion and Democracy. Oxford University Press, Oxford
Zucker I, Prendergast BJ (2020) Sex differences in pharmacokinetics predict adverse drug reactions in women. Biol Sex Differ 11:32

Fabio Macioce (Milano, 1976), PhD, is Full Professor of Philosophy of Law and Bioethics at LUMSA University, School of Law, Rome. He has held visiting positions at Cambridge University, UK (Faculty Visitor at the Centre for Law, Medicine and Life Sciences, 2018); Universidad de Valencia (Visiting Professor, Facultad de Derecho, 2017), and University of Oxford (Visiting Scholar at the Centre for Socio-Legal Studies, University of Oxford, 2014). He has collaborated since 2019 with the Council of Europe as an expert in the field of bioethics. His research interests lie in the field of individual and group vulnerability; migration and social integration; democracy, minority rights and legal pluralism; collective rights; bioethics and informed consent; law and religion; AI and human rights. In recent years, he has taken part in a number of research projects; (2019–2022) BRIC-Inail, "Risk analysis and mitigation strategies for workers' health and safety protection in contexts subject to digital transformation" (UniRoma1—Lumsa—UniTo), Unit coordinator; (2017–2020), H2020-SwafS-2016-17, "i-Consent. Improving the guidelines for Informed Consent, including vulnerable populations, under a gender perspective"—Participant; (2017–2019); ongoing projects are: (2022–2025) NHNAI—New Humanism at the time of Neurosciences and Artificial Intelligence, Unit coordinator (with prof. S. Biancu); (2023–2025) PRIN—National funding program: Vulnerabilities arising from human-robot collaboration in the workplace: ethical and legal perspectives.

Should the Reasonableness Standard Be 'Genderized'? Some Reflections from the Perspective of Personalism

Wojciech Załuski

Contents

Abstract The question of whether one ought to introduce a gender-based distinction within the so called 'reasonable person standard' does not have only theoretical character, for some courts did introduce this kind of distinction ('the reasonable woman standard') in the context of sexual harassment law, assuming as an established fact that women exhibit a lower threshold for perceiving sexual harassment than men do. The two most common objections against 'genderizing' the reasonableness standard are that it is apt to perpetuate gender stereotypes, and that it does not have a sound scientific basis. In this paper it is argued that the second objection is not plausible, but scientific theories (especially, evolutionary theory and neuroscience) which justify the claim about gender differences in perception of sexual misconduct also reveal gender differences in other mental dispositions or faculties as well, e.g., in attitude to risk, dominance assertion, or empathy. This seems to have the following normative implication: instead of limiting the reasonable woman standard only to sexual harassment law, one should, for consistency sake, *either* entirely abandon the idea of gender-differentiating the standard (if one endorses the first objection and/or if one assumes that the notion of 'reasonableness' is to be defined by the highest mental faculties which are incontrovertibly the same among men and women), *or* differentiate it in more legal contexts than only in sexual harassment law. It is argued in the paper that the first alternative, which amounts to adopting a personalist (i.e. based on philosophical view called 'personalism') interpretation of the reasonable person standard, is more convincing.

W. Załuski (✉)
Jagiellonian University, Krakow, Poland
e-mail: wojciech.zaluski@uj.edu.pl

N. Lacey et al. (eds.), *Reassessing Feminist Legal Theories*, Gender Perspectives in Law 5, https://doi.org/10.1007/978-3-031-75423-4_10

1 Introduction

The question of whether one ought to introduce a gender-based distinction within the so called 'reasonable person standard' (hereafter: RPS) has been hotly debated for quite a long time (since about the end of the 80s of the last century). This debate did not have only theoretical character, detached from legal practice. For some courts did introduce this kind of distinction ('the reasonable woman standard'—hereafter: RWS) in the context of sexual harassment law, assuming as an established fact that women exhibit a lower threshold for perceiving sexual harassment than men do.[1] However, the question arises—to be tackled in this paper—whether this distinction is justifiable.[2] I will start my considerations from providing some clarificatory remarks on RPS, which will structure my argumentation.

RPS is a comparative standard invoked to assess liability in various branches of law, e.g., in tort law, contract law, or criminal law. It works, roughly, in this way: in order to ascertain (in the context of the law of torts) whether a defendant was negligent in his/her action, the court invokes the figure of a 'reasonable person', and compares his/her imagined action with that of the defendant: if the defendant acted just like the reasonable person would have done, then the defendant is not regarded as negligent; if the defendant acted differently—with less care, then he/she is held to have been negligent. Analogously, in criminal law, the accused may invoke, e.g., the defense of duress only if his/her reaction to a threat was similar to the reaction which a reasonable person would have displayed. The usage of the standard is justified by the fact that, given the complexity and diversity of real-life situations in which the notions of negligence, duress, and the like are applied, it is not possible to determine the scope of their application by a well-defined set of *a priori* rules. It does not mean that the set cannot be constructed; it can be but only gradually, *as a result* of the application of the intentionally vague RPS (the set of rules it generates has therefore *a posteriori* character); furthermore, thus generated set is not claimed to be complete, and the rules it contains are not regarded as indefeasible. Yet, of course, RSP is not uncontroversial—it was subjected to various, more or less radical, types of criticisms.[3] In this paper I will deal with two of them,

---

[1]The landmark decision in this context is *Ellison v. Brady* (1991), in which the court ruled that "in evaluating the severity and pervasiveness of sexual harassment, we should focus on the perspective of the victim (. . .). A complete understanding of the victim's view requires (. . .) analysis of the different perspectives of men and women". On the evolution of law's regulations of sexual harassment see, e.g., Siegel (2003).

[2]It should be mentioned that there is an enormous literature on this important (practically and theoretically) issue (papers explicitly invoked in the present article constitute just a small fraction of it). So, some explanation is needed whether the next article is at all needed—whether it can bring anything new to the discussion. I believe (optimistically) that it can, since I have not encountered the explicit link (I wish to make in this paper) between the controversy over the reasonable person/ reasonable woman standard and the personalist philosophy.

[3]A particularly useful overview of these criticisms can be found, e.g., in Moran (2003), Gardner (2015) and Gardner (2019).

which, as we will see, are in fact connected to each other. According to the first one, the very term 'reasonable' is deeply ambiguous and this ambiguity cannot be eliminated. According to the second one, RPS is insensitive to the differences between men and women, and this insensitivity consists either in introducing a *de facto* male standard under the guise of gender-neutrality, or (less reprehensibly) in introducing some genderless standard, which is overly abstract and thus useless if applied to real-life situations in which, so the criticism goes, a woman's perspective is prominent.

Let me successively deal with these two criticisms. As it will turn out, the answer to the first one will constitute at the same time an answer to the second.

2 The 'Personalist' Explication of RPS

It is undeniable that RPS needs to be explicated in order to be useful. Even though, as already mentioned, it cannot be decomposed into a set of precise rules (otherwise it would be redundant), it cannot be completely 'open' in its content; its vagueness must be 'controlled', so to speak. So how can RPS be explicated? The simplest (but also inadequate, as we will see) way of determining its content is to assume that 'the reasonable person' means 'the ordinary person'; this way, therefore, consists in observing or imagining how most persons behave or would in various types of legally relevant situations, and stating that this kind of behavior, just by virtue of the fact that it is predominant, is the reasonable one. There are two obvious problems with this explication: (a) since what most people tend to do may change in time, thus reconstructed RPS would not have a stable content; (b) if 'reasonableness' is understood purely descriptively, as it is under this proposal, RPS will forfeit its normative character of being a pattern of *desirable* behavior (unless it could be demonstrated, which seems impossible, that what most people tend to do is *ipso facto* a desirable pattern of behavior); it will just mirror prevailing social norms. One alternative to this proposal was advanced by the representatives of the *Law and Economics* movement, who were trying to explicate RPS by means of the famous Judge Learned Hand Formula (which states, in the context of the law of torts, that an agent is negligent if he or she did not take precautions in a situation in which the costs of precautions were smaller than the costs of expected harm occurring in the absence of precautions). This is assuredly a valuable explication, since it respects the character of *standard* of RPS (and thus does not attempt it to reduce it to a set of precise rules), eliminates its ambiguity, and, not less importantly, respects the normative character of RPS. However, it has several shortcomings: it can be easily applied only within the law of torts (where, as a rule, the relevant costs can be quantified), and even within this branch of law it can be criticized on ethical grounds as putting on a par (in a cost-benefit analysis) the costs which the perpetrator of a tort in fact imposes on a victim, and the costs of the harm suffered by the victim. Yet I do not intend to provide a comprehensive evaluation of this explication. Rather, I would like to propose a different explication, which, as I believe, can quite easily tackle the objections raised both against the 'ordinary person' explication (the objection of non-normativity), and against the 'Judge Learned Hand Formula' explication (the objection of non-universality, and the objection of inconsistency with ethical intuitions).

The explication I wish to put forward rests on the personalist view of the human beings, proposed within the classical philosophy and developed by the twentieth century personalists, especially, Emmanuel Mounier, Jacques Maritain and Karol Wojtyła (John Paul II). It is an essential feature of the personalist view that it defines human being first and foremost in terms of reason and (free) will—his/her spiritual powers, rather than in terms of desires or instincts—his/her affective and instinctual side. Thus, it implies that that human beings occupy a distinguished place in the universe among other living beings owing to the fact that they are autonomous (in the sense that they have free will) and rational (in the sense that they are responsive to reasons and act on reasons, or at least have the capacity to act on reasons). I will now focus on those aspects of the concept of *person* (as understood within personalism) which are particularly important in the context of the analysis of RDP.

First, the concept implies the irreducibility of human being to his/her merely empirical (i.e., ascertainable by empirical sciences) mental faculties or proclivities; it posits the existence of a special faculty in human beings, viz. a rational and free will. Accordingly, human action cannot be fully described in terms of desires and beliefs as its causal factors; they play their important role of providing motives and directing action, but they do not lead to action *directly* or *on their own*: the direct cause of action is an act of will. In other words, the action is, obviously, preceded by other mental states (desires, beliefs, etc.) but they are not themselves sufficient to bring about an action; an additional—special—executive operation of the mind, attributable to the mind's part—an act of will—is necessary to generate an action. The will attests to human beings' 'capacity for transcendence', which embraces two particular capacities: to distance oneself from one's desires, propensities (the person, unlike other living entities, has an inner life—personal *depth*), and to direct one's intention to objective values. These characteristics are well captured by the definition of the human person coming from Boethius, which says that *persona est naturae rationalis individua substantia (*person is an individual substance having a rational nature). The personalist explication of RPS has direct consequences for the criminal law cases. For instance, *it implies a certain skepticism towards the defense of provocation (an institution which justifies passing a milder sentence on perpetrators of so-called crimes of passion), and thus, towards the notion of an 'irresistible impulse'. The skepticism stems from the fact that the personalist view of human beings assumes* that we are *all* (i.e., irrespective of our gender) endowed with the cognitive-volitional capacity to 'stand above' and overcome undesirable emotions, at least in the sense of preventing them from developing into fully fledged emotions, with their corresponding action tendencies. This skepticism is not radical: it does not amount to a postulate of abolishing these institutions, but to treating them with much restraint, that is, in such a way which appreciates the human capacity for self-control.

Secondly, the personalist explication of RDP is also relevant for the cases of tort law. In order to see it clearly, we need to highlight another element of the personalist picture of human beings, e.g., the faculty of prudence. According to the classical definition of prudence/practical wisdom (Latin: *prudentia*, ancient Greek: *phronesis*) provided by Cicero, prudence is *cognitio rerum appetendarum et fugiendarum*. It is therefore also a moral faculty. But I would like to focus on its non-moral components, which embrace several faculties or capacities, from the more general to the more particular.[4] The more general ones include instrumental rationality (the Aristotelian *deinotes*[5]), and what is contemporarily referred to as rationality over time, i.e. attaching sufficient importance to the future utility. Given this last feature, it can also be said that prudence is opposed, among other things, to the spontaneous/ unreflective living in the present, to 'seizing the present'. The more particular faculties/capacities that are connected to modern prudence embrace the capacity for deliberation, cautiousness, circumspection, *solertia* (clear-sightedness in the face of unexpected), memory (which gathers recollections of past decisions and their effects, thereby providing knowledge of particulars that enables making more informed decisions), foresight, docility and the consequent reliance on the judgment of other, more experienced, agents.[6] This—'thick'—account of prudence, characteristic for classical philosophy, provides a plausible, normative explication of 'reasonableness', which, as it seems, can be successfully applied in tort law. Importantly, this normative requirement does not seem to be beyond the reach of an 'ordinary' human being, it does not therefore violate the principle *impossibilum nulla obligatio est*.

Thirdly, the personalist view of human beings underlies an ethical system called "personalist ethic". The basic postulates of this ethics, derivable from the fact that human being is person and thus endowed with dignity, are twofold: the negative and the positive.[7] The negative says that person should never be treated only as a means but always also as an end (this is the personalist variant of the categorical imperative); using another person as a means always amounts to treating him/her as an object—as a something, not a someone, and this treatment may consist either in making use of him/her to realize some objective end or a subjective end which is pleasure (this second meaning has direct implications for sexual ethics, and thus for sexual harassment law[8]). The positive one asserts that each person should be affirmed for his/her own sake (*persona est affirmanda propter se ipsam*), i.e., the proper relation to each person is that of love (love in the sense of *agape/caritas*, and thus not necessarily emotional love, but love—disinterested and universal—based on an act of will). It bears stressing that this ethics *is gender-neutral* (directed to all human beings, irrespective of their sex), and realistic (imposing on human beings not

[4]See especially Aristotle (1947), Book VI, and Thomas Aquinas (1981), II-II, q. 47.

[5]Translated by W. D. Ross as "cleverness".

[6]For a more detailed analysis of prudence see Załuski and Kwarciński (2019).

[7]See Wojtyła (1960), p. 42; Wojtyła (1969), p. 87.

[8]See especially Wojtyła (1960).

very demanding rules); it can therefore be easily applied and understood. Thus, one can plausibly argue that in those cases in which the law implies a moral evaluation of the plaintiff's or the accused's behavior (e.g., in cases connected to sexual harassment), personalist ethics can be regarded as an appropriate moral reference point.

In sum, the personalist explication of RPS is immune to the first criticism mentioned in Introduction, for it provides a fairly precise—and at the same time normative—account of the reasonable person, stressing the 'shared humanity' of men and women. As a result, it should also remove the fear that "the use of gender-neutral language merely serves to mask the maleness of the standard – to turn an explicit male norm ['reasonable man standard' – W.Z] into an implicit male norm".[9] Thus, the considerations pursued in this section are also of direct relevance for the second criticism (that RPS is blind to gender differences): *the personalist view assumes that each human being, irrespective of his/her gender, is a person in an exactly the same degree, endowed with the same mental capacities of rational will, prudence, and equally capable of understanding and complying with personalist ethics*.[10] Accordingly, given this explication of RPS, there do not seem to be grounds for gender-differentiating this standard. In the next section I will consider some other arguments against this kind of differentiation.

3 Additional Arguments Against 'Genderizing' RPS

As was mentioned in Introduction, some courts introduced 'the reasonable woman standard' (RWS) in the context of sexual harassment law, assuming as an established fact that women exhibit a lower threshold for perceiving sexual harassment than men do. However, the question arises whether this separate standard is justifiable. From what has been said in the previous section devoted to the 'personalist' explication of RPS, it follows that it is not (though, of course, a number of scholars defend the gender differentiation of the reasonable person standard[11]). But it is worth

[9]Handsley (1996), p. 61.

[10]Even though some personalists admit that there may be some differences between men and women regarding their moral sensitivity (e.g., John Paul writes in his encyclical *Mulieris Dignitatem* from 1988: "It is commonly thought that women are more capable than men of paying attention to another person, and that motherhood develops this predisposition even more", and claims that women's capacity for self-sacrifice for others is greater than that of men), they nonetheless emphasize the common—and fundamental—features of men's and women's moral capacities; they would thus strongly reject either Lawrence Kohlberg's thesis (1981) that men can reach higher stages of moral development than women, or Carol Gilligan's thesis (1977) that men and women speak "in a different moral voice", that of justice and that of care, respectively (although it should be added that in her later works, Gilligan stressed—in the personalist spirit!—that by the "different voice" she did not mean the "woman voice", but, rather, a different way of moral thinking which could be adopted either by men or women).

[11]This defence may proceed on various grounds. It may be based on the biological assumption that women perceive sexual harassment in a different way than men, but it may also directly oppose this

considering some other arguments against RWS, in case the reader will not find the proposed—'personalist'—explication of RPS acceptable (as, e.g., resting, in his or her view, upon implausible metaphysical presuppositions). The most common objections against 'genderizing' RPS are the following three.[12]

The first objection says that *RWS is apt to reinforce gender stereotypes and discrimination against women*. The worry expressed by this objection seems to be justified, and thus it supports my general claim that RPS should not be gender-differentiated. Indeed, the adoption of a separate standard for women is very likely to reinforce or create the view that women, as a rule, are essentially different from men—*different*, and it is the crucial point, *in a way that is consistent with the patriarchal view of men's superiority* (as being a more rational, more poised, and psychologically stronger 'variety' of the human species than women).[13] Furthermore, this strengthening of the stereotype could occur not only among men, but also among women; as Kathleen A. Kenealy observed: "At bottom, the reasonable woman standard sends a message to women that they are inherently unreasonable. If they were objectively reasonable, a separate legal standard would not be necessary. Further, it minimizes the objective severity of a legally cognizable claim of sexual harassment".[14]

The second objection is that *contrary to the intentions of RWS's supporters, it may in practice be used by male defendants as a way of excusing their harassing behavior*. For if male and female perspectives on sexual harassment are so much different, then—as an advocate of the defendants in a sexual harassment case could claim—it cannot be expected that potential male harassers will be able to adopt (e.g.,

line of argumentation and assert that sexual harassment has in fact nothing or little to do with sexuality but is about oppression of women: the harasser's intention is to elicit in women a sense of their subordination and to stress his own sense of power. This latter kind of defence is developed, e.g., by Anita Superson (1997). However, it is not immune to the first objection discussed in this section. Furthermore, I believe that my 'personalist' interpretation of RPS provides a remedy to the problems (the tradition of discrimination of women, which may still, to a considerable degree, determine the attitude of men towards women) to which Superson and many other scholars rightly draw attention.

[12] A systematic analysis of various objections to RWS is provided by Linda L. Peterson (1999); yet she ultimately rejects them and defends this standard.

[13] According to an extreme variant of this objection (which could be defended by those postmodern thinkers who assume some radical version of social constructivism, and thus aim at 'deconstructing' the traditional categories of thought, including the categories of 'men' and 'women'), the use of gender categories in the description of the 'reasonableness standard', is prejudiced, discriminative, and above all, based on some purportedly fundamental philosophical mistake (the belief that our mental and linguistic categories have some objective 'referent' in the real world). Yet the question arises as to what the ultimate consequences of this postmodern view could be: it is dubious whether this could be a roundabout way of justifying the traditional RPS, because, for postmodernists, 'person' should also be a highly suspicious category; rather, as it seems, the view could justify the adoption of multiple, highly individualized standards (the consequence which is hardly distinguishable from dismantling the 'reasonableness' standard altogether).

[14] Kenealy (1992), p. 210.

in a working environment) their female workers' (subordinates') point of view.[15] Developing this line of defense, the advocate could claim that the defendants did not regard their behavior towards women as unwelcome or harassing; that they in fact intended it as a way of complimenting women, and that they would feel much flattered if women acted similarly towards them. Thus, assuming that gender differences in the perception of sexual harassment really exist, as they seem to do, the adoption of RWS could have in fact two contrary effects. On one hand, men's awareness (raised by the presence of RWS) that women react differently to sexual overtures than men or that (in the context of charges of rape) women tend to understand the notion of 'consent to a sexual intercourse' in a more restrictive manner than they do, could sensitize them to women's viewpoint, and thus decrease the number of sexual harassment or rape cases. Yet, on the other hand, the presence of RWS could strengthen men's belief that their own perspective is in a way justified (as being 'typically male'), and that women's perspective is somehow idiosyncratic. It is hard to say which effect would be stronger.[16] At any rate, a much more effective way of combatting men's stereotypes and sexist proclivities seems to be a genderless reasonability standard which emphasizes the common humanity of men and women. In this context one can also point at another unwelcome—and paradoxical to boot—consequence of the existence of two separate standards: if two different standards may apply to a given type of situation (e.g., behavior in a working environment), then the question arises whether it is fair to give priority to one of them (viz. RWS); and if it is assumed that to a given type of situation only one standard applies (viz. RWS), then it can be argued that, given that men find it harder than women to live up to this standard, male defendants ought to be judged more leniently than they ought

[15] As Donald C. Hubin and Karen Healy rightly noticed (in the context of their analysis of the law of rape), the very demand for two separate standards may suggest that the rift between male and female perspective is so deep that the reasonable man may not be able to "understand the very different experiences of women, and *vice versa*", Hubin and Healy (1999), p. 131.

[16] To my knowledge no systematic research comparing these two possible effects has been conducted. Yet some empirical research on RWS exists. *First*, it has been shown that RWS may activate protectionist attitudes towards women (see Wiener et al. (1997)). It should be noticed, however, that the protectionist attitude is an ambivalent effect: although it is incompatible with sexual harassment, it is fully compatible with the stereotyped view of women as a weaker, oversensitive sex. *Secondly*, the empirical research has also shown that men whose sexism is hostile rather than benevolent were not much impacted by RWS. *Thirdly*, the effects of RWS's effects on courts' decisions in sexual harassment cases were also examined; the results of this research indicated that there is "a weak relationship between whether a case followed a reasonable woman precedent-setting case and the likelihood that the court decision favored the plaintiff (Perry et al. 2004, p. 1)" (for similar conclusions see also Shoenfelt et al. (2002)). Of course, this last research does not tell us what is *ex ante* effect of the presence of RWS (i.e., the effect on the potential defendants behavior); yet it tells us that its effect on court decisions may be minimal, if any. This fact, *by itself*, seems to constitute another objection to RWS, which can, roughly, be formulated in this way: since RWS does not have any substantial impact on court decisions, and the switch to a novel standard always generates some costs (e.g., judges and citizens have to become acquainted with it), then there is no reason to introduce RWS in place of RPS. All this sounds rather speculative, since, as mentioned, there are few empirical analyses of the effects of RWS.

to be if some gender-neutral standard were adopted (and also more leniently than female defendants who sexually harassed their female subordinates). All these dilemmas vanish if we abandon the idea of 'genderizing' RPS.

The third objection states that *the postulate of gender-differentiation of RPS does not have a sound scientific basis*, i.e., there is no plausible theory which would imply that men and women perceive sexual harassment in a different way. I find this objection particularly interesting, for, as I will argue, *even though this objection is not plausible, the consequences of its implausibility also count as an argument against RWS*. Let me explain. If we take into account the achievements of evolutionary theory and neuroscience, the objection that the postulate of introducing RWS in the context of sexual harassment law lacks a solid scientific basis proves to be false. For there are good scientific arguments for the claim that *there are inddeed* some gender differences in, among other things, patterns of sexual behaviour.[17] When I speak about "scientific arguments" I mean not only empirical psychological research revealing such differences, but also biological and psychological *theories* which provide a deeper explanation of these differences.[18] For instance, evolutionary psychology supports the picture of gender differences, according to which men are: (a) more dissolute (promiscuous), and thereby less sexually discriminating than women; (b) more desirous of power (*as such* and *over the opposite sex*) than women; (c) and more aggressive than women. This picture implies, among other things, that, as evolutionary psychologists put it, there is a 'sexual strategic mismatch' between men and women: their sexual strategic are, as a rule, different. The argument for this picture consists of two parts. Its *first part* is Robert Trivers's theory of parental investment, according to which the members of the sex whose parental investment in the offspring is lower and thereby whose maximum (potential) number of offspring is higher (i.e., male sex in the human and most other species) will be less discriminating in choosing the sexual partner, more polygamously inclined, and more intensely competitive (aggressive) with other members of the same sex. This part is supposed to explain why men are more dissolute and more aggressive than women (by this kind of behaviour men, unlike women, can increase the likelihood and extent of their reproductive success),[19] but it does not explain why men are considered to be more desirous of power (*as such* and *over the opposite sex*). This last feature (the desire of power over the opposite sex) is explained by the *second part* of this argument viz. the two-element assumption that: (a) in the ancestral environments (in which human genotype was being shaped) parental investment of men in their offspring was relatively large (mainly because of

[17]Though, it is not quite clear whether the differences can be called large, medium, or rather small; but there seems to be a common agreement that the differences exist, and that they are not negligible; see, e.g., Blumenthal (1998).

[18]I do not mean to say, however, that all evolutionary theorists accept the picture presented below. But a large group of them do, viz. evolutionary psychologists. A different picture is defended, e.g., by so called evolutionary feminists (see, e.g., Hrdy 1981, 1986).

[19]On this issue see, e.g., Campbell (1995), Campbell (2013), Durrant and Ward (2015), or McDonald et al. (2012).

the prolonged helplessness of human infants) as compared the other species (though, of course, still smaller than that of women), and (b) that a man cannot be certain of his paternity of the child whom he rears. In other words, so the argument goes, since men invested relatively many resources in their offspring, but could not be certain of their paternity, they are likely to have developed an adaptation that diminished the risk of their misplaced (that is: in a child of another man) parental investment. This adaptation can be most generally described as men's will of power over their sexual partners, or as male sexual proprietariness, or as men's tendency to treat their sexual partners "as a chattel".[20] It can be decomposed into various more specific 'mental mechanisms', the most important of them being, as is claimed by evolutionary psychologists, sexual jealousy, which hyper-sensitizes men to any potential signal of women's sexual infidelity, and, when triggered off, often leads to violent behaviours. It bears stressing that evolutionary psychologists claim that women's jealousy (unlike men's) is in the first place emotional rather than sexual: it consists, above all, in sensitivity to men's emotional infidelity (emotional attachment to some other woman) rather than to men's sexual infidelity. Thus, according to evolutionary psychology, men and women value different things in their relationships: men value in the first-place sexual fidelity, while women emotional fidelity.[21] This picture also implies that there is a twofold asymmetry between the husband's and the wife's adultery: "The first is that adultery is a graver wrong to the husband than to the wife. Second, a husband's adulteries are more likely than a wife's to be casual. Evolutionary biology implies that a married man may be attracted to a woman precisely because she is not his wife, whereas a married woman may be attracted to a man because he would be a superior protector for her and her children – in other words, a better husband; therefore, the wife's adultery is a graver threat to the marriage. These considerations may explain the 'double standard': there was a time in England when the wife's adultery entitled the husband to divorce, but the husband's adultery entitled the wife only to a judicial separation unless the husband committed bigamy or there were other circumstances of aggravation".[22]

Thus, as we can see, if we restrict our attention only to the biological 'side' of human beings, disregarding the fact that they are persons (free and rational), we can indeed, quite plausibly, argue that men deserve a more lenient treatment if they manifested aggressive behaviour towards their adulterous wives (than *vice versa*), because—given the insights from evolutionary psychology—they are more likely to find themselves in a 'heat of passion' for this reason than women. But if we adopt a personalist perspective, then this kind of gender differentiation of this justification or excuse[23] will prove to be absurd (as it really is!): for, even if men tend to react more vehemently than women to the sight of sexual betrayal, this fact turns out to be

[20] See Wilson and Daly (1992).

[21] See, e.g., Buss (1998, 2003).

[22] Posner (1992), pp. 251–252.

[23] The question of whether the defence which is 'heat of passion' is a justification or excuse is a contested issue; see on this especially Dressler (1982); in a broader context (of the controversy over

irrelevant once we are recalled that they are *persons*, and thus capable, owing to their unique cognitive and volitional capacities, to control and suppress even most forceful impulses.

It should further be noticed—the point often omitted in the debate on the plausibility of RWS—that *the scientific theories (evolutionary theory and neuroscience) which justify the claim about gender differences in perception of sexual misconduct also justify the claim about gender differences in other mental dispositions or faculties*, e.g., in attitude to risk, dominance assertion, time-perception, emotionality, empathy, or status seeking.[24] This implies that, from a purely scientific point of view, RPS could—or even should (once we adopt this line of argumentation)—be gender-differentiated in many other legal contexts in addition to sexual harassment law. To give just one example: if we agree with evolutionary psychologists that men are, as a rule, more risk-loving than women, i.e., that the threshold of non-acceptable risk is, statistically speaking, higher for men than for women,[25] then one could argue that the range of dangerous actions for which women ought to be punished ought to be broader than an analogous range determined for men (since there will be a set of dangerous/risky actions which will be found acceptable by typical—'reasonable'—men, and unacceptable by typical—'-reasonable'—women). This consequence and similar ones seem preposterous. But they seem inevitable if, in the course of determining the content of the reasonableness standard, we focus our attention on some specific mental faculties and dispositions and omit the higher cognitive and volitional faculties (common for all human beings and stressed in the personalist philosophy). As can also be easily noticed, the sole focus on these specific faculties gives rise to a descriptive interpretation of the reasonableness standard, which, as argued in Introduction, is contrary to the deeper (normative) function of this standard.

4 Conclusions

I have presented several arguments for the claim that one should entirely abandon the idea of gender-differentiating the reasonable person standard. One of these arguments was a normative proposal that it is advisable to define the notion of 'reasonableness' in accordance with the personalist picture of human beings, i.e. by those mental faculties which are incontrovertibly the same among men and women, as well as by the 'gender-neutral' personalist moral duties (needless, the presupposition of this proposal is my conviction that it is *a true* picture of human nature). This proposal implies that what is common for men and women—their 'shared humanity', the fact

---

the nature of emotions) this defence is examined in Kahan and Nussbaum (1996). I've tried to develop a critique of this defence in Załuski (2021), pp. 122–128.

[24] On these differences see, e.g. Campbell (1995, 2013), Durrant and Ward (2015).

[25] See, e.g., Bribiescas (2008), pp. 116–120.

they are 'persons' (in the classical—personalist—sense of this word)—is incomparably more important than what may differentiate them. Yet it bears noticing that the personalist philosophy need not be blind to the specific ways of feeling or perceiving of men and women (assuming that there are such ways). But from fact that it may be reasonable and thus desirable to take into account gender in some circumstances (e.g., in the course of the education of the young people, or in child custody issues arising in cases of divorce) does not mean that it would be reasonable to 'genderize' the reasonableness standard.

References

Aquinas T (1981) Summa Theologica: complete English edition in five volumes, transl. By fathers of the English Dominican Province. Christian Classics, Westminster

Aristotle (1947) Nicomachean ethics (trans: Ross WD). Modern Library, New York

Blumenthal JA (1998) The reasonable woman standard: a meta-analytic review of gender differences in perceptions of sexual harassment. Law Hum Behav 22(1):33–57

Bribiescas RG (2008) Men: evolutionary and life history. Harvard University Press, Cambridge

Buss DM (1998) The psychology of human mate selection: exploring the complexity of the strategic repertoire. In: Crawford CB, Krebs DL, Mahwah NJ (eds) Handbook of evolutionary psychology: ideas, issues, and applications. Psychology Press, New York, pp 405–429

Buss DM (2003) Evolution of desire. Strategies of human mating. Basic Books, New York

Campbell A (1995) A few good men: evolutionary psychology and female adolescent aggression. Ethol Sociobiol 16:99–123

Campbell A (2013) The evolutionary psychology of women's aggression. Philos Trans Inq 6:1–30

Dressler J (1982) Rethinking heat of passion: a defense in search of a rationale. J Crim Law Criminol 73(2):421–470

Durrant R, Ward T (2015) Evolutionary criminology: towards a comprehensive explanation for crime. Academic, Amsterdam

Gardner J (2015) The many faces of the reasonable person. LQR 131:563–584

Gardner J (2019) The reasonable person standard. The International Encyclopedia of Ethics. https://onlinelibrary.wiley.com/doi/abs/10.1002/9781444367072.wbiee920

Gilligan C (1977) In a different voice: women's conceptions of self and morality. Harv Educ Rev 47(4):481–517

Handsley E (1996) The reasonable man: two case studies. Sister Law 1:53–71

Hrdy SB (1981) The woman that never evolved. Harvard University Press, Cambridge, London

Hrdy SB (1986) Empathy, polyandry, and the myth of the coy female. In: Bleier R (ed) Feminist approaches to science. Pergamon, New York, pp 119–146

Hubin DC, Haely K (1999) Rape and the reasonable man. Law Philos 18:113–139

Kahan DM, Nussbaum M (1996) Two conceptions of emotion in criminal law. Colum Law Rev 96(2):269–374

Kenealy KA (1992) Sexual harassment and the reasonable woman standard. Lab Law 8(2):203–210

Kohlberg L (1981) The philosophy of moral development. Vol. I, moral stages and the idea of justice. Harper & Row, San Francisco

McDonald MM, Navarette CD, Van Vugt M (2012) Evolution and the psychology of intergroup conflict: the male warrior hypothesis. Philos Trans R Soc 367:670–679

Moran M (2003) Rethinking the reasonable person. Oxford University Press, Oxford

Perry EL, Kuklik CT, Bourhis AC (2004) The reasonable woman standard: effects on sexual harassment court decisions. Law Hum Behav 28(1):9–27

Peterson LL (1999) The reasonableness of the reasonable person standard. PAQ 13(2):141–158

Posner R (1992) Sex and reason. Harvard University Press, Cambridge
Shoenfelt E, Maue AE, Nelson J (2002) Reasonable person versus reasonable woman: does it matter? J Gender Soc Policy Law 10(3):633–672
Siegel RB (2003) A short history of sexual harassment. In: MacKinnon C, Siegel RB (eds) Directions in sexual harassment law. Yale University Press, New Haven, pp 1–39
Superson AM (1997) Sexual harassment. In: LaFollette H (ed) Ethics in practice. Blackwell, Oxford, pp 400–409
Wiener RL, Hurt L, Russell B, Mannen K, Gasper C (1997) Perceptions of sexual harassment: the effects of gender, legal standard, and ambivalent sexism. Law Hum Behav 21(1):71–93
Wilson M, Daly M (1992) The man who mistook his wife for a Chattel. In: Barkow JH, Cosmides L, Tooby J (eds) The adapted mind. Evolutionary psychology and the generation of culture. Oxford University Press, New York, pp 289–322
Wojtyła K (John Paul II) (1960) Miłość i odpowiedzialność. Towarzystwo Naukowe KUL, Lublin
Wojtyła K (John Paul II) (1969) Osoba i czyn. Towarzystwo Naukowe KUL, Lublin
Wojtyła K (John Paul II) (1988) Mulieris Dignitatem. www.vatican.va
Załuski W (2021) The insanity defense: a philosophical analysis. Edward Elgar Publishing, Cheltenham
Załuski W, Kwarciński T (2019) The dualism of prudence. Prakseologia 161:291–314

Wojciech Załuski (b. 1978) is a Full Professor of Legal Philosophy at the Jagiellonian University (Krakow, Poland), author of many books (in English: The Limits of Naturalism: A Game-theoretic Critique of Justice as Mutual Advantage, Wolters Kluwer: Krakow, 2006; Evolutionary Theory and Legal Philosophy, Edward Elgar Publishing, 2009; Game Theory in Jurisprudence, Copernicus Center Press, 2013; Law and Evil: the Evolutionary Perspective, Edward Elgar Publishing, 2018; The Insanity Defense: A Philosophical Analysis, Edward Elgar Publishing, 2021), and of dozens of articles in legal, moral and political philosophy, as well as in moral psychology and philosophy of science.

Individual and Collective Harm in Sex Discrimination

Antonio Álvarez del Cuvillo

Contents

Abstract The concept of discrimination appeared historically as a response to the ineffectiveness of the principle of formal equality to address certain systematic inequalities between human groups that are firmly rooted in our societies, such us the subordination of women. In this sense, it is connected with the idea of substantial equality that characterizes modern democracies. However, in its specific formulation, the anti-discrimination regulation tends to use the individualistic categories of our legal ideology, that are sometimes interpreted in a formalistic way by legal operators, turning victimized groups into abstract reasons for difference in treatment. Some feminist scholars have argued that the individualist notion of discrimination, linked to the Aristotelian notion of equality, is ineffective and in many cases even counterproductive to address the situation of oppression suffered by women. In order to reconstruct a group-based notion of sex discrimination it is necessary to provide a theory on the damage caused by discriminatory conduct, articulating individual and social harm. In this way many issues can be addressed, such as the justification of affirmative action measures, the possibility of reverse discrimination, the application of the concept of discrimination by association, the difference between discrimination and stigmatization or the question of whether men can bring claims of indirect

A. Á. del Cuvillo (✉)
University of Cádiz, Cádiz, Spain
e-mail: antonio.alvarez@uca.es

N. Lacey et al. (eds.), *Reassessing Feminist Legal Theories*, Gender Perspectives in Law 5, https://doi.org/10.1007/978-3-031-75423-4_11

discrimination to challenge the application of a criterion that harms them individually and women globally.

1 Discrimination and the Guarantee of Substantive Equality

The principle of formal equality is one of the fundamental values upon which liberal democracies have been built since their inception. Indeed, the triumph of the bourgeois revolutions in the United States and Europe during the 18th and 19th centuries led to the formal proclamation of equality before the law for all citizens in the first declarations of rights and liberal constitutions. This stood in contrast to the legal inequality inherent in the estate-based societies of the *Ancien Régime*. However, a deeper analysis reveals that significant inequalities, both legal and factual, persisted in these liberal democracies due to individuals' membership in certain social groups. These inequalities were so deeply entrenched in the structure of bourgeois societies that they were taken for granted, and there was no need to explicitly mention them as exceptions to equal treatment, beyond the generic reference to "men" as subjects of citizenship.

Thus, constitutional proclamations of the principle of equality were by no means perceived as incompatible with the persistence of slavery for Black individuals or the exclusion of women from the most basic civil and political rights. These forms of oppression were seen as inherent in the natural order of things and, therefore, irrevocable. For example, for the dominant elites, granting women the right to vote was considered as absurd as granting it to minors[1]; in other words, it was believed that women could not be equated with men in their legal status due to a natural inequality inherent in the sexes. As a result, in practice, the status of citizens within the political community was exclusively restricted to white and property-owning males, excluding the vast majority of the population. Only certain individuals and organizations advocated for taking the principle of equality to its logical conclusion by extending it to women and other subordinate groups. In this regard, the well-known example of Olympe de Gouges comes to mind. In 1791, she wrote the "Declaration of the Rights of Woman and of the Female Citizen" as a response to the "Declaration of the Rights of Man and of the Citizen" of 1789.

In reality, the principle of formal equality is based on the Aristotelian idea that things that are alike should be treated alike, whereas things that are unlike should be treated differently. However, if this rule is applied purely in a formal and abstract sense, without considering the systematic inequalities that actually exist among

[1] In this regard, consider MacKinnon's reflection on the debates in the American Congress regarding the potential effects on women resulting from the introduction of the XIV Amendment to the Constitution, MacKinnon (1991) p. 1283.

human groups, its logic can justify any degradation of the social and legal position of the most vulnerable groups.[2]

Beyond this principle of formal equality, the prohibition of discrimination on various grounds, including "sex" is primarily developed in the second half of the twentieth century as a guarantee of the effective realization of universally recognized "human rights" following World War II. Indeed, the Universal Declaration of Human Rights of 1948 and the subsequent declarations of rights promulgated within the framework of the United Nations and the International Labour Organization (as well as the European Convention on Human Rights within the Council of Europe) invariably establish non-discrimination clauses based on various grounds, including sex, in relation to the exercise of all other recognized rights. Ultimately, these clauses constitute a manifestation of the "universal" nature of these rights, requiring that they be attributed to all human beings without any exclusion, restriction, or distinction based on membership in victimized social groups, contrary to what had occurred in the past. Therefore, these clauses are not primarily aimed at protecting individuals belonging to dominant social groups, who may be victims of human rights violations, but not due to their membership in certain collectives. The protection is specifically directed towards women and vulnerable minorities to explicitly indicate that human rights must also be applicable to them, both in theory and in practice. In essence, the prohibition of discrimination is a social right related to the principle of substantive equality since it aims to address the existing social inequalities that have resulted in the exclusion of a large part of the population, particularly women, from citizenship. It seeks to correct the dysfunctions that arise from the formally neutral application of the principle of equality.

However, the deliberate social purpose of the prohibition of discrimination is not always evident because it is often expressed through seemingly neutral and individualistic language. Thus, these norms avoid direct references to disadvantaged social groups, which are replaced in legal texts by abstract classifications that operate as "suspect categories". These categories are generally considered insufficient to justify certain differential treatment. For example, these clauses prohibit discrimination "on the grounds of sex", which may suggest that the aim is not so much to prevent the subordination of women, but rather to avoid the use of an irrational and, therefore, inefficient distinguishing criterion in a market-oriented society, as if the issue to be addressed were not the violation of women's dignity, but rather illogical or unjustifiable behavior.

This relative concealment of systematic social inequalities among human groups is partly due to the individualistic and formalistic nature of the dominant legal culture in Western societies. However, it is also largely explained by the political purpose of articulating greater social consensus regarding the introduction of measures that, to some extent, challenge values and principles deeply embedded in civil

[2] "If it were to be applied literally, it could be used to justify the Nuremberg laws of Adolf Hitler", Canadian Supreme Court, *Andrews v. Law Society of British Columbia*, [1989] 1 S.C.R. 143.

society, such as traditional gender norms within the patriarchal order.[3] Thus, the almost unanimous rejection of discrimination in our societies is partly explained by the fact that there is no clear and precise concept of discrimination that highlights its group-based nature. However, this individualistic formulation of anti-discrimination norms carries a significant risk of blurring and once again confusing the prohibition of discrimination with the principle of formal equality. This can effectively undermine the effectiveness of protection from the perspective of substantive equality.

For example, the concept of sexual harassment emerged in the mid-1970s within the American feminist movement to encompass a range of behaviors that women experience in the context of paid employment, which hinder their participation in the labor market on equal and dignified terms.[4] These behaviors are largely rooted in unequal power relations in both society and the workplace and, in turn, contribute to reinforcing these inequalities. For this reason, it was proposed to consider sexual harassment as a discriminatory act based on sex, thus included in the Civil Rights Act of 1964. However, judicial bodies adopted a more formalistic stance. Initially, some court rulings considered that there was no discrimination because not all women were being harmed, but only those who rejected advances from their superiors. Subsequently, it was concluded that sexual harassment is discriminatory, but through convoluted reasoning based on sexual orientation, which poses many operational problems. If it is assumed that the harasser is heterosexual and the victim is a woman, then it could be argued that sex is a determining factor in the pejorative treatment. Thus, the collective harm caused by harassment to women as a group is rendered invisible, as the focus is placed on attributing workplace significance to an inappropriate distinguishing criterion ("sex").

However, the dissolution of the specificity of the prohibition of group discrimination within the logic of formal equality is not absolute. Often, in the text of norms and in case law, the social purpose of ensuring substantive equality among human groups becomes relevant. For instance, the concept of "indirect discrimination" or "disparate impact,"[5] which necessarily involves considering the real disadvantages faced by victimized groups in society, originally emerged through judicial interpretations that went beyond a formalistic interpretation of the anti-discrimination mandate. Similarly, many legal systems expressly allow for the adoption of direct affirmative action measures that involve preferential treatment based on prohibited categories—albeit with certain limits and contradictions—which would be

[3] "But antidiscrimination law explained its decision selectively to disestablish elements of this social order without describing the system of status relations in which it was intervening; the law instead asserted that it was prohibiting arbitrary and irrational distinctions on the basis of immutable characteristics that denied persons equal opportunity [...] Silence about the structure of the larger social order was, in an important sense, a precondition of the disestablishment dynamic, a narrative necessity if antidiscrimination law was going to persuade those with privilege voluntarily to cede (some of) it", Siegel (2008).

[4] We largely follow the argument presented by Siegel (2008), pp. 8–18.

[5] The notion of "disparate impact" first appeared in the United States Supreme Court's decision *Griggs v. Duke Power Co.*, 401 U.S. 424 (1971).

impossible to accept from the strictly individualistic paradigm. Moreover, the principle of equal pay for work of "equal value"—not just for the same work—which already appeared in the ILO Constitution of 1919 and was further concretized in Convention No. 110 of 1951, already contains the seed of an assessment of work free from sexist prejudices.

As a consequence, in our modern notion of discrimination, two paradigms coexist, even though they are, in principle, mutually exclusive. Catherine MacKinnon refers to them as the "Sex differences approach" and the "Sex inequality approach,"[6] but I prefer to label them as the "individualistic perspective" and the "social perspective." The individualistic perspective, related to the Aristotelian idea of equality, considers discrimination as differential treatment that lacks justification or is expressly prohibited by law. It emphasizes the individual harm suffered by those who are subjected to pejorative treatment without objective and reasonable justification. On the other hand, the social perspective is linked to the principle of substantive equality because it aims to prevent certain behaviors from generating or reproducing a systematic situation of subordination, subjection, or oppression of specific social groups.

This work is based on the premise that the prohibition of discrimination must necessarily be viewed from the social paradigm, linked to substantive equality. Therefore, its purpose is not to abstractly proscribe the use of "sex" as a justifiable basis for differential treatment but rather to combat the structural inequalities between men and women that operate in society. However, this does not mean that the individual harm suffered by victims is irrelevant. On the contrary, to fully support the social notion of discrimination, it is essential to articulate individual harm with collective harm.

2 The Articulation of Individual Harm and Collective Harm

When we inquire about the ultimate basis of the prohibition of discrimination, two types of answers may arise: on one hand, the necessity to avoid detriment to the recipients of differential treatment (individual harm); on the other hand, the intention to combat systemic inequalities that create relationships of subordination contrary to human dignity (collective harm). Some authors argue that the prohibition of discrimination solely addresses individual harm.[7] Conversely, others refer to collective harm,[8] often avoiding the term "discrimination" due to its individualistic

---

[6]MacKinnon (1979), p. 107 and following.

[7]Foran (2019).

[8]"A view of sex discrimination less frequently adopted by courts, but which often animates their sympathies, implicitly centers upon the analysis that discrimination consists in the systematic disadvantagement of social groups [...] A rule or practice is discriminatory, in the inequality

connotations.[9] Lastly, it has been argued that the prohibition of discrimination sometimes causes harm to individual interests and other times to collective interests, or both, depending on the cases.[10] The theory we aim to support in this work is that, for a case of "discrimination on the basis of sex" to occur, both elements must be present, even if the individual or collective harm is purely potential.

In this regard, Article 1 of CEDAW may be illustrative, stating: "For the purposes of the present Convention, the term 'discrimination against women' shall mean any distinction, exclusion, or restriction made on the basis of sex which has the effect or purpose of impairing or nullifying the recognition, enjoyment, or exercise by women, irrespective of their marital status, on a basis of equality of men and women, of human rights and fundamental freedoms in the political, economic, social, cultural, civil, or any other field."

From this definition, we can deduce three constitutive elements of the concept of discrimination:

(a) Detrimental treatment resulting in individual harm ("[. . .] any distinction, exclusion, or restriction");
(b) A causal relationship between this detrimental treatment and the victim's affiliation or association with a specific social group, in this case, women ("[. . .] on the basis of sex").
(c) Collective harm to women ("[. . .] which has the effect or purpose of impairing or nullifying the recognition, enjoyment, or exercise by women [. . .] of human rights [. . .]). It should be noted that in this case, the term "women" is used in the plural, not exclusively referring to the victim of the contested treatment.

These three elements are also present in the definition of discrimination contained in Article 1.1 of ILO Convention No. 111, with one difference. In this case, the Convention is not exclusively focused on the protection of human rights, so the collective effect consists of "[. . .] nullifying or impairing equality of opportunity or treatment in employment or occupation." In essence, the discriminatory treatment

---

approach, if it participates in the systemic social deprivation of one sex because of sex. The only question for litigation is whether the policy or practice in question integrally contributes to the maintenance of an underclass or a deprived position because of gender status", MacKinnon (1979), p. 116. Also, MacKinnon (1991), pp. 1281–1328. Khaitan (2013), p. 147 claims that "[. . .] for a ground to be salient in discrimination law, it must define at least one group whose members are more likely to suffer disadvantage than those of another group defined by the same attribute".

[9]Fiss (1976), p. 197 argues that the "Equal Protection Clause" of the US Constitution should be interpreted as oriented towards a "group-disadvantaging principle," meaning that the crucial aspect is whether the contested legislation or practice tends to worsen or perpetuate the subordinate position of a specially disadvantaged group. In contrast, he presents the possibility of the individualistic perspective, which he precisely labels as the "antidiscrimination principle", Fiss (1976), pp. 108–109. Also, Young (1976), p. 197 claims that the primary focus of the struggle for emancipation should be on "oppression" rather than "discrimination", interpreted from the individualistic perspective. The latter becomes condemnable when it supports oppression and necessary when it contributes to reducing or eliminating it.

[10]Blum (2013), p. 96.

contributes to placing women in a position of disadvantage in the labor market or in employment relations.

In practice, these three elements are inseparably linked: on the one hand, the contested "treatment" cannot be dissociated from its cause ("on the basis of sex"), and on the other hand, collective harm is directly connected to both the individual treatment that contributes to its generation and the identification of the affected social group. However, this distinction is necessary for practical purposes because conduct can only be classified as discriminatory when all three elements are present simultaneously.

2.1 The Presence of Individual Harm

The phrase "distinction, exclusion, or restriction" implies that discrimination always involves a "treatment" attributable to a responsible subject, through action or omission, with a pejorative character causing harm to the recipients of the conduct. This pejorative treatment may include the denial of a benefit based on a person's sex, which is encompassed by the term "distinction," although ILO Convention No. 111 adds the clearer term "preference."

Thus, the systematic inequalities between men and women that exist in patriarchal societies cannot be legally classified as "discriminatory" unless they can be attributed to a specific responsible party due to the existence of a "treatment" causing significant harm to at least an individual. Certainly, social policies must be adopted to reduce or eliminate these inequalities. However, the legal technique of Antidiscrimination Law is not appropriate to address the problem, as it relies on the imputation of specific responsibilities to individuals or legal entities. For example, traditional gender roles may lead many women to "voluntarily" assume disproportionate domestic and caregiving tasks within the family, detrimental to their professional careers. Undoubtedly, this imbalance is a social problem that should be addressed through certain social policies, such as those that promote male co-responsibility. However, applying the prohibition of discrimination to that issue is not feasible because it would imply the possibility of resorting to the judiciary to claim legal responsibilities from one or more specific individuals. In this case, responsibility becomes diffuse throughout society as a whole, and it is not possible to "sue the patriarchy" in court.

Similarly, there may be individual behaviors that do not have sufficient relevance to be legally significant as they do not cause clearly identifiable individual harm to their recipients. However, they may still contribute to reproducing the subordination of women. For instance, this may occur with purely expressive behaviors such as the display of sexist stereotypes and prejudices or misogynistic jokes, when they cannot be classified as sexual harassment, sex-based harassment, instructions to discriminate or hate speech.[11] It also applies to gender microaggressions, pure cognitive

[11] Quinn (2017).

biases or automatic assumption of traditional roles. These acts may end up causing significant harm to specific individuals, but not on their own, rather through their social repetition or generalization, making legal responsibility diffuse throughout society. In that sense, collective harm is present, but not individual harm. For example, in an abstract context, hearing a joke about how poorly women drive may not cause significant harm to a woman. Nevertheless, living in a society where such jokes are not isolated incidents but are normalized and widespread may undermine her self-esteem, leading her to doubt her driving ability. Of course, it is appropriate to combat these behaviors, but they are not considered discriminatory because, once again, the technique of attributing specific responsibilities to individuals is not suitable. It would not only be ineffective but also counterproductive. Indeed, in the case of sexual harassment or gender-based harassment, it is possible to identify the structural connections between a series of behaviors that might have limited significance when considered in isolation. However, in these cases, the fact that all these behaviors occur within the same organization allows for assigning responsibilities to both the organization and the perpetrators.

Finally, it is not necessary to establish that the individual harm has actually materialized, but it can be purely potential, as long as it is a clearly identified damage that could affect specific individuals, even if they have not been determined yet. For this reason, the concepts of direct discrimination in Directives 2004/113/EC, 2006/56/EC, and 2010/41/EC include the conditional expression "would be treated," which refers to the possibility of suffering future harm from a given treatment. For example, a job offer that openly excludes women will undoubtedly create a disincentive for female candidates to apply in the hiring process, resulting in a clearly defined significant harm, even if it cannot be specified with concrete victims.[12]

This "potential individual harm" should not be confused with the collective harm we will address later, although they are closely related and often coincide. However, it is possible that certain behavior may cause individual harm to certain individuals characterized by their sex who are not fully determined, yet it may not contribute to generating or reproducing systematic inequalities between men and women at the same time, as we will see later.

2.2 The Presence of Collective Harm

As we have seen, anti-discrimination laws are not in place to prevent harm to individuals due to the use of irrational criteria in decision-making. In fact, there

[12]In this regard, although in relation to other grounds of discrimination, Case C-54/07, *Feryn* (ECJ 10 July 2008), paragraphs 22–25), Case C-81/12, *Asociația Accept* (ECJ 25 April 2013), paragraphs 46–47 and Case C-507/18, *NH* (ECJ 23 April 2020), paragraph 40 refer to publicly credible statements made by a person with decision-making power in the company.

can be irrational or arbitrary behaviors that are not discriminatory (for example, a dismissal based on personal antipathy). At the same time, there can be discriminatory decisions that are economically rational to the extent that they benefit the party implementing them (for example, maintaining a gender wage gap may result in cost savings). Therefore, the reason for prohibiting discrimination "on the basis of sex" is rather to combat certain systematic social inequalities between men and women that tend to place women in a socially inferior position contrary to human dignity. What is condemnable about discriminatory behavior is precisely its ability to generate, promote, or reproduce this systematic position of subordination or exclusion of women. Thus, to interpret anti-discrimination regulations in line with their purpose, it is necessary to require the presence of a social or collective harm in every case.

This harm cannot be properly understood if viewed from a purely individualistic perspective, focused solely on isolated behaviors, regardless of their structural conditions or consequences. From this standpoint, a behavior would only affect "women" when it had an impact on each and every one of this gender group, which is materially impossible.[13] In reality, the collective harm lies in the realization that the contested behavior embodies a social pattern whose generalization would contribute to generating or reproducing this group inequality contrary to human dignity. Therefore, what is intended to be prevented is the potential segregating or socially dangerous nature of certain behaviors, although the individual harm is also required in order to attribute responsibilities to an agent.

In paradigmatic cases of sex discrimination, it is not necessary to explicitly reference collective harm because it is implicit in the convergence of the other two elements. For example, if an employer decides not to promote a female employee because they believe that leadership positions should be held by men, who are presumed to have fewer family responsibilities, there is no doubt that there is individual harm (suffered by the employee excluded from promotion) and group affiliation (she was excluded because she is a woman). It is undeniable that the combination of these two factors implies that the contested behavior tends to place women in an inferior position because it actualizes or embodies a social pattern whose generalization would contribute to the subordination of women.

However, there are more complex scenarios, such as those in which the measure in question harms individuals classified as men or benefits individuals classified as women. In these cases, a deeper analysis of collective harm is necessary, as will be discussed in the following sections.

[13] See Foran (2019).

2.3 *Different Forms of Connection Between Individual and Group Harm*

The element that links individual harm with collective harm is precisely the connection between the victim of the detrimental treatment and the gender group that experiences collective harm (primarily, women). This linkage with the group can occur in various ways. For these purposes, a general distinction is often made between two types of connection with the group: direct and indirect.

Direct connection occurs when the individual held responsible is the one who immediately establishes the connection between the victims of the pejorative treatment and the gender group experiencing collective harm. This can be done openly, covertly, or unconsciously. It is not relevant for these purposes whether the active subject is motivated by psychological dispositions such as stereotypes, prejudices, and gender-based cognitive biases, or if it is simply an economically rational decision aimed at gaining a particular benefit.

On the other hand, in the case of indirect connection, the individual making the contested decision does not immediately link the victim of the detrimental treatment to the social group of women but merely applies a formally neutral criterion. Nevertheless, the application of this criterion contributes to generating collective harm to women due to the effects that gender inequalities have produced beyond the context in which the decision is made. For example, due to various factors related to gender patterns, the majority of part-time workers are women. Therefore, detrimental treatment targeting individuals with this type of contract ultimately has a disproportionate impact on women and must be justified.

However, in this context, it is crucial to emphasize that the direct or indirect connection established between the recipient of detrimental treatment and the victimized gender group does not necessarily have to be one of membership. In other words, the victim of individual harm does not have to be a member of the group that suffers collective harm. This concept is evident in cases of discrimination based on perception, discrimination by association (direct or indirect), or in considerations of retaliation when they could be assimilated to discrimination by association.

Discrimination based on perception is a form of direct discrimination in which the active party "erroneously" attributes group membership to the recipient of differential treatment. This seems less common in cases of sex discrimination because the sexual dimorphism of the human species often allows relatively clear boundaries to be drawn for each group based on the presence of specific anatomical features. However, scenarios involving intersexuality and transgender individuals can introduce variations in how a particular person is perceived as "male" or "female."

For example, let's consider a scenario where a person is assigned the "female" gender at birth due to their biological and anatomical traits, but later identifies as "male" and even, in a legal framework that allows for "gender self-determination," changes their legal gender to "male." In this case, both from a legal and personal self-perception perspective, this individual would not be considered a "woman." However, in practice, if they do not alter their anatomical features, they may still be perceived as such, experiencing systematic disadvantages associated with this classification. In this context, "sex-based discrimination" and collective harm against women will occur, even if the victim of individual harm cannot legally be considered a "woman." In conclusion, discrimination does not depend on how individuals classify themselves, but rather on how they are perceived and treated by others.

Turning to another matter, "discrimination by association" occurs when the connection with the affected social group is established through a link other than membership, often through the presence of a personal relationship.[14] At first glance, this form of discrimination may not appear particularly relevant when applied to sex discrimination because, in reality, virtually anyone has some kind of relationship with a woman. However, it's important to remember that sex-based discrimination does not only pertain to identifying a person as a "woman" but also to other circumstances associated with this classification, such as pregnancy.

Consider a scenario where a male worker has relocated to a different location from his residence to provide services for a specific company and learns that his wife has suffered an ectopic pregnancy, putting her life in danger. In this context, after notifying the company and leaving his job to return to his place of residence to care for his wife, he is subsequently terminated as a result. If it had been the woman who was terminated due to a pregnancy-related illness, there would be no doubt in labeling the behavior as sex-based discrimination. However, the dismissal of the male worker due to his relationship with a pregnant woman would also be discriminatory—in this case, by association—as there is individual harm linked to collective harm against women, as the widespread application of this pattern would ultimately place the affected women in a position of vulnerability.

On the other hand, in our opinion, association can be applied not only to personal relationships but also to other ways of connecting an individual to a group they do not belong to, such as the "black sheep" phenomenon. We use this term to refer to behaviors carried out in retaliation against a person for their disobedience to dominant gender norms or for not meeting societal expectations related to the gender assigned to them. Often, women are victims of these treatments for not considering themselves "feminine" enough, for assuming "masculine" roles, or for similar reasons. However, men can also face reprisals for displaying attitudes or behaviors that are socially associated with 'women.' In such cases, the collective harm is frequently experienced by a specific social group associated with this gender nonconformity (e.g., those characterized by diverse sexual orientations, gender identities, or gender expressions). Nevertheless, there are situations where the collective harm resulting from reprisals against a non-conforming man is actually borne by women. For example, if a man faces pejorative treatment for taking on caregiving responsibilities within his family, as these tasks are typically seen as "feminine", in this case, the punishment of the non-conforming man reinforces the existing imbalance in the distribution of these roles.

---

[14]See Case C-303/06, *Coleman* (ECJ 17 July 2008) and Case *Guberina v. Croatia*, n° 23682/13 (ECHR 22 March 2016), both related with disability.

Furthermore, in many legal systems, retaliatory actions related to discrimination complaints or legal claims are also classified as discriminatory. For instance, the termination of employment by an employer against a person who has filed a discrimination complaint, acted as a witness in a legal or administrative procedure seeking accountability for an alleged act of discrimination, or assisted the alleged victim in any way would be considered discriminatory. In such cases, the victim of retaliation undoubtedly experiences individual harm, and there is also collective harm because, if the law were to tolerate these kinds of behaviors, discrimination victims would ultimately be defenseless. This collective harm occurs even if the act subject to the initial complaint is not discriminatory, and regardless of whether the victim of retaliation belongs to the victimized social group. If the victim does not belong to that group, the case should be considered a special form of discrimination by association.

Lastly, "discrimination through association" can also be indirect.[15] This occurs when a male is disadvantaged by the application of an ostensibly neutral criterion that results in collective harm to women due to being incorporated in a feminized space. For instance, as mentioned earlier, the detrimental treatment directed at part-time workers has an adverse impact on women. The question arises as to whether a male part-time worker would have grounds to challenge this differential treatment. One might argue that he cannot claim sex-based discrimination since he is not a woman and that males are not adversely affected by the measure. However, the fact remains that the distinctive elements of discrimination still exist, with the caveat that the individual suffering harm does not belong to the group affected by collective harm.

3 Application of this Theory to Controversial Scenarios

3.1 Affirmative Action and Reverse Discrimination

As we have seen earlier, the individualistic perspective leads to a purely "symmetrical" understanding of the grounds of discrimination, which conceals the substantial purpose of anti-discrimination laws to combat the systematic inequalities suffered by women, based on the abstract notion that "sex" is a presumably irrational criterion to justify differential treatment.

Logically, this results in a paradoxical situation concerning the evaluation of affirmative action measures, which, like anti-discrimination provisions, aim to address the situation of subordination or exclusion of women but may be hindered

[15] In this context, concerning racial or ethnic discrimination, see Case C-83/14, *CHEZ Razpredelenie Bulgaria AD*, (ECJ 12 May 2011), related to a measure that disadvantaged individuals living in a predominantly Roma-populated neighborhood, even though it had not been proven that the person filing the complaint belonged to this ethnic group.

precisely by the application of anti-discrimination rules. Indeed, when these measures directly use sex (female or male) as a basis for introducing differential treatment, unequal treatment occurs that requires some form of justification. In this context, from an individualistic perspective, a suspect classification is being used to justify significant differential treatment. Therefore, the more odious sex is considered as a justificatory reason for differential treatment, the more intense the scrutiny to which affirmative action measures would be subjected.

However, from the notion of discrimination we have previously advocated, affirmative action measures can never be categorized as a form of group discrimination as long as they really tend to reduce an existing situation of systematic inequality. In this vein, Article 4.1 of CEDAW allows for the establishment of "[...] temporary special measures aimed at accelerating de facto equality between men and women." Indeed, when these measures are designed to rectify a pre-existing inequality, they cannot cause collective harm, provided they are withdrawn once the desired equality has been achieved. Similarly, within the context of the European Union, Article 157.4 of the Treaty on the Functioning of the European Union allows for the adoption of measures "[...] providing for specific advantages in order to make it easier for the underrepresented sex to pursue a vocational activity or to prevent or compensate for disadvantages in professional careers."

In many cases, affirmative action measures involve preferential treatment, which means that there may be subjects who suffer individual harm as a result of the application of these policies. These individuals can be both women or men. For example, if labor rights for balancing family and work life are provided "only for men,"—overlapping with those already established—in order to promote shared responsibility in caregiving, this might lead to some women feeling excluded from these benefits. However, it cannot be said that there is collective harm inflicted to women. On the other hand, giving preference to a woman over a male candidate of equal merit and capacity for a position in which women are underrepresented may result in individual harm to the affected male candidate but not to "men" as a whole since they continue to be the majority group.

However, in some cases, this individual harm can be disproportionate if the affirmative action measure is poorly designed. For example, if a less qualified female candidate is preferred over a clearly more qualified male candidate for a position in which women are underrepresented, we could argue that the passed-over male candidate has suffered disproportionate individual harm. In such cases, there is no "discrimination" in the strict sense—that is, in a group sense—but rather a violation of the principle of equal treatment. The issue is that the term "discrimination" has often been improperly generalized to refer to any unjustified inequality prohibited by the law. These cases of 'individual unfairness' are not equivalent to group discrimination. Therefore, the rules governing such situations must differ, regardless of how the conduct is formally labeled, as the underlying interests are distinct.[16]

[16] However, in the context of European Union law, the text of anti-discrimination regulations seems to assume a principle of equal treatment "on the grounds of sex" understood in symmetrical terms,

This does not mean that males cannot be subject to group discrimination on the basis of sex. Of course, as we have seen earlier, they can experience discrimination "by association," both direct and indirect, including the "black sheep" punishment and possible reprisals related to previous discrimination claims. Moreover, we understand that it is theoretically possible to construct a case of "reverse discrimination" in which differential treatment based on sex not only results in individual harm to a specific and identifiable male but also has a collective impact on males as a group. This is because collective harm is always hypothetical. As we have stated, to establish it, it is not necessary for the contested measure to single handedly produce a situation of group inferiority. What is condemned is its potential for segregation, to the extent that its repetition or generalization could indeed cause systematic inequalities. This means that the victimized group does not have to be necessarily a vulnerable collective; it suffices that the conduct has the potential to generate vulnerability through its generalization. For example, even if there is no apparent disadvantage for people of Jewish origin in the job market of a specific country, excluding a person from employment due to this origin is still discriminatory because its potential for segregation is undeniable, tending to produce situations contrary to human dignity.

Certainly, in the case of discrimination "on the grounds of sex," it's challenging to find situations in which specific behavior tends to create a situation of subordination or exclusion for males. This is due to the ubiquity of systems of male dominance, which implies that males, as a group opposed to women, are almost always in a privileged position, which usually prevents the production of such discriminatory behaviors. In fact, when we come across real cases of "status inversion," they are most likely related to sexist cultural patterns that are ultimately associated with the patriarchal system but can, in particular contexts, lead to systematic inequalities against men. That could be the case of a male who joins a strongly feminized workplace and experiences discriminatory harassment from his female colleagues aimed at reproducing a sexist division of productive labor that ultimately harms women. Nevertheless, in these cases, the harm suffered by women is indirect and mediated, making it easier to identify a collective harm experienced by men in a restricted social context where the usual power relations are somewhat reversed.

---

which must somehow be reconciled with the explicit admission of affirmative action measures. In general terms, the position of the Court of Justice has leaned toward a symmetrical understanding of the principle of equal treatment on the grounds of sex. In fact, in the Case C-450/93, *Kalanke*, (ECJ 17 October 1995), it explicitly stated that, since the admission of affirmative action measures is an exception to this general principle, it must be interpreted restrictively (paragraph 21). This interpretative pattern disappears in subsequent rulings, perhaps because it is recognized that affirmative action aims precisely to guarantee effective equality. Nonetheless, the normative weight of this initial decision has significantly influenced subsequent case law, perhaps due to the European Court of Justice's practice of not formally overruling previous decisions.

3.2 Indirect Discrimination

As we have noted earlier, the concept of indirect discrimination implies, by its very nature, the concurrence of collective harm. Therefore, in these cases, in contrast to direct discrimination, there must be a real, not just potential, situation of vulnerability of the affected group. Indeed, in these cases, the application of a seemingly neutral criterion produces an unfavorable outcome for a particular social group precisely due to the existing social inequalities. As a result, dominant groups cannot, under any circumstances, be victims of indirect discrimination. With regard to discrimination on the basis of sex, the ubiquity of patriarchy, to which we referred earlier, surely implies that it is impossible for men, as a collective, to be the group harmed by treatments qualified as "indirect discrimination." Of course, men as individuals can be victims of indirect discrimination, but only by association, as described earlier.

However, sometimes even the definitions of indirect discrimination use individualistic language, which generates some uncertainty regarding their practical application. For example, Article 2.1 b) of Directive 2006/54/EC defines indirect discrimination as follows: "[. . .] where an apparently neutral provision, criterion or practice would put persons of one sex at a particular disadvantage compared with persons of the other sex, unless that provision, criterion or practice is objectively justified by a legitimate aim, and the means of achieving that aim are appropriate and necessary." In this case, there is no explicit reference to the contribution of the conduct to the production or maintenance of the systematic inequalities affecting women. Instead, the emphasis is placed on individuals "of one sex" who suffer a particular disadvantage compared to those "of the other".

This has led some author to argue that indirect discrimination is applied symmetrically,[17] which is problematic because, in that case, not only affirmative action measures based on direct gender group attribution should be subject to particular scrutiny but also indirectly-based affirmative action measures, that is to say, those equal opportunity measures derived from the application of the gender mainstreaming principle aimed at combating systematic inequalities affecting women but without directly using gender membership as a criterion for preferential treatment. In our opinion, this perspective is incorrect because it conflicts with the gender mainstreaming principle that can be found, for example, in Article 29 of the aforementioned Directive.

Finally, collective harm becomes relevant in the application of the test for indirect discrimination. In the European context, this test includes, among other elements, a strict proportionality requirement, which involves a comparison between the benefit achieved by implementing the measure for a legitimate purpose and the disadvantage suffered by women as a group. In this context, it is necessary to identify and clarify the extent of collective harm to carry out the weighing of interests. However, on some occasions, the contested measure is judged exclusively in individualistic terms,

[17] Foran (2019).

without taking into consideration its effects on group inequality. For example, the judgments of the European Court of Justice regarding the prohibition of wearing the "Islamic veil" in the workplace, while formally invoking the institution of indirect discrimination,[18] have practically focused on the individual perspective of "religious freedom" rather than from the perspective of group discrimination. Thus, it is understood that business interests can come into conflict with the right of Muslim women to express their religious beliefs, without highlighting the negative impact that the generalization of the ban on wearing the Islamic veil at work could have on the integration of Muslim women into the labor market.

4 Conclusion

The prohibition of sex discrimination arises to address the systematic vulnerability experienced by women due to the social implementation of patriarchal structures. However, this purpose is often distorted by the use of individualistic language in the drafting of anti-discrimination laws, as well as in academic and judicial arguments. In this context, to restore the underlying purpose of the prohibition of sex discrimination, it is necessary to emphasize its social dimension, which implies that there should always be an identification of collective harm in discriminatory behavior. However, this social perspective cannot go so far as to equate legal discrimination with any systematic inequality, as this legal framework requires the attribution of legal responsibilities to specific individuals. Therefore, to qualify an action as discriminatory, it is also necessary the existence of a detrimental treatment that would produce individual harm, either real or potential, to specific individuals.

The element that connects individual harm with collective harm is a relationship of connection, either direct or indirect, between the individual victim of pejorative treatment and the gender group affected by the measure, which in most cases will be the female collective. This connection is usually the victim's belonging to the victimized group. However, situations of "discrimination by association," both direct and indirect, can also occur. As a result, it is possible for a male to be a victim of sex discrimination in cases where the victimized group is women.

Identifying cases in which discriminatory treatment harms "males" as a group is more challenging. This only occurs in exceptional cases, often ultimately related to the application of patriarchal patterns, in particular contexts where the usual power relations appear reversed. Often, affirmative action measures that result in individual harm to males are labeled as "reverse discrimination." However, in such cases, there is no genuine collective harm, although certain poorly formulated measures may be disproportionate and, thus, contrary to the principle of equal treatment, but they do

[18] Cases C-157/15, *Achbita*, (ECJ 14 March 2017), C-804/18 and C-341/19, *Wabe*, (ECJ 15 July 2021), C-344/20, *SCRL*, (ECJ 13 October 2022) and C-148/22, *Commune D'Ans*, (ECJ 28 November 2023).

not constitute cases of genuine group discrimination. Unfortunately, the term "discrimination" is often used to refer to any differential treatment which is not properly justified, but this notion should be distinguished from the concept of group discrimination.

Finally, collective harm is a defining element in cases of indirect discrimination, where real vulnerability of the group, not just potential vulnerability, must be required. Therefore, males can only be victims of indirect discrimination when collective harm to women is identified. Furthermore, it is necessary to properly identify collective harm to balance it in the proportionality test specific to indirect discrimination.

References

Blum L (2013) Racial and other asymmetries: a problem for the protected categories framework for anti-discrimination thought. In: Hellman D, Moreau S (eds) Philosophical foundations of discrimination law. Oxford University Press, Oxford, pp 182–199

Fiss O (1976) Groups and the equal protection clause. Philos Public Aff 5:107–177

Foran MP (2019) Discrimination as an individual wrong. Oxford J Leg Stud 39(4):901–929

Khaitan T (2013) Prelude to a theory of discrimination law. In: Hellman D, Moreau S (eds) Philosophical foundations of discrimination law. Oxford University Press, Oxford, pp 182–199

MacKinnon C (1979) Sexual harassment of working women. Yale University Press, New Haven

MacKinnon C (1991) Reflections on sex equality under law. Yale Law J 100(5):1281–1328

Quinn P (2017) The problem of stigmatizing expressions: the limits of anti-discrimination approaches. Int J Discrim Law 17(1):23–50

Siegel RB (2008) Introduction: a short history of sexual harassment. In: MacKinnon C, Siegel RB (eds) Directions in sexual harassment law. Yale University Press, New Haven, pp 1–39

Young IM (1990) Justice and the politics of difference. Princeton University Press, Princeton

Antonio Álvarez del Cuvillo is an Associate Professor of Labour and Social Security Law at the University of Cádiz (Spain) He holds a dual undergraduate degree in Law and Social Anthropology so he is very interested in interdisciplinary approaches. He has authored numerous papers regarding discrimination on different topics such as the concept of discrimination, the legal implications of the concept of gender, discrimination of immigrants and foreign people, the concept of race, affirmative action, reverse discrimination, burden of proof in discrimination cases, sexual and gender-based harassment, or gender discrimination and collective bargaining. He has been the Principal Investigator on an Interdisciplinary research project on sexual harassment in the public universities.

The manufacturer's authorised representative in the EU is Springer Nature Customer Service Centre GmbH, Europaplatz 3, 69115 Heidelberg, Germany. If you have any concerns regarding our products, please contact ProductSafety@springernature.com

Printed and bound by CPI Group (UK) Ltd, Croydon, CR0 4YY
01/10/2026
02225909-0004